Hart Crane: The Patterns of His Poetry

Hart Crane:
The Patterns of His Poetry
M. D. Uroff

UNIVERSITY OF ILLINOIS PRESS
Urbana Chicago London

Publication of this work was supported in part by a grant from the Andrew W. Mellon Foundation.

LIBRARY OF CONGRESS CATALOGING IN PUBLICATION DATA

Uroff, Margaret Dickie.
    Hart Crane: the patterns of his poetry.

    Includes bibliographical references.
    1. Crane, Hart, 1899–1932—Criticism and
interpretation.   I. Title.
PS3505.R272Z798   811'.5'2   74–8906
ISBN 0–252–00393–4

To Dorothy Sweet and Henry Hodgeson Dickie

Acknowledgments

I am indebted to Carol Thomas Neely and Sherman Paul for careful and helpful comments on this book. And I am grateful to Benjamin Uroff, who agreed not to read the manuscript and helped in every other way too.

An early version of Chapter Two appeared as "The Imagery of Violence in Hart Crane's Poetry" in *American Literature* (May 1971).

M.D.U.

Contents

chapter one: Introduction

Hart Crane's long poem, *The Bridge,* has never lacked serious readers. From its publication it has been the subject of discussion, attack, justification, and finally careful explication. The same is not true of the bulk of Crane's work, his lyric poems. Although they have been judged even by the most negative critics of *The Bridge* as among his best work, the lyric poems have only recently attracted the kind of close critical attention granted to Crane's self-styled epic, and even now they are separated from *The Bridge* for examination and discussed almost entirely in isolation from it. This divisive emphasis is an unfortunate but perhaps understandable fact of literary history. From the outset *The Bridge* posed certain unique and difficult problems of interpretation, problems which fascinated Crane's readers in the 1920s and 1930s and drew their attention away from his short poems. For example, the structure of *The Bridge,* its place in the epic tradition, its treatment of the myth of America, all have occasioned considerable critical controversy of a kind that is not directly applicable to the lyric poems. The lyrics have been neglected not because they are inferior to *The Bridge* but because they appear totally unrelated to it. The approach to Crane through *The Bridge* was established by his earliest critics, Yvor Winters and Allen Tate, who had praised Crane's first volume of lyric poems when it appeared but who found *The Bridge* paradoxically both more significant and seriously flawed. They tended to revise their original estimates of Crane's value in terms of his long poem.[1] Their criticism of Crane has been answered by lengthy analyses of *The Bridge* which have given that poem a central place in Crane's work. Although Tate and Winters both called it a collection of lyrics, neither they nor their followers developed that insight by attaching *The Bridge* to Crane's lyric poems. Instead, the efforts to explore the structure and meaning of the long poem have isolated it from Crane's other work.

The excessive emphasis given *The Bridge* is not entirely the work of Crane's readers. He himself made extravagant claims for the intentions of the poem; he worked on sections of it during most of his creative life; and if in the end he recognized that *The Bridge* was not perfectly realized and that perhaps his lyric poetry was his best work, he nonetheless invested a great amount of creative energy and literary hope in *The Bridge*. Crane seemed to regard *The Bridge* during much of his life as his major achievement and as a work in some ways different from his lyrics. In a sense, then, his readers have simply followed his lead, and, in fact, it is astonishing to see how responsive Crane's critics have been to his claims for the poem.

It is easy to understand why Crane himself distinguished *The Bridge* from his lyrics. It was more ambitious than his other work, and he hoped that it would be more significant. He first considered

1. See Allen Tate, "Foreword," *White Buildings* (New York: Boni & Liveright, 1926), and *Reactionary Essays on Poetry and Ideas* (New York: Charles Scribner's Sons, 1936). In a review of *White Buildings* Yvor Winters calls Crane "among the five or six greatest poets writing in English." See Winters, "Hart Crane's Poems," *Poetry*, XXX (Apr. 1927), 47–51. For Winters's attack on *The Bridge*, see his "The Progress of Hart Crane," *Poetry*, XXXVI (June 1930), 153–165, and *In Defense of Reason* (New York: Swallow Press and William Morrow, 1947). In his new edition of Hart Crane's poems Brom Weber claims that Crane's reputation is still encumbered with the ideological and literary conflicts of the 1920s and 1930s of which the most dire effect is "the excessive emphasis placed on *The Bridge*" and an "unwarranted slighting of his other poems." See Weber, "Introduction," *The Complete Poems and Selected Letters and Prose of Hart Crane*

writing a long poem of a new and unique construction in 1923 when he was working on the poems of his first volume, *White Buildings*. Two events inspired his early ideas about *The Bridge*: his own composition of a three-part poem, "For the Marriage of Faustus and Helen," and his reading of T. S. Eliot's poetry. "For the Marriage of Faustus and Helen" was, Crane felt, something entirely original. He claimed that it was not only something different from anything he had tried before but also "a conscious pseudo-symphonic construction toward an abstract beauty" never before attempted in English poetry.[2] He was encouraged in this belief by his friends' warm response to the poem, and upon completing it, he began to think of another long poem that would develop more fully the "tendencies" in "For the Marriage of Faustus and Helen."[3] That new long poem was *The Bridge*, and as he worked on it in the course of the next seven years, he tended to minimize its genetic connection to the earlier poem and to emphasize its entirely new achievement. The second initiating inspiration for *The Bridge* came from Crane's reading of *The Waste Land*. Although he had probably conceived of *The Bridge* before he read Eliot's poem, that work was a significant factor in Crane's early ruminations on his long poem.[4] He was very im-

---

(New York: Doubleday, 1966), pp. xi–xvii (hereafter cited as *The Complete Poems*).

2. *The Letters of Hart Crane*, ed. Brom Weber (New York: Hermitage House, 1952), p. 92. When he was writing "For the Marriage of Faustus and Helen," he wrote to his friend Gorham Munson about the poem: "At any rate, it is something entirely new in English poetry, so far as I know. The jazz rhythms in that first verse are something I have been impotently wishing to 'do' for many a day. . . . However, I have considerable ambitions in this opus, as I have told you." See *Letters*, p. 89.

3. *Letters*, p. 118.

4. He told Munson, "There is no one writing in English who can command so much respect, to my mind, as Eliot. However, I take Eliot as a point of departure toward an almost complete reverse of direction. His pessimism is amply justified, in his own case. But I would apply as much of his erudition and technique as I can absorb and assemble toward a more positive, or (if [I] must put it so in a sceptical age) ecstatic goal. I should not think of this if a kind of rhythm and ecstasy were not (at odd moments, and rare!) a very real thing to me. I feel that Eliot ignores certain spiritual events and possibilities as real and powerful now as, say, in the time of Blake." See *Letters*, pp. 114–115.

pressed by the importance of *The Waste Land* at the same time that he felt the need to offer a counter-statement to it. His composition of "For the Marriage of Faustus and Helen" had assured him that he could write an original and ambitious long poem; then his reading of *The Waste Land* convinced him that he should answer Eliot and that to do so he would have to create a poem as startlingly new as the one he sought to counter. His insistence on the originality of *The Bridge* and on its distinction from his other work may then be simply attributed to his ambition. If he separated *The Bridge* from his lyric poems, he also separated its aims from Eliot's poem and from most of what had been done in English poetry. It was, in his mind, a totally unique composition.

If we can understand why Crane distinguished *The Bridge* from his lyric poems, it is not so easy to explain why his readers have made the same division. To be sure, *The Bridge* as a long poem about America seems to be totally unrelated to the intensely personal experience explored in the lyrics. Also, as we have said, the problems of structure and meaning presented by *The Bridge* appear quite irrelevant to the shorter poems. However, the separation of Crane's work by genre has led to an unnecessarily bifurcated view of his career. The earliest and most dire effect of this division was the assessment of Crane as a lyric genius who denied his best talent by trying to write an epic poem. Although this judgment has been overturned, it is still common to describe *The Bridge* as a magnificent failure and thereby to justify Crane's lyric power while acknowledging his severe limitations. A more recent result of the division of Crane's work is the view that the lyrics prepared Crane to write *The Bridge*.[5] This position is not entirely true to the facts of

5. Both R. W. B. Lewis and Sherman Paul bridge the gap between their discussion of the lyric poems and their consideration of *The Bridge* with a brief comment that Crane was made ready for his long work by his composition of the lyrics. In talking about the intensely creative spurt in which Crane produced a large portion of *The Bridge*, Lewis says, "This was Crane's *mensis mirabilis*, what the whole period of the visionary lyric had prepared him for." See R. W. B. Lewis, *The Poetry of Hart Crane* (Princeton, N.J.: Princeton University Press, 1967), p. 215. Paul says, "From that distance, as poetic accomplishment, the 'Voyages' affirm the honesty and resolution of the human spirit. And this, even more than

his career. He published *White Buildings* in 1926, *The Bridge* in 1930, and at the time of his death in 1932 he had a projected volume of lyric poems. Crane started thinking about *The Bridge* when he was still writing the poems for the first collection, and he continued to work on sections of it to the date of its publication, by which time he had composed most of the lyric poems of what was to be a new volume. So the actual composition of most of his poetry took place during a relatively short period of time. And even during this time his creative periods were remarkably infrequent and resulted in clusters of poems, some designed for inclusion in *The Bridge* and in the same cluster some quite independent of the longer work. The point is that it is impossible to separate Crane's poetry into strict periods and to regard *The Bridge* as his mature work for which his lyrics were the preparation. His life was short, his productive life very short; he matured as a poet early, and aside from his very early poetry his work is of one piece.

A career such as Crane's seems to demand a reading of his work as a whole, and in recent years his entire collection has been given a careful and discriminating line-by-line examination. There still remains to be explored, however, the common ground between the lyric and epic poems, and this study is designed to examine not simply the connective links between Crane's two genres but the imaginative patterns that are repeated throughout his poetry and thus may be said to typify it. Abandoning the division by genre, one can see in Crane's poetry as a whole a recurrence of patterns and can explore more fully the ways in which Crane's imagination worked. Crane has been regarded as a poet of broken efforts, of varied creative aims, but a study of his poetry reveals that his is

---

the skillful use of the 'logic of metaphor,' which he demonstrated in single poems and now extended as the unifying thematic element of a narrative sequence of poems, gave Crane the creative assurance he needed to complete his task." See Sherman Paul, *Hart's Bridge* (Urbana: University of Illinois Press, 1972), p. 165. Both these comments come at the end of extensive and sensitive discussions of Crane's lyric poems and may be regarded simply as a means of shifting focus to *The Bridge*. Certainly they are not the only connections Lewis and Paul make between the lyrics and the epic; but the fact that both critics make sequential connections here suggests the difficulties of dividing Crane's work for analysis.

rather a work of unusual continuity, of patterns recurring with obsessive frequency. Although Crane made great claims for the originality and ambition of *The Bridge,* it is the product of the same imagination that produced the lyrics, and its connections with them are multiple. Some poetic concerns dominate his work from beginning to end and seek expression in varied patterns throughout his career. One formulation may serve to illuminate another as Crane developed and explored and repeated them. Other concerns, while evident elsewhere in his poetry, are concentrated in a particular group of poems and may be studied most effectively by reference to that group.

The poet whose consciousness is the center of Crane's imaginative world defines himself again and again by two separate and in some ways opposing patterns of impulses: the impulse to violence and the impulse to possession. These are the two extreme responses of the creative self aware of its isolation yet agonizingly moved to enter into communion with the larger life around it. As soon as Crane discovered his poetic vocation, which was almost coincident with his discovery of self, he saw also the connection between art and violence. To create is to violate the certainties of the world, to free oneself and to move beyond all accepted limits; but it is also to suffer the violence of self-expenditure as well as the torment of the world's scorn. In his apprentice poems Crane imagines the artist as the supreme sufferer. "Up the chasm-walls of my bleeding heart / Humanity pecks, claws, sobs and climbs," he wrote in the early poem "The Hive." And in another adolescent poem, "The Moth That God Made Blind," Crane sets forth the fable of a moth specially favored and specially damned by his blindness, which allows him to fly into the sun, to see "Great horizons and systems and shores," but which also causes him to be burned and destroyed by that sight.[6] Like the moth, as Crane admits in the last stanza, the poet's "eyes have hugged beauty and winged life's brief spell," but he shares the moth's fate. In these early works Crane insists upon the suffering and violence that attend the creative act. Humanity claws,

6. See Paul's illuminating discussion of this poem in *Hart's Bridge,* pp. 10–15.

the sun burns, and the winged spirit that would triumph cannot escape this torment.

But as Crane's poetic powers developed, so did his confidence in the victory to be won from the violence of art. Although he imagined himself throughout his career as violated, burning, breaking, and in agony, he came to regard his suffering as purgative, redemptive, worthy. The attitudinizing and maudlin self-pity of his apprentice works give way to a deeper awareness of the artist's strength to endure. The suffering and self-expenditure of the poet lead, Crane came to see, not to exhaustion and defeat but to a new vision. The poet who unleashes his imaginative force spends it, but he also breaks through the deadened and restrictive forms of the world, releases the life hidden within them, and achieves thereby a new freedom and an apprehension of the world that is an expansion of ordinary consciousness. The poetic act is thus liberating. The "white buildings" of poetry, unlike the stultifying enclosures of the city's skyscrapers, are open to the light. To dwell in them is to be free. The bells of the imagination "break down their tower; / And swing I know not where," Crane said in a late poem, "The Broken Tower," where he celebrates the liberating and barrier-breaking power of the imagination.

The poet's suffering sets him off from other men who are *"untwisted by the love of things / irreconcilable."* Yet it is this suffering, this extreme responsiveness to his own psychic turmoil and to the torment of experience, that ennobles while it isolates him. This is the pattern of Crane's self-portrait in several poems, and it is also the pattern imposed on other poets he treats. Whitman is addressed in "Cape Hatteras" as one who has seen "And passed that Barrier that none escapes— / But knows it leastwise as death-strife." Emily Dickinson is imagined as "transmuting silence with that stilly note / Of pain." Poe, too, is one who has been probed by death and whose vision remains still bright in eyes "like agate lanterns." Melville is the "fabulous shadow." Crane saw in these American artists a community of sufferers and survivors to which he attached himself. Art is the victorious, if violent, strife with death and silence.

The pattern of violence in Crane's poetry is intricately interwoven with a second pattern: the urge for possession. Violence is a means to possession. To violate the world and thus possess it is one way of imaginative access to an otherwise resistant reality. The fire that burns in Crane's poems, the wind that razes "All but bright stones wherein our smiling plays," the bells that break down the tower, all are analogues of the imagination's violent power to wrest from experience a new and purified meaning. But the poet who per-petrates violence is also consumed by an unassuagable lust and agonized by his loneliness. In his isolation and suffering he is tor-mented by a desire to possess the miraculous spirit that has the power to transform the ugliness and torpor of the quotidian world and the unbearable solitude of his own experience into something whole, perfect, pure. This spirit is imagined in Crane's poetry as an elusive female figure.[7] To possess her is to claim her gift of beauty, grace, vision, poetry.

The pursuit of this seductive but tantalizingly remote figure is traced in three of Crane's best series of poems: "For the Marriage of Faustus and Helen," "Voyages," and the section of *The Bridge* entitled "Powhatan's Daughter." The pattern repeated in varia-tions in these long poems starts with a dreamlike vision of a beatific presence who inspires the poet with feelings of love and insight and harmony but who fades or disappears almost as soon as the poet senses her illuminating powers. She is awesome, and the poet is overpowered by his initial glimpse of her. Although he desires an intimate contact with her, he realizes that this exalted figure cannot be possessed, that, in fact, she possesses him. Still he longs for her. Energized by her presence, yet frightfully lonely and un-certain of his own powers, the poet sets out on a quest for her. She eludes him, and in the course of his pursuit he vents his frustration and rage, purifies himself of his purely sexual desires, and survives to claim, if not the object of his desires, the reward of new life and vision that she bestows.

7. In "Voyages" the figure is not given a strict sexual identity; since it is asso-ciated with the female sea and a goddess, we may assume it is a female.

The female figure that Crane seeks is no ordinary mortal. Her presence is "Reflective conversion of all things." Union with her promises to answer the "wide spindrift gaze toward paradise." She makes *"eyes wide, undoubtful | dark | drink the dawn."* The tribute that she demands is the whole life of her lover: the "Lavish heart" "spent beyond repair," "this single change," "The silken skilled transmemberment of song," the man who "Surpassed the circumstance, danced out the siege!" Her gifts are "gold-shod prophecies of heaven," "Creation's blithe and petalled word," "the torrent and the singing tree."

The dream of possession that this figure inspires arises from the poet's anguished desire for wholeness and vitality in a life he experiences as broken and fatally incomplete. No human union could fulfill his needs. He wants not a mortal lover but an immortal love. By exalting the object of his devotion, he makes her inaccessible, "unsearchable," and at the same time more intensely desirable. Service to her involves suffering and destruction. Yet, as this figure is associated with dawn, with light, with springtime, she is imagined as possessing regenerative powers. The poet's love for her is purifying. It lifts him from his lowly and mortal condition, endows him with the will to endure every torment for her sake, and prepares him to receive her vital gift. By his devotion, he is transformed and the world he inhabits is restored to its original beauty. The song with which the poet celebrates this beatific presence is the reward she grants and also the sign of devotion to her. It is testimony of the imagination's power to transmute suffering into beauty, to span beyond despair. To pursue this elusive figure is to call into the world her miraculous and transforming spirit.

The third pattern evident in Crane's poetry is that of flight, a pattern involved in much of his poetic action. In his poems of violence the poet races from all restrictions, moves through purgatorial fires, breaks barriers. His desire for possession propels him toward pursuit, hurries him along in his quest, and leads him to moments of ecstatic transport. The poet himself seems driven to flee, compelled by forces at the depth of his psyche. But he also experiences flight as a new and liberating sensation. His moments of most intense consciousness are caught in images of ascension, of spanning, of weightlessness. If patterns of flight serve to express certain psychic situations in Crane's poetry, they are also used in what seems a totally different way to detail the sensations of the twentieth century. Flight was, Crane felt, the revolutionizing experience of the modern world. The speed attainable in the conveyances of the machine age excited Crane's imagination with a new sense of illimitable power while it terrified him with its destructive potential. The airplane gave man "a Sanskrit charge / To conjugate infinity's dim marge— / Anew . . . !" It opened up the "star-glistered salver of infinity." If man was consumed by the immensity of space, he was still "launched in abysmal cupolas of space, / Toward endless terminals, Easters of speeding light." Crane described the train that "strides the dew— / Straddles the hill, a dance of wheel on wheel." Even the demonic subway, "tunnels that re-wind themselves," appears as it "yawns the quickest promise home." For Crane, the technological bridge also is motion: "Through the bound cable strands, the arching path / Upward, veering with light, the flight of strings." In a sense, Crane's vision of the modern world as a realm of speed is intimately connected with his own psychic movement. He had absorbed the shocks of the machine age. He claimed, "The modern artist needs gigantic assimilative capacities, emotion,—and the greatest of *all—vision.* 'Striated with nuances, nervosities, that we are heir to'—is more than a casual observation for me. . . . It is to the pulse of a greater dynamism that my work must revolve. Something terribly fierce and yet gentle."[8]

In *The Bridge,* particularly, Crane returns again and again to treat modern means of transportation. He sensed their liberating speed as well as their destructive drive. He was not willing, like Eliot, to lament the advent of the machine age. In his poetry he develops a pattern of speed and flight that attempts to reconcile the

8. *Letters,* p. 129.

dynamism of the machine with cosmic motion. He felt that the new insights of pure science as well as the modes of transportation made possible by applied science had so revolutionized man's relationship to the world that he entered into a new consciousness of it, and it was this new consciousness that he sought to celebrate.

Flight is not the only experience of the modern world in Crane's poetry. The dynamism of speed was exhilarating, but Crane also sensed moments of stasis, times when he felt rooted in space, enclosed in a world of hardened forms, oppressed by the resistant bulk of the material world. The modern mechanical world appeared to him in some moods as a "prison crypt / Of canyoned traffic," a labyrinth, "mashed and shapeless debris," the subway's box. For the poet who felt in his most creative periods like a voyager in a world of speed, movement is knowledge and stasis is imaginative paralysis. Images of stasis occur throughout Crane's poetry to describe moments when he feels balked, dejected, trapped, uncreative, but these moments are usually transitory in the process of the poems and give way quickly to movement. However, Crane did write a series of poems devoted to the poet's sense of stasis. These poems are unusual in Crane's work because they were written, if not as a group, at least during a relatively short period of time, and they are set off from his other work not only by their pattern of stasis but by their subject as well. They were inspired by a stay in the summer of 1926 at the Crane family house on Isle of Pines, and they treat the tropical island landscape. From a scene resplendent with life, Crane chose to describe sterile plants, fruitless trees, the island quarry, all static images. These are Crane's most objective poems, poems about objects, and the pattern of stasis they develop suggests the terror Crane felt at living in a world that could not be absorbed into his consciousness, that could not be rendered subjective. Although Crane was, as he said, striated with the nervosities of the technological world, he still found its space receptive to his transforming imagination. But the natural landscape of this foreign island impinged upon his consciousness as a space that would not be possessed by the poet, and his poems about it describe the sense of psychic assault experienced in this strange and resistant world.

Violence and possession, flight and stasis, these are the alternating and inextricably intertwined patterns in Crane's poetry. The tension between them is extreme, yet it is tautly held by the work's intensity of feeling and the powerful control of Crane's artistry. There was in Crane's imagination a fervent longing to see these patterns as part of a larger pattern, to see his intensely private sensations as cosmically meaningful. As he develops each pattern, he attempts to expand its significance beyond the immediate experience and to give it a larger value. In his violence and suffering the poet spends himself, Crane imagines, to win for the world the "bright logic" of the imagination. His desire for possession moves beyond the beautiful object of his dreams and expresses his longing to call into the world the spirit of beauty and harmony. The pattern of flight traces not only the speed and destruction of the machine age but the vast potential for a new perspective of time and space, "New verities, new inklings." Even Crane's poems of stasis trace a pattern, however terrifying, which he senses operating in the world.

Throughout Crane's poetry from beginning to end is the persistent effort to give direct expressive form to those moments of intense consciousness in which he felt he had attained the "pattern's mastery." The last pattern of his poetry to be explored details the poet's sense of mastery. To describe it, he uses terms of religious, liturgical, and ritualistic significance, but he detaches them from their orthodox and dogmatic meaning, uses them freshly to detail the sense of awe that attended the greatest flights of his imagination. In this process Crane's intention is not so much to revitalize the outworn language of religious belief as it is to affirm and celebrate his own conception of the creative power, of Creation's power. At the same time he is anxious to know if his word is "scored / Of that tribunal monarch of the air," if it is "cognate" of the "Word." The pattern of mastery, developed in poem after poem, expresses both Crane's confidence in his own powers to glean the meaning of the universe and his anxious desire to have his meaning confirmed by an answer from beyond himself. Unlike traditional religious poets, Crane did not have the assuring belief in God's presence, the sense of reciprocity between the human and the divine. Although feelings of awe and mastery are direct and overpowering in his poems, the meaning of those feelings is questioned even while it is being affirmed. While this is Crane's most overarching and celebratory pattern, it is also his most tentative. In it he poses directly the central question of the modern poet: can it be true?

These five patterns may be understood as Crane's persistent efforts to give form to the deepest and most complex urgings of his imagination. He called poetry "the articulation of the contemporary human consciousness *sub specie aeternitatis.*" These patterns are that articulation. Contemporary human consciousness was, Crane felt, the consciousness of the machine world, which "can not act creatively in our lives until, like the unconscious nervous responses of our bodies, its connotations emanate from within." And he felt that the supreme qualifications for the modern poet were his extraordinary capacity for surrender to the sensations of urban life and his ability to "convert this experience into positive terms."[9] For this reason an understanding of Crane depends upon an examination of the emanations from within and the process by which he converted them into the patterns of his poetry.

He constructed his poems, he said, "on the organic principle of a 'logic of metaphor,' which antedates our so-called pure logic, and which is the genetic basis of all speech, hence consciousness and thought-extension."[10] The logic Crane describes may also be called the logic of the imagination, which operates not according to the laws of rationality but creatively according to its own laws. For support, he cited Coleridge: "The key to the process of free creative activity which Coleridge gave us in his *Lectures on Shakespeare* exposes the responsibilities of every poet, modern or ancient, and

---

9. "Modern Poetry," *The Complete Poems,* pp. 260, 262.
10. "General Aims and Theories," *The Complete Poems,* p. 221.

cannot be improved upon. 'No work of true genius,' he says, 'dares want its appropriate form, neither indeed is there any danger of this. As it must not, so genius can not, be lawless: for it is even this that constitutes its genius—*the power of acting creatively under laws of its own origination.*'"[11] The works of genius create, as they arise from, a "field of added consciousness and increased perceptions," Crane said. They are free from "already evolved and exploited sequences of imagery and logic."[12]

In using "the logic of metaphor," Crane said he was manipulating "the more imponderable phenomena of psychic motives," relying on the "dynamics of inferential mention," risking criticism "in the conquest of consciousness," and giving "form to the living stuff of the imagination."[13] In talking about his construction of *The Bridge*, he says, "It has taken a great deal of energy—which has not been so difficult to summon as the necessary patience to wait, simply wait much of the time—until my instincts assured me that I had assembled my materials in proper order for the final welding into their natural form."[14] The work involved in gathering materials and welding them together is linked with an instinctual assurance that comes from patience. Certainly this explanation seems to be an adequate description of his own progress on *The Bridge* over a number of years. But it also points directly to the creative logic of the imagination. Such logic does not move forward on the basis of previously proved points. It works back and forth by the power of words to rebound against each other, to summon up other words, to activate latent meanings in themselves and the groups they form, to suggest and evoke associations.

Crane's imagination worked through the materials of his poems, as he says:

It is my hope to go *through* the combined materials of the poem, using our "real" world somewhat as a spring-board, and to give the

11. "Modern Poetry," *The Complete Poems*, p. 260.
12. "A Letter to Harriet Monroe," *The Complete Poems*, p. 237.
13. "General Aims and Theories," *The Complete Poems*, p. 222.
14. *Letters*, p. 305.

poem *as a whole* an orbit or predetermined direction of its own. . . .
Such a poem is at least a stab at a truth, and to such an extent may
be differentiated from other kinds of poetry and called "absolute."
Its evocation will not be toward decoration or amusement, but
rather toward a state of consciousness, an "innocence" (Blake)
or absolute beauty. In this condition there may be discoverable under
new forms certain spiritual illuminations, shining with a morality
essentialized from experience directly, and not from previous precepts or preconceptions. It is as though a poem gave the reader as he
left it a single, new *word*, never before spoken and impossible to
actually enunciate, but self-evident as an active principle in the
reader's consciousness henceforward.[15]

In this ambitious endeavor Crane realized that he courted misunderstanding. By going beyond rationality, reality, previous preconceptions, Crane frees his poems from reference to an order
external to them, but he places a double burden on internal patterns
and order. In moving outside the limits of pure logic, Crane has
to make the logic of the imagination apparent and meaningful in
his poetic structure, and he felt he could do this. He says, "certain
aesthetic experience . . . can be called absolute, inasmuch as it
approximates a formally convincing statement of a conception or
apprehension of life that gains our unquestioning assent, and under
the conditions of which our imagination is unable to suggest a
further detail consistent with the design of the aesthetic whole."[16]
Crane's insistence on the absolute aesthetic experience as his poetic
objective underscores his sense of the special workings of the imagination as pure, complete, free from restrictions.[17] The product of

15. "General Aims and Theories," *The Complete Poems*, pp. 220–221.
16. *Ibid.*, p. 219.
17. Crane's use of the term "absolute" has led to some misunderstanding of his
poetic aims. For L. S. Dembo, the term implies a "quest for a logos in which the
Absolute that he has known in his imagination will be made intelligible to the
world." See Dembo, *Hart Crane's "Sanskrit Charge"* (Ithaca, N.Y.: Cornell
University Press, 1960), p. 9. What Crane means by this term seems to me to be
different from Dembo's Absolute. Crane uses aesthetic terms. Dembo understands
Crane to mean that "an Absolute exists that manifests itself in several forms; if
these forms are 'apprehended' by the poet through the imagination, which alone
can bring on the special 'state of consciousness,' then they will reveal to him the

the imagination is for him *"formally* convincing" insofar as it is well designed. In these statements Crane pleads for a reading of the design or patterns of his work. He claimed that "new conditions of life germinate new forms of spiritual articulation," and he felt that his work expressed these new forms.[18]

Crane called poetry an "architectural art," and he understood that his art would endure only through the soundness of its form.[19] He himself responded to art in this way, as he makes clear in a comment on Plato: "What you admire in Plato as 'divine sanity' is the architecture of his logic. Plato doesn't live today because of the intrinsic 'truth' of his statements: their only living truth today consists in the 'fact' of their harmonious relationship to each other in the context of his organization of them. This grace partakes of poetry."[20] By this comment Crane means not that Plato's philosophy is not true but that his appreciation of it depends on an apprehension of its harmony, the truth of form. While the philosopher might have cared more for the "intrinsic 'truth'" of his work, as Crane is well aware, the poet responds to its architecture, the pattern of its logic. The truth of any work resides, for the poet, in the intricate, complete, and coherent field of meaning that is created. And Crane holds his own work to the same high test. He realized that what he was trying to do was very difficult. He knew, too, how often he failed to attain his own goal. Accused of "'psychological gaming,'" Crane was at pains to justify his own sincerity and to explain its basis in an absolute fidelity to his psychic exploration.[21] In his exploration of new areas of consciousness Crane had no model or

---

nature of the Absolute itself ('spiritual illuminations')" (pp. 8–9). Dembo is careful not to give the term any orthodox religious significance, nor does he imply that Crane held any religious belief, but he still seems to identify the Absolute as something outside the poet and not something that arises from within. I would agree with Crane that the inner workings of the imagination are in some sense absolute.

18. "General Aims and Theories," *The Complete Poems*, p. 222.
19. "Modern Poetry," *The Complete Poems*, p. 260.
20. *Letters*, p. 238.
21. *Ibid.*, p. 239.

signposts.[22] He created the new patterns of his own consciousness, and in them we may see the "divine sanity," the architecture of his imagination's logic.[23]

22. A. D. Van Nostrand has focused on the "span of consciousness" in *The Bridge*. He sees the poem as a romantic cosmology, a recurrent form in American literature. See Van Nostrand, *Everyman His Own Poet* (New York: McGraw-Hill, 1968), pp. 63–81.

23. In an article John Unterecker sketched the psychological, spiritual, and aesthetic patterns in Crane's poetry. Although he did not develop his insights, his terms are very close to my own. See Unterecker, "The Architecture of *The Bridge*," *Wisconsin Studies in Contemporary Literature*, III (Spring–Summer 1962), 5–20. More recently Heinrich Ickstadt has examined an important group of images in "Possessions," "Recitative," "Legend," "Lachrymae Christi," "Voyages II and VI," "Passage," and "Proem: To Brooklyn Bridge," which expresses the central experience of "totality." He sees these images as different representations of the consciousness of the lyrical self. See Heinrich Ickstadt, *Dichterische Erfahrung und Metaphernstruktur* (Heidelberg: Carl Winter Universitätsverlag, 1970).

chapter two: The Poet as Violator

Hart Crane's first dream was to be a poet, and to be a poet, he imagined, was to live in a world of dreams where violence, suffered and perpetrated, was the obsessive pattern. He was sure of this idea from the beginning, long before he had actually written much poetry; he never abandoned it, although his tone and attitude toward it changed as he matured. The pattern of violence in his poetry defines the poet's role and reveals Crane's developing and deepening sensitivity to the poetic situation.

It is not inappropriate that his first published poem bears as its title the identification assigned to Oscar Wilde by Reading Gaol, since Crane's earliest poems depict the poet as a victim of the world's cruelty, imprisoned, abandoned, closeted, scorned, but still dreaming his dreams, in fact venting his dreams upon the world in response to its neglect. Although its language is inflated and its sentiment maudlin, "C 33" describes not only Wilde but the position of the poet in Crane's youthful imagination:

> He has woven rose-vines
> About the empty heart of night,
> And vented his long mellowed wines
> Of dreaming on the desert white

With searing sophistry.
And he tended with far truths he would form
The transient bosoms from the thorny tree.

Here the poet as prisoner is still the dreamer and truth-sayer. He suffers from the pain of isolation and from the aridity of the world's sophistry, yet he is still devoted to a creative and fecund principle. In fact, he suffers for his devotion. His purpose is "O Materna! to enrich thy gold head / And wavering shoulders with a new light shed." This feminine principle, a familiar figure in Crane's poetry from beginning to end, "Can trace paths tear-wet, and forget all blight." She is the spirit of poetry. In service to her, the poet realizes his own power to transform the emptiness and sterility of the world. The poet weaves and forms and enriches. The feminine principle that inspires these creative acts also responds to them and comforts the suffering poet.

In two other early poems Crane depicts the poet as isolated, this time of his own choice, yet still in some way tormented. The poet finds in the modern industrial city of "Porphyro in Akron" no need for his own powers:

O City, your axles need not the oil of song.
I will whisper words to myself
And put them in my pockets.

The direction of this poem is not clear, since the poet feels both detached from the city and its factories and drawn to the "raisin-jack" and conviviality of immigrant communal life. This company, presumably composed of the city's factory workers, is more congenial than his mother's middle-class "stuffy parlour" with which he contrasts it. However, the poem concludes, "in this town, poetry's a / Bedroom occupation." The poet's sense of isolation dominates the poem despite his social connections with the immigrants and his own family life.

"The Bridge of Estador" takes quite a different approach to the modern metropolis. The optative mood of "The Bridge of Estador," in which the poet walks "high on the bridge" "Where no one has ever been before," is revealed in the poet's vision of a sun-lapped lake and the sunlight on a laborer's gashed hand (a peculiar moment of shared suffering and communion). For this poet from his elevated position, beauty seems to be found everywhere, both in the pastoral setting and in the industrial scene. Yet even in this moment of self-assurance the poet is aware that the sunlit vision is not the only one:

> I do not know what you'll see,—your vision
> May slumber yet in the moon, awaiting
> Far consummations of the tides to throw
> Clean on the shore some wreck of dreams. . . .

Written at the outset of his career, "The Bridge of Estador" expresses the poet's simultaneous wonder and fear. The speaker in this poem anticipates that time will bring pain and loss and perhaps a different vision. He is committed nonetheless to his position, his poetic stance high on the bridge that overarches the world, and to whatever vision he attains there. Only a young poet could have entrusted himself so completely to the moonlit world and the moon-driven tides of his poetic future. By identifying himself in the last stanza as "Pierrot," "Beauty's fool," Crane accepts both the suffering and the vision of the poet. He accepts the suffering for the vision because, as he suggests in the lines quoted above, perhaps the vision must await the "wreck of dreams."

The speaker's exalted position in "The Bridge of Estador" is not a frequent pose in Crane's early poetry. More often his characters occupy an enclosed and restricted place. In "Black Tambourine" Crane describes a black man in a cellar where "Gnats toss in the shadow of a bottle, / And a roach spans a crevice in the floor." In this squalid underground the black man is "forlorn," shut out by the "world's closed door." Unlike Aesop, who, "driven to pondering, found / Heaven with the tortoise and the hare," this man cannot escape from his suffering, the "dark" "mid-kingdom" of his experience. He is arrested, constrained, trapped. His tambourine, the instrument with which he might have transformed his torment into song, is "black," "stuck on the wall," silent. The black man is an outcast and a victim of the world's injustice, but he is even more a silenced musician, and in both roles his situation is close to the modern poet's. The restriction and enclosure of this poem describe both the victimization of the black man and the paralysis of the creative spirit. As the case of Aesop suggests, the two situations are not necessarily related as cause and effect. They exist side by side and reinforce each other in this poem as they did in the black moments of Crane's moods.

The artist as exile is actually the subject of "Praise for an Urn," a memorial to Ernest Nelson, a man who gave up poetry and painting to support himself by lithographic work. Nelson, a Norwegian, was an exile from his native land but he was even more, as Crane said, "one of many broken against the stupidity of American life."[1] Nelson's thoughts are "Delicate riders of the storm" which, like Crane's own memorial words, will be lost to the world. The most fully drawn indictment of the modern world is in "Chaplinesque," in which Crane sees in the dramatic genius of Charlie Chaplin a representative of "the futile gesture of the poet in U.S.A., today."[2] The fury of the street that has crowded out human emotions as well as poetry and the policeman who pursues Chaplin at every turn with the "doom of that inevitable thumb" have forced the poet to take the tramp's comic route of camouflage and sidesteps. The poet must become a clown to preserve his innocence and surprise. He must be content with "random consolations" and "fine collapses" in a world of "lonely alleys" and an "empty trash can." Behind his smirks, however, is the "grail of laughter," whose quest is vitally serious. It is a quest prompted by love and by the heart which still loves the world that has abandoned it. If the modern

---

1. *Letters,* p. 93.
2. *Ibid.,* p. 66. R. W. B. Lewis, following the lead of Wallace Fowlie, has associated the image of Chaplin with the archetype of the poet as clown, or the poet and Everyman as Fool, evident in a long tradition of French literature and in the comic spirit of Walt Whitman as well. See Wallace Fowlie, *Love in Literature* (Bloomington: Indiana University Press, 1965), pp. 128–138, and Lewis, *Poetry of Hart Crane,* pp. 45–79.

questor is clownish, it is not only that Everyman in the eyes of God is a clown but that the way of the artist in the "dull squint" of the modern world must always appear grotesque.

Crane abandoned early the image of the poet victimized by an insensitive world; he did not, however, abandon the imagery of violence and suffering. Rather, he used it for a different purpose. At first Crane imagined the poet's suffering as imposed from without; in his more mature work it arises from within. In his earliest works he had emphasized the pitiful and lonely condition of the outcast or the isolated poet; in his later works he shifted his attention to the poet's inner turmoil and violent creative activity. His early pieces treat characters that are silent, dead, confined, or clowning, all in some way deflected from their artistic purpose. Only in "The Bridge of Estador" does the poet occupy an exalted position, and even there he is aware that time may cause him suffering. The early poems describe passive victims, sometimes actual people whom Crane met as he served an apprenticeship in his father's business enterprises, but always figures who shared in his mind the poet's isolation and suffering. In his more mature works Crane drops the mask of victim and outcast and becomes instead a performer. He may still suffer but his pain is of a different nature. It stems from his extreme sensitivity to experience, from his self-exposure, from his agonizing desire to confront his inner turmoil and release it in art. The cruelty of the world is never so great, Crane learned, as the cruelty of art and of the consciousness that seeks its form in art. The pain of the artist is the pain of self-discovery, of formulating what for most people remains forever unknown. As a man, Crane lived an anguished life; as a poet, he probed the depth of that suffering and sought to transform it into art.

The high purpose allotted the poet in Crane's apprentice pieces is at odds with his victimized state. If the poet's powers are as great as Crane claims them to be even in these early works, then they cannot be easily constrained by the world. The poet's vision cannot be deflected by the world's "dull squint"; his "far truths" must extend beyond the world's "searing sophistry." Crane had made this point only by implication in his early works. As he matured, he came to treat it more directly. The creative powers of the poet become his subject. In his later works the poet comes out of hiding and performs in public. No longer the violated, the poet becomes the violator of the world's dull certainties. Whereas Crane had first imagined the poet as abandoned by the world, now he pictured the poet as abandoning the world by going beyond its limits in a creative act. Propelled by the turbulent power of his imagination, the poet threatens all boundaries, all accepted forms and restrictions. He will create a new world in the "white buildings" of his poetry. It will be no safe retreat from suffering and violence but an open arena where these sensations are confronted and purified into art. Crane refuses to be confined by a world not of his own making, and he is willing to expend all his poetic energy in the creation of his own imaginative world. The suffering in his later poetry derives from the pain of his own psychic distress and creative urge. The violence is the transforming power of art.

The pattern of creative activity in Crane's mature poems may be traced in his recurrent use of fire, wind, and acts of breakage. The fire that consumes and purifies, the wind that razes the world, the breaking of all bounds, are all analogues for the poet's imaginative process. They are not peculiar to Crane; M. H. Abrams has noted their significance in the English Romantic poets and has traced their history to antiquity.[3] But Crane's particular use of them departs from tradition in its emphasis on their decreative and purifying properties. The Romantics used the lamp or fire as an analogy for the mind because it suited their notions of the active role of the mind in the creative process; the mind-flame shed light upon the world and did not merely reflect an image. Fire sheds light in Crane's poetry as well, but it also consumes and purifies. The fire of the creative process is always close in Crane's mind to

3. M. H. Abrams, "The Correspondent Breeze: A Romantic Metaphor," in *English Romantic Poets,* ed. M. H. Abrams (New York: Oxford University Press, 1960), and *The Mirror and the Lamp* (New York: Oxford University Press, 1953).

lust that is released only in consummation, to passion that retained for Crane its original meaning of suffering and is purified only by death. Crane frequently uses the word "possession" to describe the imaginative act at its climax, and this word carries an obvious sexual significance. Intertwined with these meanings is the idea of the poet who loves the world and is burned by it, who burns up and purifies his life in art, who is destroyed and still seeks to destroy all that restricts his imagination.

The wind as a metaphor for creative activity is another borrowing from the Romantics. For them, the wind is destroyer *and* preserver; for Crane it is chiefly a destroyer, in the sense that it consumes and purifies. In Romantic poetry it is, as Abrams has noted, a "correspondent breeze"; the actual wind playing upon the landscape correlates with the complex subjective process of renewal in the poet. The west wind that scatters the dead leaves and new seed for Shelley is at the start the natural wind, and the analogy between the wind and the poet's inspiration, the new seed and the poet's poems, binds the ode together. The wind in Crane's poetry does not belong to the seasons of fall and spring or to the cycle of rebirth. It is always a catastrophic wind, the hurricane or the monsoon, that plays through Crane's lyric poems. It levels the world, yet it refreshes too. As Crane says in "Possessions," it razes "All but bright stones wherein our smiling plays." It destroys everything but the poet's bright world, or it makes way for the free play of the poet's feelings. Crane's wind, like the imagination it analogizes, is a liberating force.

Finally, in a number of poems, especially poems about memory, Crane imagines the creative act as one of breakage, of breaking open and revealing the inner energy and pure or perfected meaning of life. Often this breakage is associated with the purifying fire or the leveling wind, but in its cleaving and sundering it is also distinct from the fire and wind.

In the opening poem of Crane's first volume of poetry, the powers of the purifying fire are extolled as the source of creative activity. "Legend" is the story of Crane's artistry, and it details the pattern of consummation and purification which is characteristic of his imaginative act. Not, as its place might suggest, an early poem, it expresses a confidence unknown in his apprentice work.[4] By the the time Crane wrote "Legend" in 1925, he had realized his imaginative powers and had abandoned the victim's pose. Gone from "Legend" are even the "meek adjustments" of "Chaplinesque," the poet's maudlin self-pity that caused him to admit that he could "still love the world" despite its cruelty. "Legend" is not the story of a saint's life; it is the story of the poet's life. But, like the saint, the poet's suffering is purposeful, and, like the saint too, the poet lives for that purpose. The poem is, as the last line states, the legend of "youth," of vitality and creativity.

"Legend" opens with a brief comment on a passing scene of hectic activity:

> As silent as a mirror is believed
> Realities plunge in silence by . . .

Between the silence out of which they come and the silence into which they rush in this two-line stanza, the "Realities" occupy a brief but explosive space. They are both the chaotic movement of the poet's experiences, which he will string, as he says later in the poem, into a "constant harmony," and momentary flashes of that harmony. His immediate reaction to them is a confident assertion: "I am not ready for repentance; / Nor to match regrets." Whatever the force of the "Realities," the poet does not shrink from them or from the silence that surrounds them. He goes on to explain:

> For the moth
> Bends no more than the still
> Imploring flame. And tremorous
> In the white falling flakes

4. The self-assertion of "Legend" may be compared to the self-denial of an early poem, "Legende," where the poet says, "even my vision will be erased / As a cameo the waves claim again." This earlier legend also recounts the effect of a love affair which has ended and left only "The tossing loneliness of many nights." The poet's loss in "Legende" is complete. In "Legend," however, there is no loss but a redemption of experience through art.

> Kisses are,—
> The only worth all granting.

The image of the moth and the flame describes the fatal attraction between the poet and the plunging "Realities," the poet's delicate sensibility and the passion that threatens to consume it. The moth, which had served Crane in a very early poem as a symbol of the daring if doomed free spirit, here again stands for the poet who plays with fire, a dangerous yet enchanting element. But here, if the moth is drawn to the flame, the flame seems also to seek out the moth, and in their mutual desire for each other they form a patterned relationship which has its value, as the next stanza makes clear:

> It is to be learned—
> This cleaving and this burning,
> But only by the one who
> Spends out himself again.

Bending and imploring, cleaving and burning, the moth and the flame enact their ritual of attraction and torment. It is a ritual familiar to the poet, who knows that if he bends to the flame, he will be burned, and yet he bends because it is the "only worth all granting." He does not retreat to regret or repentance but, in an image that carries sexual connotations, "spends out himself again." And again and again, as the next stanza continues:

> Twice and twice
> (Again the smoking souvenir,
> Bleeding eidolon!) and yet again.
> Until the bright logic is won
> Unwhispering as a mirror
> Is believed.

Unlike the moth, who has only one flirtation with the fire and then if it veers too close is destroyed completely, the poet learns, has learned, and will forever return to learn the fire's "bright logic."

The fire does not destroy the poet; it burns him and torments him and never ceases to allure him. Yet it is by enduring this repeated ritual of burning that he will win the prize, the poetic image. The legend of Crane's art is one of purification, of the cleaving, burning, and spending of life in order to produce art. The parallel construction of the poem's opening lines, where "Realities plunge" "As silent as a mirror is believed," and the moment when the "bright logic is won / Unwhispering as a mirror / Is believed," underscores the poet's confidence in his intuition and in his purifying imagination. His first brief glimmer of "Realities" is an intuitive awareness of the reality of the imagination, which is confirmed not by regretting its brevity but by seeking it ceaselessly in experience. The "bright logic" that is won in this process is the logic of the imagination, bright not with reflection but with the purifying fires of vision. It is believable, something in which the poet intuitively believes and something he has subsequently won from the violence of experience. Out of this new silence, the "Unwhispering" which has nothing to do with dumbness but is rather the silence of awe expressed here synaesthetically as brightness, comes the poet's word. In the last stanza the poem moves to its climax:

> Then, drop by caustic drop, a perfect cry
> Shall string some constant harmony,—
> Relentless caper for all those who step
> The legend of their youth into the noon.

The "perfect cry" is the poet's response to his suffering. It is not a howl of pain or a repentant lament but a proclamation of victory. His cry is perfect, purified of imperfections, and so constant, not plunging by but steadfast. But, most important of all, the perfect cry is the poem that arises from suffering endured and transformed into art. It strings together and orders the separate and stinging expenditures of self. This kind of art is a caper, a performance, and, like the twelfth-century juggler's caper, it is relentless in its demands on the performer. In spending out himself and stepping into the noon, the poet yields himself completely to the fire that burns and purifies, and in this sacrificial act he wins from the fire itself the "bright logic" of vision.

"Legend" is a central poem in describing Crane's artistic method and draws together many of the elements that appear in other poems written around the same time, between 1923 and 1925. Although some of these poems warrant the charge that their language is too secretive to be meaningful, on the whole they actually reveal again and again the secret of Crane's art. Taken together, these poems demonstrate the importance of suffering and violence in the imaginative pattern of his work.

In "Possessions" the poet is also in agony, "sifting / One moment in sacrifice (the direst)." But where in "Legend" he had willingly endured his torment, here he seems to doubt its value and at the same time to be unable to escape it. The poem opens in what Sherman Paul calls an accent of mocking bravado: "Witness now this trust!"[5] The poet's trust here is specifically in sexual activity and the purification of his lust through consummation, but his experience does not seem to bear witness to his trust. He knows but one moment of sexual release "Through a thousand nights the flesh / Assaults outright for bolts that linger / Hidden." He is possessed by a desire that finds no object, and "this fixed stone of lust" frustrates and maddens him. In the next stanza he continues the imperative mood of the first line in the same tone of self-mocking. "Accumulate such moments to an hour: / Account the total of this trembling tabulation," the poet says, as if to suggest that such an account would prove simply the folly of his trust. Yet he persists, not in the confident mood of "Legend" but in desperation, driven by his sexual desire to "take up the stone," and in this moment of anguish he says:

> I hold it up against a disk of light—
> I, turning, turning on smoked forking spires,
> The city's stubborn lives, desires.

5. Paul, *Hart's Bridge*, p. 110.

He no longer seeks a sexual partner; he seeks rather to vent his sexual rage even if it must be a solitary act. Consumed himself with erotic desire, tormented by his sexual failure in a city of lust, still the poet pleads for release from his sexual agony and for its transformation into something pure. By holding his lust up to the light, by exposing it, he can write the "page whose blind sum finally burns / Record of rage and partial appetites." The "piteous admissions" of his frustrations are "spilt" into the poem, released at last, and the poet awaits at the end the witness of his outsetting trust:

> The pure possession, the inclusive cloud
> Whose heart is fire shall come,—the white wind rase
> All but bright stones wherein our smiling plays.

The poem is the "pure possession"; on its page the agonies of his life are purified. The images of torture in "Possessions" are all sexual, in fact, phallic, and suggest the homoerotic nature of the poet's suffering. What he seeks to consume, raze, burn out, is the sexual rage that burns him. Finding no object for his desire in the city, he creates instead a poetic object.

The "inclusive cloud" and the "white wind" are emblems of the psychic storm that rages in this poem. They destroy everything but the "bright stones wherein our smiling plays," that is, everything but the brilliant objects of the imagination. Like the "bright logic" of "Legend," the "bright stones" here gain their radiance from the destructive white wind and from the consuming and purifying fire. In this poem Crane describes the source of his imaginative power and the way in which it works. It derives from his constant submission to suffering and from his unwillingness to be completely destroyed by it. His trust in the regenerative power of the imagination wins in the end a victory over suffering. The area wherein the poet's "smiling plays" is the poem, the "pure possession" in which his anguish is purged and transformed. The destruction is ultimately imagined as creative. Against the "Record of rage" and the "trembling tabulation" of his experience, the poet sets the poem, whose "blind sum" is not an addition to his experience but a complete consummation and revision of it.

The analogy of art with consummation is far-reaching in Crane's poetry and finds a quite different expression in "Lachrymae Christi." Many of the ideas of the earlier poems crystallize in this poem where the consummation is both literal and symbolic, and the artist who destroys to create is seen as a figure like Christ and Dionysus. The passion, death, and resurrection of Christ, the disappearance and return of the fertility god Dionysus, and the suffering and destruction that result in artistic creation all meld together in one symbolic pattern in this poem.[6] Here the crucified Christ becomes Dionysus burned at the stake; however, the chief result of the suffering and death of the gods is artistic, the eternal life not of the soul but of poetry and music.[7] The suffering has, Crane says, "cleared my tongue," recalled him to music. "Betrayed stones slowly speak," and the poet hears and sees in a moment of synaesthesia "Names peeling from Thine eyes." Crane regards this pattern of suffering, death, and rebirth as the only way of achieving meaning in life, and he associates the poet with Christ and Dionysus not only because the poet, like them, is victimized but because the poet's calling is a holy one. Only by spending himself, by purifying himself through fire, does the artist save himself and the unworthy world. Art is itself passion, death, and resurrection. It arises for Crane out of human suffering, requires the sacrifice of life, and is redeeming because it achieves an absolute experience beyond the imperfections of time.

Art is a release from life's pain in "Lachrymae Christi," and

6. For an extended discussion of the significance of Dionysus in modern poetry, see Monroe K. Spears, *Dionysus and the City* (New York: Oxford University Press, 1970). Spears discusses Crane's use of the figure.

7. Crane's use of religious imagery will be discussed more fully later, but here Elizabeth Jennings's comment is pertinent: "Crane employed many Christian words, signs and symbols. But, as with Rilke, he removed these things from the realm of strict orthodoxy and gave them a free life of their own. His imagination unyoked them from the bondage of dogma in order to liberate them for a visionary but less easily defined activity." See Elizabeth Jennings, *Every Changing Shape* (London: Andre Deutsch, 1961), p. 232.

images of transmutation and release (dissolving, opening, recalling, retrieving, unbinding) form the basic pattern of this poem. One image or scene dissolves into another as the poem progresses. The poem starts in springtime, but, far from the worlds of Christ and Dionysus, the opening scene is set in a modern mill town. There the pattern of release begins. The mill and the machinery inside are dissolved by the moon's rather technological "benzine / Rinsings." Having cleared the landscape of the mill, the poet turns in the second stanza to the springtime hillside where some kind of sacrifice is going on as the "fox's teeth" and thorns "freshen on the year's / First blood." And it is the bloodletting, the suffering and killing perhaps of the sheep, that releases the song where "the nights opening / Chant pyramids." The sacrificed sheep becomes by extension the Nazarene, whose death is associated with the "compulsion of the year," the springtime rites of Dionysus; the tears of Christ become the wine of the title and the grail becomes the "grail / Of earth." The "unyielding smile" of the machine in the modern world has become by the end of the poem the "Unmangled target smile" of Dionysus-Christ, and the process of the poem has been one of transformation and of releasing the meaning dormant in the world. By associating the mill with the wool it spins and the wool with the sheep and the sheep with the sacrificial lamb and the lamb with Christ and Christ with the symbol of suffering and dying and rebirth, the poet unmangles the machine world. The whole process of development in the poem is one of absorbing the complex and multiple meanings of the words into one permanent meaning, of purifying life into art.

The fire that burns Dionysus and thus purifies and renews the world appears at various junctures in Crane's work. In "The Dance" section of *The Bridge* the Indian sachem, Maquokeeta, performs a ritual dance and then, with the poet, is burned at the stake as a sacrifice to restore the earth's fertility and to release "the torrent and the singing tree," the fructifying rain and the eternal song that attends it. Again in *The Bridge* God reveals himself to Columbus and the modern subway voyager as a "Hand of Fire."

In "Ave Maria" the fiery corposant and destructive volcano are God's greetings to Columbus, whose suffering not only at the hands of the old world but in pursuit of his own true view of the new world makes him another version of the artist. He, too, is an exile from the world and creates his own world by overruling the accepted version of the real world. Another victim in *The Bridge* is Edgar Allan Poe, whose burned body appears in the modern subway of "The Tunnel":

> Whose body smokes along the bitten rails,
> Bursts from a smoldering bundle far behind
> In back forks of the chasms of the brain,—
> Puffs from a riven stump far out behind
> In interborough fissures of the mind . . . ?

In Crane's view Poe was victimized by a world that did not understand artists. But this world is destined to burn itself out, and what is left after this sacrificial fire will be God's "Hand of Fire," which annoints his true son, the artist.

Violence in Crane's poetry is not directed solely against the agonies of frustration that the world imposes upon the poet. Another poem of this period, "Passage," describes the poet's desire to rid himself of his memory because it is a "Casual louse"; it covers up, weaves together, gathers experience that the poet wants to uncover, unbind, scatter. As the poet leaves his memory in the ravine, "Dangerously the summer burned." Here the burning is a self-immolation in which his memory of the childhood season of summer is destroyed in the hope that the poet will be released from its hold upon him and thus from time. But his imagination, symbolized here again as the wind, "Died speaking through the ages." The imagination cannot destroy its material without destroying itself. In a sense, all the poet has is his memory, the real world. The poet returns in the second half of the poem to the ravine, psychologically appropriate as the resting place of memory, "To argue with the laurel." The laurel as the emblem of honor and fame is also the emblem of time and of art, and it is only by confronting it that one escapes the "iron coffin." Art that aims at purity is art that is always destined to fall short of its highest ideal. The imperfect world of time and memory, the imperfect vehicle of words, must be purified and perfected, but they cannot be annihilated by the poet. It is only through time and memory and words that we come to apprehend the eternal and wordless world. So the poet here is "turned about and back" to his "too well-known biography"; he cannot destroy it entirely without destroying all attempts to improve that biography through art. The poem ends in questions:

> What fountains did I hear? what icy speeches?
> Memory, committed to the page, had broke.

The poet does not know what he has learned, what forces overflowing into fountains he has released, but his memory has broken in the writing. The last line is rather puzzling, but if we are to take Crane's word that memory is for him a "Casual louse" that "Aprons rocks," it is possible to consider its breaking a good thing.

The wind that fails in "Passage" and rises at the end of "Possessions" plays also in "Recitative," but with a greater force than in the other poems. Once again it is a purifying wind, but in this poem it is also an abiding wind, not like the dying wind of "Passage" or the catastrophic wind of "Possessions." Still, it symbolizes here as in the other poems the imagination's power of transformation. In the middle stanza the poet explains this process:

> Look steadily—how the wind feasts and spins
> The brain's disk shivered against lust. Then watch
> While darkness, like an ape's face, falls away,
> And gradually white buildings answer day.

The poet seems to be describing a sleight-of-hand trick, a vanishing act, and his opening words in various stanzas ("Regard," "Inquire," "Look steadily") are designed to draw attention to the magic of the transformation. Here, as in "Possessions," the wind is a counter-force to lust. In "Possessions" the poet, tormented by his sexual desires, had been "Wounded by apprehensions out of speech"; his fears and frustrations had silenced his poetry. Not until the leveling white wind stirs at the end of the poem is the poet released from his anguish. In "Recitative" the brain is "shivered" against lust, a nice verb which suggests both a shattering into splinters and a fearful trembling, and in both senses the suffering and destruction of the man consumed with lust. The wind, the inspiriting power of the imagination, is again curative as it sets the brain in motion once more. It is also purifying and light-giving. Under its power the "ape's face," that aspect of man which is merely bestial and stupid, "falls away," and with it goes darkness and creative paralysis. In its place the "white buildings" of the created object are revealed. Like the "bright logic" of "Legend" and the "bright stones" of "Possessions," the "white buildings" are radiant with the power of the imagination, both destructive and creative. As the wind blows through Crane's inner landscape, it destroys the paralytic power of lust and liberates the poet's higher spirit from its grasp. At the same time the wind heralds a new day, a new light, new "white buildings" for the poet.

The three stanzas preceding this middle and crucial stanza detail the poet's suffering in a world of duplicity, his agonizing desire for unity, and his painful awareness of duality. The poet seems to be addressing an audience. In fact, Crane explains his purpose in "Recitative" in these terms. He says in a letter to Allen Tate: "Imagine the poet, say, on a platform speaking it. The audience is one half of Humanity, Man (in the sense of Blake) and the poet the other. Also, the poet sees himself in the audience as in a mirror. Also, the audience sees itself, in part, in the poet. Against this paradoxical DUALITY is posed the UNITY, or the conception of it (as you get it) in the last verse. In another sense, the poet is *talking to himself* all the way through the poem."[8] The theme of duality dominates the first two stanzas in the image of a mirror, the "Janus-faced" "capture" of the poet's point, the "Twin shadowed

8. *Letters*, p. 176.

halves" that torment him. The divisions in this poem are multiple, as Crane's letter indicates; they split man from man, man from himself, the poet from his audience, the body from the mind. But the imagination has a power to heal and unite all these divisions. It is not simply an inner force inspiring the poet and releasing him from his private suffering; it has a public power as well, energizing the poet's audience, uniting them with each other and the poet. The "white buildings" serve not only the poet but also his audience as proof of the certainty and endurance of the imagination in a divided and broken world. Although the remaining three stanzas do not minimize the torment and constriction of such a world, the tone in these stanzas is one of trust and assurance. "Let the same nameless gulf beleaguer us," "let her ribs palisade / Wrenched gold of Nineveh," the poet says. He willingly accepts the conditions of the modern world and of the divided self because he knows now that

> The bridge swings over salvage, beyond wharves;
> A wind abides the ensign of your will . . .

The connective bridge and the bright buildings are poetic constructs, works of the imagination which swing over and beyond the world of fragments. They are not only whole and complete themselves; they also provide the means of achieving wholeness. The bridge that swings over salvage and the buildings that answer day are visions that release us into a new dimension beyond the torment and confinement of the modern metropolis. The wind abides and inspires. If it does not, as in "Possessions," raze the world, it nonetheless inspires us to bypass the wrecks.

The last stanza opens with an image of unity:

> In alternating bells have you not heard
> All hours clapped dense into a single stride?

The question arises more from the poet's wonderment than from his desire for a confirming answer. And he invites his audience to share with him his new-found sense of wholeness. He says, "let us walk through time with equal pride." The bells' "single stride" is a model for the communion of all men. The purpose of the poet in "Recitative" is to unite the divided world, the divided self, the isolated poet, and he accomplishes his aim through art and through the revivifying powers of the imagination. Crane's claims for the restorative and unifying power of the imagination are vast in "Recitative." The wind that abides his will not only inspires the poet but revitalizes the whole community of man. Crane was to make this point more elaborately in "For the Marriage of Faustus and Helen" and *The Bridge,* and it is crucial to his concept of creativity.

The wind in these early poems is symbolic; it blows chiefly on Crane's interior landscape. However, Crane spent the fall of 1926 in the Caribbean and lived through a real hurricane which must have convinced him of the rightness of his choice of symbols. He made the hurricane the subject of two poems and a fragment of a poem, none totally successful but all interesting as expressions of the ecstasy that destruction aroused in Crane. The hurricane filled him with the same raptures that the wind storms inspired in Shelley and Wordsworth. As it uprooted trees, washed out roads, and destroyed houses, Crane watched with exhilaration. The morning after the storm was one of celebration, dancing, cleaning up, and mingling with the sailors who had come to the rescue.[9]

The details of this particular hurricane are presented in a very straightforward form in "Eternity," which rises from mere accounting only by the brilliance of its inclusiveness and the excitement of the recorder. The scene described is one of confusion and destruction in which everything has been blown about and randomly strewn over the landscape; but the world's upending actually energizes the poet, who rushes from place to place with the wind's willfulness exclaiming over the damage. The poem moves from exclamation point to exclamation point as the speaker surveys

9. See John Unterecker, *Voyager: A Life of Hart Crane* (New York: Farrar, Straus and Giroux, 1969), p. 456.

the whole scene from house to town to beyond the sea and back again to house, town, and seaside bar. The death and destruction "didn't so much matter," the poet tells us, as the sheer power of the cyclone, the "memoried night / Of screaming rain—Eternity!" The destructive winds have razed the landscape in the night, but the morning brings a new kind of life. The roof of the house has reached Yucatan, the streets are full of injured people, "cotted negroes" are housed in the only building, the wharf is "unsandwiched," Havana is rumored "halfway under water with fires," the "sinking carcass" of the mule is "death predestined," and the atmosphere is "dense with carrion hazes." "Everything gone—or strewn in riddled grace." But the grace of the destruction is a new and lavish life: a "frantic peacock," the "ogre sun" that licks "the grass, as black as patent / Leather, which the rimed white wind had glazed." Then appears "the strange gratuity of horses" with "one, white," "Like a vast phantom maned." The white horse recalls the apocalypse, the destruction of this world and the building up of a new one, but here it seems to be, like the white wind, a symbol of the imagination.

For the poet, the night of storm has been forever "memoried" because he has seen with his own eyes a natural analogue of the poet's way. To turn the whole world upside down, to uproot and unsandwich old certainties, to funnel like the tornado into the universe with an imaginative energy that will release the secret of eternity, the "riddled grace" of the world, is the poet's role. At the end of the poem the poet is celebrating the storm at a bar; others in town set about the humdrum tasks of burying the dead and rebuilding the houses. In fact, the poet too has "shoveled and sweated," but his real response to the storm is to celebrate its primeval energy.

A more poeticized rendition of the events of "Eternity" is "The Hurricane," where again the destruction of the winds is the prime subject:

> Nought stayeth, nought now bideth
> But's smithereened apart!

But this "chisel wind" is also liberating as "Scripture flee'th stone" under its power. It uproots ("e'en boulders now out-leap / Rock sockets, levin-lathered!"), it purifies ("Rescindeth flesh from bone"), and it destroys ("summits crashing / Whip sea-kelp screaming on blond / Sky-seethe, dense heaven dashing—"). All this release and destruction is described in the most constrained and artificially poetic language, yet there is a sense in which the inflated rhetoric of its apostrophe is a fitting medium for this aeolian gambade and for its inspiriting effects upon the poet.

Among Crane's poetic effects was one more treatment of the hurricane, "The Return," a four-line footnote on the power of the wind, which, in the sea storm it creates, "spouted, sheared / Back into bosom—me—her, into natal power. . . ." The poem is a confusion of heterosexual symbolism and rampant phallicism (campanile, spout, "column kiss") and of the suicidal urge that emerged in Crane's imagination from time to time, but in the hurricane at sea Crane also saw the "natal power" of the universe, the dynamism that created the world and was the model of the poet's creative activity. What Crane admired in the cyclonic force of the Caribbean wind was its primitive energy, which he saw as sacred. The wind that foretells eternity, releases Scripture, and returns us to natal power destroys the old world only to create the new and purer world, and so, like the fire, it is purgative.

The violence of poetic vision is the subject of the last poem Crane wrote before he committed suicide. Read as his epitaph, "The Broken Tower" has been given elaborate significance.[10] The brokenness of the title and of the major symbol in the poem has been generally regarded as Crane's indictment of the modern world and a summary of the kind of poetry he could write. However, given the background of violence and destruction in his

10. Marius Bewley first set forth the interpretation of the poem as Crane's own recognition that the tower of absolute vision was too high to climb in his art. Here, according to Bewley, Crane expresses most clearly his sense that a Platonic vision of the world is never realizable in art and he must content himself with the limits and distortions of mortal vision. See Marius Bewley, "Hart Crane's Last Poem," *Accent*, XIX (Spring 1959), 75–85.

poetry, it is possible to assume that the brokenness is salutary. The tower has been broken by the bells, and the brokenness is part of the victory of the poet over the concrete and obdurate world and also part of the victory of the poem over the constricted and enclosed self. As early as "Recitative" Crane had urged the poet to "leave the tower"; here, at the end of his life, he describes this action:

> The bells, I say, the bells break down their tower;
> And swing I know not where. Their tongues engrave
> Membrane through marrow, my long-scattered score
> Of broken intervals . . . And I, their sexton slave!

The tower has been broken by the music of the poetic bells, not by the world. In an earlier version the bells "sing" and "Their tongues engrave / My terror mid the unharnessed skies." It is the overpowering and outpouring and barrier-breaking poetic energy that survives. The poet says he has "entered the broken world" and in a sense it is the shattered modern world, the world of time and imperfection, but it is also the world that he has broken, the world whose message he has released from its prison, from its dead form. At the end of "The Broken Tower" the poet reconstructs a tower, not the constricting church bell tower or the stone tower but the tower of poetry within the "matrix of the heart." The poem ends:

> And builds, within, a tower that is not stone
> (Not stone can jacket heaven)—but slip
> Of pebbles,—visible wings of silence sown
> In azure circles, widening as they dip
>
> The matrix of the heart, lift down the eye
> That shrines the quiet lake and swells a tower . . .
> The commodious, tall decorum of that sky
> Unseals her earth, and lifts love in its shower.

The broken tower and the chiming bells that break it symbolize many things poetically here: the constriction of mortality and the immortal song of the poet, the limits of words and the music that transcends them, the obdurate world and the life that is released poetically from it, the isolation of the poet and the love that destroys that isolation.

Breaking and razing and destroying are not negative actions for Crane; they are always the way to affirmation.[11] As in "Possessions," where the white wind razes all but "bright stones," so here there remains to the poet the "slip / Of pebbles," his enduring poetry. And the poetic act in "The Broken Tower," as in "Possessions," is somehow conjoined with the sex act. Tormented by his lust, the speaker in "Possessions" says:

> I know the screen, the distant flying taps
> And stabbing medley that sways—
> And the mercy, feminine, that stays
> As though prepared.

In "The Broken Tower" the same torment is expressed and the same sweet feminine figure appears:

> The steep encroachments of my blood left me
> No answer (could blood hold such a lofty tower
> As flings the question true?)—or is it she
> Whose sweet mortality stirs latent power?

The woman in the later poems acts creatively (as she does not in "Possessions") upon his passion as she arouses in him not only sexual but poetic power as well.

Hovering on the fringes of this poem about poetry and love and sex is also some notion about Crane's life or memory. Lewis has noted the echoes and reminders of earlier poems in "The Broken

---

11. Here Crane is close to William Carlos Williams, who also celebrated the poetic power that breaks through restrictions and generates new growth. Williams said in "A Sort of a Song," "Saxifrage is my flower that splits / the rocks." In *Spring and All*, originally published in 1923, Williams defines the imagination in terms congenial to Crane: "The imagination, intoxicated by prohibitions, rises to drunken heights to destroy the world. Let it rage, let it kill. The imagination is supreme. To it all our works forever, from the remotest past to the farthest future, have been, are and will be dedicated. . . . To it now we come to dedicate our secret project: the annihilation of every human creature on the face of the earth. . . . None to remain; nothing but the lower vertebrates, the mollusks, insects and plants. Then at last will the world be made anew." See William Carlos Williams, *Spring & All* (Columbus, Ohio: Frontier Press, 1970), pp. 5–6.

Tower"; in fact, he sees it as a recapitulation of Crane's poetic moments and visionary achievements.[12] Certainly his past life was on his mind as he wrote regretfully about "the knell / Of a spent day" in the first stanza. In commenting on the role of memory in Crane's poetry, Herbert Leibowitz refers to this poem: "His restless memory continually brings forth questions he cannot answer. Memory recalls his 'long-scattered score / Of broken intervals,' his betrayals of himself and his muse, his seasons in hell; but it also brings back, and adds, 'The angelus of wars my chest evokes,' those elating times he 'entered the broken world / To trace the visionary company of love,' and found that the word he poured *was* cognate with his finest imaginings."[13]

It is true that the poet's memory of his personal life is disturbing. The "curse of sundered parentage," as he said in "Quaker Hill," as well as his homosexual proclivities made of his life a series of "broken intervals." But it is also true that by reshaping the fragments of his life into poetry, he seeks to heal the brokenness and to reveal what is through the creative process made "original now, and pure." If "sundered parentage" is a curse, it also "unfolds a new destiny to fill," and it was this new destiny that Crane sought in poetry.

Another version of this process is seen in the "Van Winkle" section of *The Bridge*:

> So memory, that strikes a rhyme out of a box,
> Or splits a random smell of flowers through glass—
> Is it the whip stripped from the lilac tree
> One day in spring my father took to me,
> Or is it the Sabbatical, unconscious smile
> My mother almost brought me once from church
> And once only, as I recall—?

This passage demonstrates the way in which Crane uses memory. Memory strikes a rhyme out of a box. He remembers and he writes.

12. Lewis, *Poetry of Hart Crane*, p. 411.
13. Herbert A. Leibowitz, *Hart Crane* (New York: Columbia University Press, 1968), pp. 119–120.

The striking of a rhyme is occasioned by the memory of the father's whipping.[14] The sense of pain and loss experienced as a child and remembered as an adult causes the poet to create, to strike in quite a different way. Like the question at the end of "Passage," the question the poet asks here is posed as a surmise. Perhaps it is this deepest psychic hurt that causes him to write poetry. His memory is of his father's striking him and the split he recognized even as a child in his mother's affections, but Crane realizes also that as he uses his memory poetically, it can strike and split creatively. The poetry of memory has the power to release the poet from the boxed-in sense of his life, from a constricting self-enclosure. The revelations of his memories are painful but perhaps, Crane suggests, liberating.

In "Repose of Rivers," another poem of memory, Crane again forms into a pattern the various elements he had used in the poems just discussed. The wind that gathers its force in the monsoon, the scalding heat of his hectic activity that is matched by the city's torment and the Caribbean summer, images familiar enough now in Crane's poetry, work here in a strangely reminiscent way, as if the poet were recalling not simply actual scenes but the entire landscape of his life and his poetry. The occasion of the poem perhaps does most to explain its reflective and nostalgic tone. It was written when Crane returned to his family's house on Isle of Pines to work on *The Bridge*. The return accounts for the Proustian sensations he experienced, his sense of something forgotten and now remembered, evoked by feelings that are recovered from the landscape of their source. But his mood, unusually receptive to such reminiscences, derived also from a writing block. When he wrote "Repose of Rivers," he had not been able to start work on *The*

14. Thomas Vogler calls these two of the most important memories in the whole poem. He says that Crane "may even be asking the psychological question whether this is the source of his need to find now, in his adult life, some means of assimilating this early experience into a pattern of benignity." See Thomas A. Vogler, *Preludes to Vision* (Berkeley and Los Angeles: Unversity of California Press, 1971), p. 159.

Bridge, and his sense of creative failure may have contributed to the muted tone.[15]

The image of the wind that usually is the herald of a new imaginative life in Crane's poetry and rises most often at the climax of the poem opens this one with its "slow sound," its "seething, steady leveling of the marshes." In its slow and steady movement it does not appear to be either a destructive or a purifying wind. As the poet listens to it, his memory is stirred by it, but he actually recalls scenes sheltered from its refreshing force: the "steep alcoves" that drew him "into hades almost," the "black gorge," "the singular nestings in the hills." He says, "How much I would have bartered!" And in this exclamation he expresses the regret that he has dwelt so long away from the wind. Yet he also recalls

> The pond I entered once and quickly fled—
> I remember now its singing willow rim.

Here is a fleeting moment of joy. At the start of the poem the willows had carried a slow sound; now they are transformed by the poet's memory into singing trees, responsive to the wind's movement, as the poet himself is now responsive. As in "Passage," he joins the entrainments of the wind, following its course finally to the restorative sea. The way is, as always, through the torment of the city, but its direction is toward a vision:

> And finally, in that memory all things nurse;
> After the city that I finally passed
> With scalding unguents spread and smoking darts
> The monsoon cut across the delta
> At gulf gates . . . There, beyond the dykes
>
> I heard wind flaking sapphire, like this summer,
> And willows could not hold more steady sound.

The monsoon, a seasonal wind of the Indian Ocean, is a symbol of the release enacted in this poem. It blows in from the sea, and at

15. I would not go so far as R. W. B. Lewis, who claims that the poem is auto-elegiac, although his reading of the poem is at every point instructive. See Lewis, *Poetry of Hart Crane,* pp. 211–215.

the same time it attracts the poet's attention to the sea, and the vision he achieves is again brilliant. The image of waves in "flaking sapphire" is, as Paul suggests, "an image of cool gemlike beauty, of precious brightness, that is visual as well as aural."[16] It belongs to the series of bright images that symbolize in Crane's poetry the imagination's effects: the "bright logic" of "Legend," "the bright stones" of "Possessions," the "white buildings" of "Recitative." The "flaking sapphire" is here more closely tied to the natural scene, the wind's rippling action on the water. Its brilliance and refreshment are contrasted to the "noon's / Tyranny" on land where mammoth turtles "Yielded, while sun-silt rippled them / Asunder...." The poet says at the start that "age had brought me to the sea," but it is only by retracing his journey in his memory through the contrasting experience of "hades" that the poet is able to bring himself imaginatively to the sea and the wind's inspiriting power. Once again in Crane's poetry the process of regeneration is through suffering and pain, here remembered and outlived.

In commenting on this passage, Elizabeth Jennings says, "If his poetry often seems at white heat, it is never chaotic; there is no sense of sprawling or anarchy. . . . What he often achieves most triumphantly is a sense of tamed violence."[17] She is right in identifying the sensations in this ending as tamed violence, but it does not seem to me the characteristic mood of Crane's poetry. "Repose of Rivers" is an unusually tamed poem because it is a work of memory, and it details not the chaos and anarchy of immediately lived experience but the recollection of a journey that seems finally purposeful. The penultimate stanza of "Repose of Rivers" is reminiscent of the point in "Legend" where the poet seems actually to be enduring the torment which will release his poem. The "scalding unguents" and "smoking darts" are as vividly imagined as their exact counterparts in "Legend," "the smoking souvenir" and "Bleeding eidolon," but in "Legend" the poet insists that he must

16. Paul, *Hart's Bridge*, p. 108.
17. Jennings, *Every Changing Shape*, p. 230.

endure again and again this suffering while in "Repose of Rivers" he suggests that he has finally passed beyond it. The monsoon that cuts across the delta seems to cut off the poet from his torment, and he reaches finally a place of repose. But repose, as Paul suggests, seems to involve deprivation.[18] Despite the triumphant movement of this poem, the ending contains within it a kind of finality. One suspects that this poet will not step the legend of his youth back into the noon.

The imagery of razing, burning, and breaking is central to Crane's poetry.[19] Violence is deeply ingrained in his imagination. His apprehension of life in the modern metropolitan world was of torment, brokenness, burning, and destruction, but there was no easy retreat for him into the sanctuary of his own heart; there, too, was a torture chamber of consuming lust, unassuaged desire, broken efforts. In a sense, the agonies of the world and the agonies of his heart were one, and he saw himself tormented equally by the smoking darts without and the stabbing medley within. Suffering is the pattern of his life and art, and he came to regard it not only as inevitable but as desirable. Suffering, he told his mother, is a real purification, and only through suffering, he felt, could any true happiness be realized.[20] What he meant by that statement is made clear in the poetry just surveyed. To be consumed by lust until lust burns itself out and leaves the "pure possession" is to suffer and be purified. To break one's memory is to expose moments of deep

18. Paul, *Hart's Bridge,* p. 109.

19. These images call to mind the whole tradition of apocalyptic literature. In fact, in a recent survey R. W. B. Lewis has associated Crane with this tradition and particularly with what M. H. Abrams has identified among the English Romantic poets as "apocalypses of imagination." The old millennial hope is shifted from history to the mind, from external action to the imaginative act, and the marriage between the Lamb and the New Jerusalem of the biblical apocalyse becomes a marriage between subject and object, between mind and nature, which creates a new world out of the old world of sense. See Lewis, "Days of Wrath and Laughter," in R. W. B. Lewis, *Trials of the Word* (New Haven, Conn.: Yale University Press, 1965), pp. 201–202. However, the emphasis in Crane is always on the actual torment, on the process of purification rather than on the revelation.

20. *Letters,* p. 164.

psychic pain, but it is also to "strike a rhyme." To raze the world is to cause suffering, but it also reveals the "bright stones" of the imagination.

Suffering for Crane is not action; it involves no choice. It cannot be averted. It is neither dramatic nor tragic. Nor, on the other hand, is suffering in Crane's mind absurd like Sisyphus's travail. It is rather the symbol of the poet's serious calling. Others do not suffer in the same way; there are those, Crane felt, *"untwisted by the love of things irreconcilable."* They live in a "dimensional" world. But the poet is twisted; he does suffer because he longs for an undimensional and unbounded world. Suffering in Crane's poetry is then regarded not as the shared condition of man but as the special condition of the poet. While the poet may be aware that others suffer, he is most concerned with his own experience and with its function in the creative process. Although the anguish in Crane's poems seems to stem from fairly common sources (lust, loss, unrequited love), it always functions as part of the uncommon creative act. Crane's poetic images are fired into brilliance by his anguish. The "bright stones" and "flaking sapphire" are effects of the imagination won only through torment and the expense of spirit. In one poem, at least, Crane associates the poet's suffering with the passion and death of Christ and Dionysus, and he imagines it as a holy sacrifice which will release a new meaning and a new life for the world. Usually, however, the poet-sufferer in Crane's work is not divine but human, tormented by his isolation and twisted by his love, yet still in some way specially marked by his pain.

Crane does not regret his suffering nor does he try to evade it. But he certainly does not seek it either. He does not submit to torment in order to purify the flesh. Rather, the pattern of suffering in his poems suggests that he is a lavish poet who will not spare himself even when he realizes that his experience will be a torment. He spends out himself again and again because he cannot save himself. He is possessed by emotions which overpower him, and only as they expend themselves, only as they exhaust him, is he purified of them. The purity won in this process is not a childlike innocence but an emptiness, a consummation, in which the poet is made ready for the arrival of imaginative insight. The creative act is a pattern of repeated torment, self-expenditure, frenzy, and release. The "pure possession" of the imagination is attained only by passing straight through and moving beyond the pain of experience. Imaginative inspiration is not a guiding spirit through that pain; it is rather the survivor's reward. The inspiriting wind, the light-giving fire, the revelatory breakage, all analogues of the imagination's regenerative force, appear in Crane's poetry only after much suffering. They visit only the contrite and exhausted spirit. However, in their coming they transform the poet.

The poems surveyed in this chapter end at the very moment that seems most interesting, the moment in which the "bright logic" is won. These poems are condensed versions of the poet's legend. In three long poems Crane worked out in more elaborate detail the patterned movement of the poet inspired by the brilliance of the imagination. This pattern, discussed in the next chapter, details more intricately the "pure possession."

chapter three: The Poet as Possessor

Beyond suffering and violence in Crane's consciousness is the more powerful desire for the "pure possession," a desire to be "possessed" by the poetic spirit and at the same time to possess the muse and through her the world, the word, the poem. The pattern of the poet as violator is linked in his poetry to the dream of the poet as possessor, and in a sense discussion of one cannot avoid mention of the other. But in various poems the power of one dream absorbs the other, and even in the simultaneity of these impulses it is possible to describe the dominance of one. Yoking violence and possession evokes certain erotic connotations present in the relationship between the poet and the muse. While other poets have worshipped the muse, Crane, agonized by his desire for her, pursues her wildly, longs to know her, and suffers miserably because she eludes him. The ideas of violence and possession coalesce in Crane's mature poetry around three feminine figures: Helen in "For the Marriage of Faustus and Helen," the unnamed beloved and the sea in "Voyages," and Pocahontas in "Powhatan's Daughter," Section II of *The Bridge*.

Ostensibly these three figures stand for beauty, and to possess beauty is to possess much more, to possess in Crane's view all that is most sacred to the poet: light, harmony, unity, even the song with which to celebrate beauty. But these figures are not so easily possessed; in fact, they seem to be perversely elusive, tantalizingly remote, and even cruelly indifferent to the poet. Their pursuit is torment; it leads to destruction and yet paradoxically to a rebirth. These figures may be identified as feminine since two of them have feminine names, but in Crane's consciousness they exist chiefly as demon spirits. Although they are connected with beauty, they are themselves frequently imaged as Medusa-like figures. Helen is "in final chains," and in one view she is replaced by the "incunabula of the divine grotesque." Pocahontas appears with "Time like a serpent down her shoulder, dark, / And space, an eaglet's wing, laid on her hair." The unnamed figure in "Voyages" is called "Prodigal" and identified chiefly by a tormenting absence. As muses, all three figures are remarkably silent: Helen is identified with "hiatus," in "Voyages" the figure's breath is "sealed by the ghosts I do not know," and Pocahontas is a "speechless dream of snow." Also, despite the passionate heat of the poet, the figure he pursues remains cold and pure. Yet she persists in his dream as a tantalizing smile that attracts and torments him. Finally, this beautiful object demands as her tribute the destruction of her pursuer. Only through his destruction is the song he longs to sing released from him.

In each of these three poems or series of poems, the figure appears first to the poet in a dream or in a dreamlike moment of ecstasy as in "Voyages," and he is puzzled not only by her identity but by her relationship to him. He touches her, holds her, but does not possess her, although he imagines that he could consummate his passion for her. But, almost immediately, she withdraws, and the pain of her withdrawal is immensely energizing to him. It leads to a resurgence of vitality which impels him to search her out, and this quest forms the structure of the poems that follow. As he pursues her, she becomes transmuted into the atmosphere, one with the elements, until the whole world in which he moves is a dreamlike landscape of beckoning arms and hands, smiles and tears, in which the elements are permeated with this demon spirit. The solitary poet at first identifies himself with the elements, transfers his lust to the land and sea, until he is absorbed completely in their frenzy. In the course of the search the feminine muse and the masculine poet who desires her form a rhythmic pattern in which not so much sexual consummation is the object as the poet's desire for the eternal continuance of the state of ecstasy and pain which the search entails. In one sense the poet's fantasy, dramatized as a desire for the physical possession of a woman and then transferred to a landscape animated by sexual passion, is a fantasy of eroticism in which the poet indulges his unbridled passion. When the poet seeks to be married to beauty as in the title of "For the Marriage of Faustus and Helen," what he seeks ultimately is not the union of man and woman, fact and fancy, the imagination and beauty, the real and ideal worlds, but the ecstatic and frenzied arousal of his own psychic powers to that harmonious instant of complete "possession." Only in this moment is his passion purified.

This dream of being possessed or of self-possession becomes then neither a willful surrender to sensations nor the self-indulgent thrills of an aesthete, nor can it be simply described as the veiled projection of his homosexuality. The pattern of this dream is developed and repeated because Crane associates it not merely with his own apotheosis but with the beatification of the whole world. The poet possessed is the poet as possessor. His imaginative powers are vitalized not for some private ecstatic orgy but for the release of the world from its deadened and death-dealing state. Helen is not simply the projection of Crane's private erotic fantasy; she is imagined as the counter-force to destruction, and, as such, she is the creative spirit which animates the poet's imaginative world. In "Voyages" the figure becomes a goddess who transforms the cold and threatening world into Belle Isle. And in "Powhatan's Daughter" Pocahontas is associated with the vitalism of the American continent, lost in the mythic past and recovered by the poet to prevail against the dead present. By examining the three works closely, it is possible to describe the elaborate and intricate pattern of this fantasy and to understand its central place in Crane's consciousness.

"For the Marriage of Faustus and Helen"

This three-part work, written in 1922 and 1923, is the first long and ambitious poem Crane attempted, and, despite its imperfections, it is important as his first formulation of the dream of possession. In the poetical trappings of its title and epigraph it shows certain unassimilated influences of T. S. Eliot, but in this series of poems Crane also found his own poetic voice, and the power of the work is quite independent of its influences. Part I opens with a daytime view of the poet's mind "Divided by accepted multitudes." The poet lives in the crowded city, suffers the "stacked partitions" of the business day, and shares the fragmentation and divisiveness of city life, although even here his "mind is brushed by sparrow wings." He is, however alienated, still receptive to hints from another world. City-bound as he is, he imagines that the "wings flash out equivocations," glimmers of release from the deceptions of the city. But it is only in "the graduate opacities of evening" that the poet is freed from the city world, which is dissolved into "somewhere / Virginal perhaps, less fragmentary, cool." Unlike the certainty of the daytime description, the evening's details are tentatively given. It is a world of possibility as yet unrealized, and the change from day to night is set off by three italicized lines:

> *There is the world dimensional for*
> *those untwisted by the love of things*
> *irreconcilable . . .*

These lines, borrowed from "The Bridge of Estador," where the poet says "some are twisted with the love / Of things irreconcilable," contain two meanings.[1] In one sense Crane seems to be

---

1. Paul examines the submerged meanings in the imagery of the stanza which precedes these lines and makes some useful suggestions about the double thrust of

summarizing the dimensional city world of "memoranda, baseball scores," and "stock quotations," and to be suggesting that there is a world that can be measured and defined in a rational, mathematical way which is perfectly satisfactory to those *"untwisted"* by a desire for things that cannot be reconciled in this way. At the same time, in these three lines he suggests that there is another dimension beyond the rational world, and in what Lewis notes as the slight stress on the word *"There,"* he points to that dimension, that magnitude, which cannot be so easily confined.[2] It is this dimension that the poet enters in the night, although it is a gradual transfer and at first the poet feels "lost yet poised in traffic." Still, in this state of suspended animation he feels that here he might find Helen's eyes, "flickering with those prefigurations," flashing like her harbinger, the sparrow.

Despite his hope, Helen appears to him first not as a spirit released from the world but as one at least partially attached to it, "Half-riant before the jerky window frame" where her hands "count the nights / Stippled with pink and green advertisements." She is not very appealing, and as the ugly world frames her, the poet must exert his imaginative power to envision her beauty. Only in his dream is his vision bright, as the poet says:

> Imminent in his dream, none better knows
> The white wafer cheek of love, or offers words
> Lightly as moonlight on the eaves meets snow.

The vision flickering earlier in the poem becomes a dream of whiteness against the dark and of purity: the poet associates himself with the moonlight and the lady with the snow, and, like the snow, she is white and cold.

However, in the next stanza the identification with the elements is reversed, and the spirit of beauty is associated with the sky while the poet is absorbed by the earth:

---

words like "rebuffed," "margins," and "convoy." He does not pursue the submerged meaning in these lines, however. See Paul, *Hart's Bridge,* pp. 66–67.

2. Lewis, *Poetry of Hart Crane,* p. 93.

> Reflective conversion of all things
> At your deep blush, when ecstasies thread
> The limbs and belly, when rainbows spread
> Impinging on the throat and sides . . .
> Inevitable, the body of the world
> Weeps in inventive dust for the hiatus
> That winks above it, bluet in your breasts.

The blush and wink of the sky woman mark her as warm and sensual as well as coy and tantalizing, and quite distinct from the cold and pure spirit of snow. Not only is the poet sensuously responsive to her but his state of ecstasy charges the whole atmosphere of his world. While his gift of words had been first imagined as the dim light of the moon, it is now refracted into a rainbow. The body of the world with which he now associates himself becomes "inventive dust" through the inspiration of the female deity, and his passion is released in weeping. But this orgiastic release is vented on a void as the woman becomes a "hiatus," and through the flower in her breast, the bluet, also known as innocence, she retains her virginal associations. But the shifting female image energizes him. It is to this elusive and virginal Helen and to the world of purity and solitude she demands that he pledges himself. His imagination desires to move beyond the city with its "million brittle, bloodshot eyes":

> White, through white cities passed on to assume
> That world which comes to each of us alone.

He longs for an ecstatic state inspired by Helen but enjoyed alone. Helen has been imagined as known by other lovers and even possessed at last "in final chains," but ideally only the poet can truly know her and possess her in the chastity of his passion and adoration. Only the poet can respond to Helen's beauty because only the poet is capable of a pure response to beauty.

The Helen that Crane meets in his dream is a complex image of the feminine ideal. In her coyness and attractiveness she appears to be the traditional Helen, slightly romanticized; yet she is also

Helen spiritualized and recast as an image of purity whom the poet simultaneously adores and wishes to possess, and in the end she is represented as a figure who arouses a passion that is permitted because it is unconsummatable. As the symbol of beauty, Helen in this part of the poem is envisioned as flickering, cold, remote, chaste, and unmarriable. These attributes are given to Helen by the poet, whose attitude toward her is chivalric. He lifts his arms to her and prays to her to "Accept a lone eye riveted to your plane." Helen here seems to belong to the tradition of courtly love. The poet's devotion to her will bring him into contact with an ideal world; it will be an instructive passion. The erotic enthusiasms she inspires in him will be beaten out, spent, until they are purified into an ideal and eternal love that will "beat, continuous, to hour-less days— / One inconspicuous, glowing orb of praise." The plane of Helen is an exalted one, purposefully exalted by the poet, who raises it above the city world of "steel and soil." In his devotion to that plane the poet tries to elevate himself from his lowly, mortal, and metropolitan condition. By putting the woman out of reach, he intensifies his pleasure as well as his suffering. He is caught between the fragmentary real world that he spurns and the whole and harmonic world of Helen, who spurns him.

The tension between his pure devotion and his sensuous desire collapses in the "guilty song" of Part II. He dances out the ecstasies of limb and belly that arise accidentally in his dream of Part I. Curiously enough, he moves upward, away from the crowded daytime curbs to a roof garden, but the atmosphere is, if anything, more frenetic there. The "metallic paradises" of these "gardened skies" resound with "snarling hails of melody." Here everything is permitted, and the restraints of his devotion to Helen are removed. But here again he is alone, dancing by himself. He addresses a woman who has become a "divine grotesque," a siren, with the idea that "you may fall downstairs with me" or "plaintively scud past shores." The woman in this poem is only someone he could take but does not. Her accessibility makes her undesirable. She is "Striated with nuances, nervosities / That we are heir to," not remote and cool but tormented like the poet. To possess her would be to yield to his baser needs. She smiles at him and he confesses that he cannot frown at her, but it is a guilty admission. In his fantasy he imagines that the aerial realm of the sky woman has merged with the poet's earthly realm, but the merger is unsatisfying.

The hiatus that winks above the earth, the sky realm of Helen as the spirit of beauty, is assaulted in Part III by the poet now turned into a modern fighter pilot who becomes the "Capped arbiter of beauty." In a sense, the gunman in the airplane releases the sexual rage and violence that has built up in this poem against the hiatus of the female sky spirit. In a fury of destruction the poet as pilot mounts and saddles the sky and shakes "down vertical / Repeated play of fire." The poet associates himself with the gunman as he says, "We know, eternal gunman, our flesh remembers." And, indeed, his flesh remembers the tormenting ecstasy, inspired by Helen in Part I, that can know its only release in death. But as soon as he confesses his memories, partakes of the ritual rape, he recovers his voice as a poet and the true lover of ideal beauty and dissociates himself from the gunman:

> We did not ask for that, but have survived,
> And will persist to speak again before
> All stubble streets that have not curved
> To memory, or known the ominous lifted arm
> That lowers down the arc of Helen's brow
> To saturate with blessing and dismay.

The arms that he pledged in Part I to lift in praise of Helen have become ominous in their association with the gunman, and yet he recovers from his fantasy of violence to

> Laugh out the meager penance of their days
> Who dare not share with us the breath released,
> The substance drilled and spent beyond repair
> For golden, or the shadow of gold hair.

His laughter is a psychic release, a venting of his feeling on the tantalizing "Half-riant" female spirit. Through destruction and assault he has spent his passion, possessed the golden spirit, released his poem. The mood here and in the stanza that precedes it recalls the creative destruction of "Legend," where the poet yields to the fire to win its "bright logic." In a letter to Waldo Frank, Crane underscores this connection in describing Part III as "Dionysian in its attitude, the creator and the eternal destroyer dance arm in arm, etc., all ending in a restatement of the imagination."[3] The extent to which the poet must dance with destruction is made clear in his admission:

> The lavish heart shall always have to leaven
> And spread with bells and voices, and atone
> The abating shadows of our conscript dust.

The lavish heart is the poet's heart pledged to Helen's purity yet not immune to the destructions of the world and the flesh. It is also the heart that persists and speaks again its "continuous" praise even in the midst of destruction. The supplication to Helen in Part I is one means of worshipping her. Another act of devotion is the self-expenditure of the poet, who spends himself beyond repair in the quest of Helen and thus spreads with "bells and voices" the void. The lavish heart does not despair of seeking beauty through and beyond the actual war-torn world. The lover of beauty has always had to overcome death by yielding to a purifying fire. The plight of the modern poet is, Crane insists here against Eliot's testimony, the plight of all poets throughout the ages. The creative act always takes place in the shadow of death. Crane reinforces his point by including in his poem reference to what seemed to his generation the unprecedented horror of the aerial warfare of World War I. We have survived even that, he boasts, and suggests that the survival must be imaginative as well as physical. He does not minimize the horror, nor on the other hand is he silenced by it. He accepts the actual violence of war as he accepts the violence that arises in his psyche in response to his pursuit of beauty. However,

3. *Letters*, p. 121.

the violence of war is destructive while the violence of art is creative. The poem ends in praise:

> Distinctly praise the years, whose volatile
> Blamed bleeding hands extend and thresh the height
> The imagination spans beyond despair,
> Outpacing bargain, vocable and prayer.

The "Blamed bleeding hands" are guilty of the bloodshed of
modern warfare, but they are also the hands of those that have
suffered and survived. They are, like the "Bleeding eidolon" of
"Legend," symbols of suffering. They join the poet's lifted arms
of Part I in an act of supplication. Once again Crane enacts a ritual
of sacrifice and purification. The action here is reminiscent of the
moment in "Possessions" where he purifies his lust by holding it up
"against a disk of light," and it also recalls the prayer to the sacrificed god in "Lachrymae Christi" to "Lift up in lilac-emerald
breath the grail / Of earth again."

What is being praised here is the poet's persistent imagination,
the years of devotion to beauty, the suffering endured and survived
in its quest, and its ultimately elevating effect. Threshing the
heights, the poet repeats his pledge of Part I to follow "companion
ways / That beat, continuous, to hourless days." The way has not
been without its torment and fury. It has been no easy transcendent
path but by acts of blame and bleeding, violence and destruction.
The imagination that desires so much and despairs precisely because its aims are so high and pure still "spans beyond" and out-
paces all other means of access to that height. The poet is elevated
by his devotion to the exalted Helen, whose heights still inspire
him.

The pattern of this series of poems works out from a fleeting
moment of erotic ecstasy, which the poet attempts first to imagine
as a state of intense purity, and then reveals as a grotesque dance,
and finally transforms into a fury of destruction which releases
him into a new affirmation. Although the title calls for a marriage

between Faustus, whom Crane describes in his letters as the imaginative man, and Helen, the spirit of beauty, the only actor in the poem is the poet, and the marriage is the achievement of a new state of release and elevation. Devotion to Helen leads not to her possession but rather to the possession of imaginative powers. In her service the poet is able to unbind his throat, release his breath. The poem, for all its torment, is a hymn of praise from the poet to his liberated and liberating imagination. The "glowing orb of praise" of Part I, the glee and "Blest excursion" of Part II, and the imagination that "spans beyond despair" in Part III express the delight the poet experiences in his erotic dream. There is no letdown in this poem; it whirls always upward into new heights of ecstasy. In expressing his frenzied desire, his song becomes "Three-winged and gold-shod prophecies of heaven." The "hiatus" of the heavens, the void that tantalized him in the beginning of the poem, is filled by the imaginative powers of poetry. It is this power to "spread with bells and voices" the emptiness of the world that is the ultimate triumph of this poem.

"Voyages"

"Voyages" is another expression of the recurrent dream of possession. Although it was written only shortly after "For the Marriage of Faustus and Helen" in 1924 and 1925 and includes in fact parts of poems composed as early as 1922 and 1923, it is a much more complex rendition of Crane's obsessive dream. The pattern persists: the poet starts his musing in the daylight realm of bitter fact, then enters his dream and describes an ecstatic moment which he longs to perpetuate but which fades almost instantly; this withdrawal energizes him to pursue not only the elusive object of his passion but the fading instant of possession; as he submits to the elements of his dream, he suffers and is thus transformed and renewed. But the tone of this poem is quite different from the tone of "For the Marriage of Faustus and Helen." The earlier poem had been celebratory, a brazen whipping up of frustration and fury vented upon a void. In "Voyages" the mood is less frenzied, more meditative. The poet seems to be charting the directions of his voyages, describing the new world of his consciousness at the very moment that he is discovering it. The self-congratulatory statements of "For the Marriage of Faustus and Helen" give way here to self-inquiry, a careful and tentative probing of the depths of the poet's sensations. He is possessed by his dream and yet he seems to be evoking it through his poems.

In "For the Marriage of Faustus and Helen" too many lines are extractable; that is, they operate as summary statements quite separate from the movement of the poems. The final stanzas of Parts I and III, for example, are tacked on to the poems as pledges of devotion to a state of ecstasy which if realized would be so all-consuming as to make the statements unnecessary. In fact, the conclusiveness of these stanzas works against the continuum of the poem, stalls the imaginative formulation of the movement. In "Voyages," however, the movement is embodied in fluid imagery and continues almost without interruption of the summarizing kind found in "For the Marriage of Faustus and Helen."

In order to read the six poems of "Voyages" as a sequence, however, it is necessary first to understand the nature of the movement. There are certain syntactical continuities, for example, between "Voyages I" and "Voyages II" and between "Voyages III" and "Voyages IV," in which the ending of one poem leads directly into the opening of the next poem. All six poems are united by a single voice speaking, by a common fund of images of sea and flowers, and by the common themes of love and death. Finally, in "Voyages VI" elements in the preceding poems are recapitulated and integrated, and it is probably correct to say that no single poem has its total meaning alone without reference to the other poems. But the six poems are not joined in any logical or chronological sequence. While the poem moves from the boys on the shore in "Voyages I" to the mature man at sea under "stranger skies" in "Voyages VI," the progression is no simple outward journey from innocence to experience. What the man realizes in "Voyages VI" about the destructive nature of the sea, he has already known in "Voyages I" where he warns the boys that "The bottom of the sea is cruel." What he has learned at the end of the poems is that the sea is also kind and beneficent and restorative; this lesson is a return to the state of innocence enjoyed in some ways by the boys playing next to the sea in the beginning. The voyager has come back to himself, and the development is a psychological one, to a new awareness of what he has already known.

Gone from "Voyages" are the city scenes and the details of aerial combat that framed "For the Marriage of Faustus and Helen." "Voyages" draws its imagery from nature. This difference accounts in part for the change in intensity. Crane's double effort to transpose the rhythms of jazz into verse and to find a correlative " 'of ancient days' " for modern symbols in "For the Marriage of Faustus and Helen" gives to that poem a certain strained and frenetic quality that is absent from "Voyages."[4] However, the world of "Voyages" provides no pastoral retreat from the divisive and war-torn city of "For the Marriage of Faustus and Helen." The nature imagery of "Voyages" describes the same desire, yearning, and struggle evidenced in the earlier poem. If anything, the sea is a setting more divisive and destructive than the "stacked partitions" of the city and the "speediest destruction" of the fighter plane. That the sea is alluring as well as dangerous gives to "Voyages" a dimension lacking in "For the Marriage of Faustus and Helen." The longing to escape the confines of the city and the relief in surviving the war are relatively unmixed emotions as compared to the poet's attraction to and fear of the destructive and sustaining sea. In his involvement with the sea of "Voyages" the poet confronts at a deeper level the intricacies of his psychic makeup. The alienating effects of modern life attributed to the city in the early poem are rendered more intimate and immediate in "Voyages," where the alienation is identified in the experience of love itself. The poet in the natural world of "Voyages" is permeated with fear, loss, self-doubt. The sea is even more engulfing than the modern metropolis.

4. *Ibid.*, pp. 89, 120–122.

If it is also sustaining as the city is not, it exacts its toll. In addition, the sea in "Voyages" is an erotic presence as well as a setting, and the poet's contact with it is intricate.

"Voyages" is a love poem. While "For the Marriage of Faustus and Helen" is concerned with the quest for beauty in the modern world, "Voyages" details the search in the interior world of the poet's psyche. Although inspired by the most passionate affair of Crane's life, his intense involvement with a young sailor, "Voyages" is an exploration of the experience of beatific love rather than a narrative of an actual love affair.[5] Although the presence of the loved one is felt at certain points in the sequence, there is only one lover in the poem. He is the speaker, and what he evokes is not a progression of events, not a story of his involvement with another person, but the nature of his involvement with love. The dominant mood of this erotic fantasy is expectation; the speaker is always on the perilous and so delightful brink of possession, of ecstasy, of submission, of self-integration, and the ecstatic instant glows and fades in the poem.

In describing the love affair which inspired these poems, Crane wrote to Waldo Frank: "I have seen the Word made Flesh. I mean nothing less, and I know now that there is such a thing as indestructibility. In the deepest sense, where flesh became transformed through intensity of response to counter-response, where sex was beaten out, where a purity of joy was reached that included tears."[6] "Voyages" deals with that purity of joy, the sensational and imaginative state of the lover-voyager. The focus of the poem is on the transformation which occurs in a love that is imagined as ecstasy. While Helen in "For the Marriage of Faustus and Helen" is given a name and reference outside the poet, she appears only as

---

5. Lewis suggests that "Voyages" belongs to the age-old tradition of romance in which "the experience of earthly love reaches its peak of excitement only to be broken off by the departure or death of the beloved, whereupon the poet-lover finds consolation and a more permanent kind of gratification in a vision of transcendent beauty or of God or paradise; and in his own poetic narrative of the entire affair." See Lewis, *Poetry of Hart Crane*, pp. 150–151.

6. *Letters*, p. 181.

an image in his dream, and, like the figure in Poe's "To Helen," she is not the woman but the spirit of beauty which the poet summons up. In "Voyages" the person addressed is given even less tangible identity; this person figures only as the power that evokes the poet's response.

Crane called "Voyages" sea poems as well as love poems, and the image of the sea becomes the dominant sexual figure in the poem. Although Joseph Warren Beach has convincingly demonstrated the extent to which the language of *Moby Dick* played upon Crane's imagination in the writing of "Voyages," Crane's sea voyage is a dream in which the hefty fact of Melville's seafaring is dissipated.[7] Crane's adventure is inward and erotic, and in the landlessness of his voyage Crane discovers not only a medium to express the deepest truths of his consciousness but also an image on which to transfer his longing and dread. The distance between the sea and the poet expands and contracts in the poems as his dream unfolds; the sea is at once a model to emulate, a rival to fear, the protector and destroyer of his voyage, a participant with the poet in his erotic fantasy, and a tyrant overruling him. The sea is predominantly imaged as a woman in the poem, yet she is a woman of a particular kind, and occasionally she assumes a masculine identity. At all times she is an ambiguous element. She is aggressive and dominant and still seductive and alluring, regal and terrifying yet fecund and coy. The man is totally engulfed by her charms as well as her terrors. Enraptured as she is in her own eroticism, she serves as a symbol of love as ecstasy. At the same time she is the goddess of love who exacts a demanding homage. But she also usurps the role of poet as she becomes identified in her sentences, themes, bells, signature, and imaged Word. She is symbol and symbolizer, scene and actress, possessed and possessor. The poet longs to mingle with her, participate in her raptures, yet he alternately imitates her, recoils from her, and submits to her.

7. See Joseph Warren Beach, "Hart Crane and *Moby Dick*," *Western Review*, XX (Spring 1956), 183–196. For a discussion of the sea as both an erotically attractive, seductive woman and the cruel mother, see Paul, *Hart's Bridge*, pp. 143–149.

The series of six poems opens with an early poem Crane first contemplated entitling "Poster." "There is nothing more profound in it than a 'stop, look and listen' sign," he explained.[8] As the opening poem of this powerful series, however, it assumes a deeper significance. It is the poet's view of the sea from his settled position on the shore, and it provides a contrast just as the opening lines of "For the Marriage of Faustus and Helen" reveal the daytime vision of the poet in contrast to the dream he is about to enter. Viewed from the certainty of the land, "The bottom of the sea is cruel." Although it may appear as innocent and playful in the "fresh ruffles" of its surf as the children whom the poet sees digging in the sand along its shore, it is actually terrifying:

> The sun beats lightning on the waves,
> The waves fold thunder on the sand.

The poet's warning to the children is:

> O brilliant kids, frisk with your dog,
> Fondle your shells and sticks, bleached
> By time and the elements; but there is a line
> You must not cross nor ever trust beyond it
> Spry cordage of your bodies to caresses
> Too lichen-faithful from too wide a breast.
> The bottom of the sea is cruel.

As a straightforward statement the last line is reasonable enough, and yet almost everything in the short poem contradicts the warning. The children themselves are no more innocent than the sea. They "flay each other with sand" and "They have contrived a conquest for shell shucks." They are engaged in a kind of combat with each other and the elements. In contrast to their activity the caresses of the sea appear pleasurable. The poet's warning expresses not so much a lament for childhood as a rational fear of the delightful seduction of the sea and of experience.[9] Yet the flaying of the

8. *Letters*, p. 99.
9. For an alternative reading of this poem, see Brom Weber, *Hart Crane* (New York: Bodley Press, 1948), pp. 105–106.

children and the thunder on the sand drown out this warning and prove its ineffectiveness even as it is uttered. The busy and grasping hands of the children are transformed in later "Voyages" into the benedictory hands of the sea and into "the pieties of lovers' hands," and so the departure from childhood is revealed finally as beneficent. M. L. Rosenthal has commented, "This first poem is, thus, an overture in which the speaker advises his more childlike self (symbolized by the 'bright striped urchins' near the water) not to take the risks he knows he *will* take. The intriguing thing the speaker has to tell us here is that adult love and life's terror are for him synonymous. It is pity, for himself, of what will become of him in the ensuing 'voyages' that makes the three stanzas of this overture so poignant."[10] But the frisky, flaying "brilliant kids" are themselves closer to what the speaker calls the cruelty of the sea than the adult speaker; his well-intentioned warning cuts equally against the spontaneity of their conquests and the terror of the elements. It is the fear-bound and rational mind that would draw lines, circumscribe play, and imagine bodies as "cordage" and breasts as cruel.

As if in reconsideration, "Voyages II" opens with another view of the sea:

> —And yet this great wink of eternity,
> Of rimless floods, unfettered leewardings,
> Samite sheeted and processioned where
> Her undinal vast belly moonward bends,
> Laughing the wrapt inflections of our love;

All lines or boundaries are obliterated in this dream vision, and the associational process of the poem itself suggests that the poet has released himself from his land-bound fear and has succumbed to the flow of the sea. A. Alvarez points out that the "action of the verse is difficult to plot; indeed, at first sight it seems to be made up only of a number of questionably connected phrases describing the

10. M. L. Rosenthal, *The Modern Poets* (New York: Oxford University Press, 1960), p. 179.

sea. But seen from closer up it becomes clearer how the connections were made: how 'wink' brought 'rimless,' which moved, with a jump, into 'unfettered'; how there is a connection between the curve of the sea's eye and the curve of her 'belly'; how 'sheeted,' 'belly' and 'love' interact, and how the 'great wink' turns into laughter."[11] But the associations also work through a series of oppositions: "unfettered" and "processioned," "Samite sheeted" and "undinal vast belly." The image of the sea contains here a double aspect, perhaps a duplicity. Symbolized as a woman, she is both sprite and queen, free spirit and controlling power. In both aspects she is equally frightening and alluring. As a sprite, she offers the poet an example of blissful love-making, a spiritual embodiment of the rhythmic and natural movement of sea and moon. Yet her "vast" belly suggests immediately the immensity of her powers and recalls her "rimless" and "unfettered" nature that need follow no regular rhythm. As a queen, the sea seems to be controlled and orderly and so dependable; but, as the second stanza indicates, she is also imperious and may be as whimsical as the sprite. The poet says:

> Take this Sea, whose diapason knells
> On scrolls of silver snowy sentences,
> The sceptred terror of whose sessions rends
> As her demeanors motion well or ill,
> All but the pieties of lovers' hands.

This sea is the queen of death who rules by the scepter; her sessions (and, reading back, her processions) are terrifying. She is known by knells and "snowy sentences," cold edicts that foretell death. Yet she is ambiguous: she may "motion well or ill." And, despite her terrifying power, she has, the poet imagines even while he fears her, no control over lovers. The poet's injunction at the opening, "Take this Sea," seems to contradict everything he says about this powerful force which cannot be taken, accepted, pos-

11. A. Alvarez, *The Shaping Spirit* (London: Chatto and Windus, 1958), pp. 116–117.

sessed. Yet the poet's phrase suggests that he will take to the sea, accept her perilous conditions.

The sea's majestic and formal quality is sustained in the next stanza, where her bells salute in a courtly gesture the stars, but the floral imagery of the stanza opens a new dimension of the sea: her generative and voluptuous nature. The "poinsettia meadows of her tides" evoke by brilliant contrast to the whiteness of the preceding stanza her passionate side; combined with the "crocus lustres of the stars," they transform the sea's terrifying court of love and death into a garden paradise.

In this garden, as the music of the poem is stilled into "Adagios of islands," the poet senses that at this moment the sea motions well. Yet he is aware even in this instant of assurance that the tide could change, the garden could become a cold court again. He says to his beloved: "O my Prodigal, / Complete the dark confessions her veins spell." His desire is to hasten, a desire which he repeats with added intensity to his lover, who seems unaware of the threatening tides. In this moment of blissful expectation the poet sees the sea once more as a voluptuous woman, known by her "veins" that spell not "snowy sentences" but "dark confessions." She is the dark lady, erotically seductive yet also in quite a different way possibly destructive. Her "turning shoulders wind the hours" and her "palms / Pass superscription of bent foam and wave." In her winding and bending the sea seems to enclose the lovers in a protective embrace, yet as she winds the hours and bends the waves, she also reminds the poet of the tides that may change at any moment. He is moved by the urgency of time to

> Hasten, while they are true,—sleep, death, desire,
> Close round one instant in one floating flower.

In this reversal of the normal sex act the poet underscores a desire which should never be closed and so completed, not a desire for sleep and death but a desire inspired by expectant love, a desire that is itself fulfilling as it elevates and enraptures the poet. The poet seeks the preservation, not the consummation, of love, symbol-

ized in the fragile floating flower. It is a wish for release from the
fear of tides and time, from his own sense of urgency, and from the
need to complete the act of love. This longing calls forth the impassioned plea of the last stanza:

> Bind us in time, O Seasons clear, and awe.
> O minstrel galleons of Carib fire,
> Bequeath us to no earthly shore until
> Is answered in the vortex of our grave
> The seal's wide spindrift gaze toward paradise.

This supplication contains all the oppositions in the poem. The
poet does not want to emerge from the sea because his experience
there has not been and never can be completed. He has glimpsed
there in "one instant" the "one floating flower," a fleeting hint of
beauty and unity, sustained by the force that destroys everything
else. He has not consummated his love, but he has known the
ecstasy of desire. He wants to remain always at that moment of
expectation, not the moment of sleep and death but the moment
of desire. He longs to remain unbound in a state of erotic and
psychic excitement. Yet at the same time he longs to be bound,
somehow reshaped and made whole again, a longing that works
against his wish to be held forever in solution. He also wants to be
bound in time *and* awe, two more contradictory desires in which
the pull of tidal rhythms is countered by the pull of timelessness.
He wants to be bound by awe in time, a binding which is no bond
but eternally fluid and sustaining. Finally, the poet fuses here, as in
"Voyages VI," fire and water. The "Carib fire" and the sea are
opposing elements, joined only in their annihilating powers, and
yet it is to these forces that the poet paradoxically prays for pro-
tection. The "minstrel galleons of Carib fire" are emblems of the
poet's song and his passion, burning magically within the water of
his dream world. The ships are also symbols of the voyaging lover
whose passion burns in the tantalizing and threatening female
sea; she could destroy him with her vortex and yet in this mysterious and heightened moment she sustains him.

In manuscript versions of this poem the sea is a secondary lover, emulating the sex play of the human lovers, but in the final version the sea assumes the dominant role and the poet's lover is less strongly realized. The poet transfers the rhythm of his passion to the sea and thus distances himself from it at the same time that he reveals through the sea the consuming torment and raptures of his desires.[12]

"Voyages III" and "IV" work out the identification the poet has made with the sea. In "Voyages III" the poet remains at sea still in a mood of expectation, sustained by the sea's "Infinite consanguinity." As in Part II of "For the Marriage of Faustus and Helen," the poet here is alone, and the power of the movement derives from his loneliness. But, unlike the roof-garden dance in Part II, the action here is not a grotesque experience; rather, it reverses the torturous "sleep, death, desire" of "Voyages II" and leads from desire to a death that is a release not into sleep but into new voyaging and desire. In the first stanza the poet associates his own sustained journey with the motion of the sea. His desire for his absent lover is mirrored in the sea's own movement toward union with the sky:

> Infinite consanguinity it bears—
> This tendered theme of you that light
> Retrieves from sea plains where the sky
> Resigns a breast that every wave enthrones;
> While ribboned water lanes I wind
> Are laved and scattered with no stroke
> Wide from your side, whereto this hour
> The sea lifts, also, reliquary hands.

The consanguinity, the "tendered theme" (a pun on the tenderness of the sea's offerings), are made concrete in the eroticism of the sea, now masculine, regally and actively mounting the sky, which becomes passive and feminine. This masculine sea is tender and protective, unlike the coy and cruel feminine sea of his earlier

---

12. For a discussion of the revisions of "Voyages II," see Leibowitz, *Hart Crane*, pp. 86–90.

voyage, and the poet winds the ribboned water around himself in language that recalls both the sea's winding action in "Voyages II" and his plea there to be bound. The laving, scattering, lifting sea is in its gentle stroking movement pleasurable to him, and, distracted from his winding, he submits to his unravelment in the vast, seductive elemental force.

He descends trustingly deeper into the sea to a fantasy world:

> And so, admitted through black swollen gates
> That must arrest all distance otherwise,—
> Past whirling pillars and lithe pediments,
> Light wrestling there incessantly with light,
> Star kissing star through wave on wave unto
> Your body rocking!

The gates of the surface of the sea, ominous and deformed, are magically transformed into "whirling pillars" and "lithe pediments." Moving in this subsurface realm, the poet imagines that all nature participates in a saturnalia of passion. In a turn on the pathetic fallacy the poet describes his moment of possession as an orgiastic scene in which like mates with like. While the waves and the light had on the surface of the sea been consorting with each other, here in this underworld they vent their passion for themselves. In the wrestling and kissing of the light and stars, the poet expresses his own dream, that purity of joy, where sex is beaten out and the rage of lust is purified. This confrontation with the dark and secret sexuality revealed in the recesses of the sea elicits from the poet an acknowledgment of a death which does not consume him but proves instead the indestructability of his love. Submitting to the rocking waves and their tender care, he says:

> and where death, if shed,
> Presumes no carnage, but this single change,—
> Upon the steep floor flung from dawn to dawn
> The silken skilled transmemberment of song;
>
> Permit me voyage, love, into your hands . . .

These words, so unlike the agonized plea at the end of "Voyages II," intertwine in a new pattern elements that had figured in fragmentary ways in the two previous poems: death, carnage, the steep floor of the sea, dawn, hands, but most of all the "transmemberment of song." All the threatening qualities of the sea are metamorphosed here in this final peaceful submission. The bottom of the sea that had seemed cruel to the speaker on shore now becomes on closer contact a cradle, "flung from dawn to dawn." The sleep is the sleep of eternal bliss and eternal light. Death, associated with terror and dissolution in "Voyages II," becomes a "single change," a transformation rather than a consummation. The lover achieves a sense of unity and wholeness through his response to love. The rending and dismembering sea becomes a "transmemberment" in which destructiveness is transcended by the poet's creative song. His frantic desire to be bound at the end of "Voyages II" is replaced here with a humble plea for submission to the "hands" of the sea. The hands, clutching and grasping in "Voyages I" and solemnized into pieties in "Voyages II," here become the protective hands of love. The voyage which had been forestalled in the first poem and threatened by the perilous sea in the second poem is now readily accepted.

The poet is possessed by the destructive and creative force of love, and this moment of possession is the climax of the powerful poetic series of "Voyages." "Voyages III" is a celebration of love's transforming power, a hymn to erotic desire that "Presumes no carnage" because it has no object. In this poem the poet's beloved is absent, unnecessary because the poem is not written to him or about him; it is a poem about the state of love, not about love for someone but about love itself, about the single lover's consciousness intensified by love. Sex has been beaten out in this poem; the desire that is lust is transformed into an ecstatic state. The fear of time's destructive power is overcome in this change. The terrifying sense of the rimless sea is transcended as the poet feels the limitless power of love purified and chastened. The horror of the white death-dealing sea is transmuted into the light the poet "Retrieves from sea plains." The poem ends with the single plea: "Permit me voyage, love, into your hands. . . ." And what the poet seeks again, although in a much calmer mood, is the continuance of this state of bliss and rapture which is the condition of love and of the song that would celebrate it.

The opening lines of "Voyages IV" appear to continue syntactically from the ending of "Voyages III": "Permit me voyage, love, into your hands . . . / Whose counted smile of hours and days, suppose / I know as spectrum of the sea." The poet is sustained by the sea, which he describes as a stream of love in which all opposites are joined in unity. The smiling sea reflects the poet's new-found happiness and his consequent trust of voyaging. The smiling image picks up the positive aspects of the laughing sea in "Voyages II"; there the laughter could have been taunting as well as approving. Now the poet accepts, as he has been accepted by, the whole spectrum of the sea, its circle in which all oppositions are enclosed. The sea moves "from palms to the severe / Chilled albatross's white immutability," and includes in its circles all the divisions that had tormented the poet-lover earlier: the benedictory palms and terrifying snowy sentences of "Voyages II," love and death, growth and changelessness, green and white. In this stream of love the poet finds himself sustained, "singing, this mortality alone / Through clay aflow immortally to you." In the flowing and singing of his song, the poet's mortal love is released and transformed into his immortal poem. The ecstasy of this moment is sustained in the next stanza, where the poet claims in a riot of feeling:

> All fragrance irrefragibly, and claim
> Madly meeting logically in this hour
> And region that is ours to wreathe again,
> Portending eyes and lips and making told
> The chancel port and portion of our June—

The fragrance of the floating flower of "Voyages II" is proclaimed indestructible as the poet's breath of song combines with the incense of love. The essence, in which the song and the love intermingle, is intoxicating and the poet is maddened and "possessed" by its power. The "one instant" becomes an "hour / And region," a whole atmosphere suffused with fragrance. The last two lines with their triple emphasis on "port" ("Portending," "port," "portion") suggest that the poet is approaching the end of his voyaging. The "chancel port" is the place where love is hallowed. But in making told the port, the poet is also making port, consummating his love, and for this poet, that portends death, love's end. Therefore, he moves quickly away from this haven. He "resigns" the "harbor shoulders." The love he celebrates is not the love sanctioned at the marriage altar but the love for which he "Must first be lost in fatal tides to tell." It is the love that knows no port, that is expressed only in voyaging "For islands where must lead inviolably / Blue latitudes." The poet's pledge of love is made "In signature of the incarnate word," in an acknowledgment of the word made flesh, the spirit of love revealed in the person of the beloved, but also of the flesh made word, the physical experience of love transformed into poetry. This kind of love demands a resignation of the safe harbor, a submission to "fatal tides," but its rewards are "widening noon" and "bright insinuations," an expansion rather than a completion of desire. The poem closes with a reaffirmation of this mood of delightful anticipation:

> In this expectant, still exclaim receive
> The secret oar and petals of all love.

But in "Voyages V" the poet emerges from the sea to the shore and to a puzzling feeling of alienation, betrayal, and treachery. Nature takes on a hardened quality, and all the fluid, soothing qualities of the sea are marmorealized into a world that threatens the poet:

> Infrangible and lonely, smooth as though cast
> Together in one merciless white blade—
> The bay estuaries fleck the hard sky limits.
>
> —As if too brittle or too clear to touch!

The sea's transcendent glow has become a parodic "frozen trackless smile," and the "tidal wedge" of its movement tortures the poet. Strangely enough, the poet finds himself in the company of a lover who is now physically present but spiritually absent. The poet feels himself betrayed by the lover whose hand he cannot touch, whose eyes are "already in the slant of drifting foam," whose breath is "sealed by the ghosts" he does not know. The world has become a tomb for the poet as he awakens abruptly from the peaceful sleep of his dream:

> The cables of our sleep so swiftly filed,
> Already hang, shred ends from remembered stars.

The expectations aroused by his imaginative voyaging make this moment doubly treacherous. He exclaims, "I dreamed / Nothing so flagless as this piracy." In the end the poet enjoins his lover to a sleep that is merely forgetting, a retreat into himself, a resignation to his loss and loneliness. His passion has spent itself, and in the opening of "Voyages VI" he finds himself blinded and alone in a sea which is, like the land in the preceding poem, a prison. The coldness of the sea is emblematic of the poet's psychic state:

> Where icy and bright dungeons lift
> Of swimmers their lost morning eyes,
> And ocean rivers, churning, shift
> Green borders under stranger skies.

In a state of darkness and confusion the poet throws himself upon the mercy of the savage sea:

> O rivers mingling toward the sky
> And harbor of the phoenix' breast—
> My eyes pressed black against the prow,
> —Thy derelict and blinded guest
>
> Waiting, afire, what name, unspoke,
> I cannot claim: let thy waves rear
> More savage than the death of kings,
> Some splintered garland for the seer.

Describing himself as a swimmer and yet afire, struggling with waters that can dissolve him and at the same time paradoxically burning within those waters, the poet points in one sense to his total annihilation but in another sense to the magic of his situation and to a new moment of possession made possible through his identification with these opposing elements. The poet's designation of himself as "afire" recalls the moment of ecstatic desire in "Voyages II" when he prayed to the "minstrel galleons of Carib fire" to bind him in time and sustain him at sea. Here the elements which had been exterior to the poet in "Voyages II" are identified with him, and like the phoenix he prepares for a new birth through this painful consummation. The poet moves beyond the seasons to which he had appealed in the earlier poem, beyond time and the threatening destructiveness of the elements, to a timeless world in which opposites fuse and he is released from the torments of his contradictory desires.

The movement toward unity and possession is through storms that symbolize not only the poet's inner turbulence but the violence that precedes creation. The inspiriting wind and the thundering rain rush in upon the deathlike scene to stir the "seer" with energy and vitality and annoint him with a new life, a new life which comes from above, sent from the sky, realm of the gods:

> Beyond siroccos harvesting
> The solstice thunders, crept away,
> Like a cliff swinging or a sail
> Flung into April's inmost day—
>
> Creation's blithe and petalled word
> To the lounged goddess when she rose
> Conceding dialogue with eyes
> That smile unsearchable repose—

This entire scene can be interpreted as erotic. The poet, afire with his passion, releases it, and from the turbulence of consummation he moves toward a state of bliss and peace. As the icy dungeons of the winter sea release their paralytic grip on the world and move

into the new rhythm of spring, the savage waves themselves lose
their fatal power; in their swinging, flinging movement they become again the fluid, undulating, and sustaining medium of the
blissful dream. The sea resumes its feminine identity, but, unlike
the lustful and seductive undinal sprite of the poet's earlier dream,
this female sea is a goddess who is imagined as "lounged" and in
repose. This queen of the sea rules not in "sceptred terror" nor with
"scrolls of silver snowy sentences" but through "dialogue" and
smiles, calling forth "Creation's blithe and petalled word." Perhaps
this figure is Amphitrite, queen of the sea, but she is certainly a
beneficent spirit whose embrace is life-giving. The female sea that
had tormented the poet in earlier voyages was wildly erotic, and
as he observed her insatiable love-making he felt frightened and
threatened. Now this feminine goddess turns to him and com-
munes with him, and he entrusts himself to her guidance. And in
the poem's final stanzas she reveals to him the vision of harmony
he had desired:

> Still fervid covenant, Belle Isle,
> —Unfolded floating dais before
> Which rainbows twine continual hair—
> Belle Isle, white echo of the oar!
>
> The imaged Word, it is, that holds
> Hushed willows anchored in its glow.
> It is the unbetrayable reply
> Whose accent no farewell can know.

Elements that had figured in the earlier poems are here intertwined
in a new and harmonious pattern. The covenant the poet had made
in "Voyages II" is still fervid but is totally removed from the perilous world of time and the seasons as the rainbow indicates a divine
annointment of the scene. "Adagios of islands" which the poet
had glimpsed momentarily in his early voyage become stilled into
the beatific Belle Isle. The image of hair, the "argosy of your
bright hair" of "Voyages V," and the "secret oar and petals of all
love" of "Voyages IV" are retrieved from loss and darkness in this

luminous scene. The "incarnate word" of "Voyages IV" is divested of its flesh and possible carnage through the purification of this voyage.[13]

To read these last stanzas against "Voyages I" is to understand the nature of the voyaging in these poems. The thunder and lightning that had reminded the poet in the first poem of the terrors of nature have released their storm and been transformed into rainbows. The cruel bottom of the sea which the poet had feared at first anchors in this vision the "imaged Word." The "lichen-faithful" caresses of the sea which seemed to be death-dealing to the landed poet actually are creative as they sustain the "petalled word." The line the poet warned the children not to cross becomes upon the crossing a "floating dais." The poet of "Voyages I" had seen nature not only as treacherous but as static and hardened; in "Voyages VI" the natural world is dynamic and fluid and creative. "Voyages I" is a daylight view of the world which seems terrifying to rational reflection. Yet in his dream of voyaging, his "sleep, death, desire," he plunges into the destructive element, experiences the death he had feared, and rises from it to be beatifically possessed. The sea is the world of dreams and love which the poet wishes to avoid at the outset of his voyage because he recognizes in its thunder and lightning wild forces that threaten to destroy him. To encounter these forces is dangerous, and yet only through this confrontation, only by descent to the cruel depth of his consciousness, is the poet transformed.

The Belle Isle to which the poet's voyaging leads him is "white echo of the oar," that purity of joy to which Crane referred in his letter about the love affair that inspired these poems. The "secret oar and petals of all love" had in "Voyages IV" obvious sexual overtones. Here sex is beaten out and love is the "petalled word" and "white echo of the oar," no longer secret yet manifested not in

13. Evelyn Hinz is not convinced of the beauty of this scene. She sees Belle Isle, the poetic ideal, as perhaps a false promise. In her reading the speaker in "Voyages VI" appreciates the destructiveness of the perfection of pure art. See Evelyn J. Hinz, "Hart Crane's 'Voyages' Reconsidered," *Contemporary Literature*, XIII (Summer 1972), 315–333.

flesh but in words and echoes, in the poet's own song, his symbolic apprehension of the world. The whiteness of his vision here recalls the passage in Part I of "For the Marriage of Faustus and Helen" where the poet moves

> White, through white cities passed on to assume
> That world which comes to each of us alone.

And both passages are repeated in the final lines of "Possessions":

> Upon the page whose blind sum finally burns
> Record of rage and partial appetites.
> The pure possession, the inclusive cloud
> Whose heart is fire shall come,—the white wind rase
> All but bright stones wherein our smiling plays.

The world that comes to each of us alone, the pure possession, is the Belle Isle of Crane's erotic dreams of voyaging. His is no voyage to another person. Rather, his voyaging and his desire are for possession not of someone else but of something permanent, eternal, harmonious. His desire is white and pure in its final ecstasy, and its issue is poetic creation. His voyage has been a ritual of purification in which the partial appetites of his desire and lust are dissolved; what remains is their passion and vitality transmuted into poetry.

"Voyages" traces the pattern of possession. Its movement is not outward but inward, deep into the poet's psyche. Although the poet reaches in this exploration a "purity of joy," he also touches in these depths the anxieties, fears, and desires that torment him. The love affair that inspired these voyages assured him, Crane said, that there was such a thing as indestructibility, but the very need for that assurance derived from his sense that passion and lust could destroy him. The peril of his voyage images the precarious, dangerous, threatening, and finally miraculous experience of love as Crane knew it. The feeling that flesh could be transformed, that sex could be beaten out, embodies a deep desire for that transformation, a guilty sense that flesh and sex must be purified. "Beaten out," the phrase Crane chooses to describe this change, suggests the violence he imagined as part of the process. It recalls also the sea's "beating leagues of monotone," the motion steadied from turbulence into the rhythm that would perhaps contain the poet.

The sea, characterized as both a sensuous spirit and a frigid tyrant, and the poet's lover, both a prodigal and a pirate, each manifest the double nature of passion in Crane's experience. The seductive attraction of the spirit and the prodigal hides within it the dangers and treachery of the tyrant and the pirate. The desire to possess the prize won from love and voyaging leaves the poet vulnerable to loss and betrayal. The fear of love is the fear that it is associated with death only. To love is to court destruction. The sprite, the queen, the prodigal, the pirate, all are manifestations of the fatal demands of love. Yet to seek love and beauty in spite of this knowledge is to seek not a relationship of mutual giving but a state of purity which precludes mutuality. To desire the "unsearchable repose," "the unbetrayable reply," is to seek not the gifts of human, changing, corruptible, sexual love but the gifts of the spirit, which are totally removed from that love. The awareness that there could be a continuity between human love and a sense of eternal harmony is missing in Crane's poetry, where sexuality does not lead to union with another person and where harmony is so awesomely elevated that it seems beyond human attainment. To consort with the "sceptred terror" is to submit to her demands. The "unbetrayable reply" is attained only as a concession from the goddess in whose service the poet must suffer, be rendered blind and dumb. The poet, her "derelict and blinded guest" in "Voyages VI," is in the end possessed by the "lounged goddess" of the sea and of love.

"Voyages" is a more intricate and intimate formulation of the dream of possession than "For the Marriage of Faustus and Helen." The three parts of the earlier poem include the evocation of beauty, the dance or sensual culmination, and the final victory of the imagination over destruction. In "Voyages" each of these parts is developed more fully: beauty is still evoked but its terror as well as its splendor are described; the sensual culmination approaches

and recedes in scenes mixed with delight and anxiety; the triumph
of the imagination is celebrated but not in the lavish terms of "For
the Marriage of Faustus and Helen." The stress in "Voyages" on
the dark and tormented side of passion derives from a fuller realization of the "possession," the madness, that drove Crane toward
the pure possession of art. But here, too, as in "For the Marriage of
Faustus and Helen," Crane seeks to express a vision beyond his
private suffering and anguish, an affirmation of love over death.

"Powhatan's Daughter"

"Powhatan's Daughter," the five poems which are numbered as
the second section of *The Bridge* and actually make up about one-
third of the long work, repeat again in richly symbolic terms the
dream of possession which Crane had worked out in "For the
Marriage of Faustus and Helen" and "Voyages."[14] Here again
the poet is dreaming, and his dream is by now familiar: an erotic yet
elusive experience with a spirit whose disappearance launches the
poet on a perilous voyage in which he seeks not only the repetition
of his mysterious experience but submission to that ecstatic moment
in which he first imagined the possibility of being totally possessed.
This voyage is frustrating for the poet. He undergoes a ritual death
from which he rises to a state of pure possession; he is then overpowered by his passion and integrated by the vision of totality that
attends it.

Crane made for this section of *The Bridge* the longest extended
explanation of his aims and designs, and it is worth digressing from
our examination of this obsessive pattern in his poetry to examine
his intentions, not so much for what they reveal about the poems as
for what they reveal about his conceptual efforts to elevate his
private dream to universal significance. He had made the effort
before. In "For the Marriage of Faustus and Helen," he had tried

---

14. In a different context Thomas A. Vogler associates the quest in "Powhatan's
Daughter" with the quest in "For the Marriage of Faustus and Helen." His entire
discussion of *The Bridge* as a prelude to epic vision is interesting. See Vogler,
Preludes to Vision, pp. 142–196.

to give his private fantasy a universal relevance by uniting his desire for Helen to the desire of modern man for survival in a war-torn world. In "Voyages" he had moved, as is evident from an examination of his first worksheets, from an embarrassingly specific record of his affair with a young sailor to a universal statement about "all love" in which his private voyage becomes a symbolic voyage. But it is in "Powhatan's Daughter" that his desire to give his private dream a larger meaning reaches its supreme expression. As the central section of *The Bridge*, "Powhatan's Daughter" assumes a vital significance in the myth of America. Her pursuit is not merely the pursuit of the elusive female but the pursuit of the body of the continent which she represents. In a letter to his benefactor, Otto Kahn, he explained his intentions in these terms:

> At the risk of complicating your appreciation of Part II ("Powhatan's Daughter"), I nevertheless feel impelled to mention a few of my deliberate intentions in this part of the poem, and to give some description of my general method of construction. Powhatan's daughter, or Pocahontas, is the mythological nature-symbol chosen to represent the physical body of the continent, or the soil. She here takes on much the same role as the traditional Hertha of ancient Teutonic mythology. The five sub-sections of Part II are mainly concerned with a gradual exploration of this "body" whose first possessor was the Indian. It seemed altogether ineffective from the poetic standpoint to approach this material from the purely chronological angle—beginning with, say, the landing of "The Mayflower," continuing with a résumé of the Revolution through the conquest of the West, etc. One can get that viewpoint in any history primer. What I am after is an assimilation of this experience, a more organic panorama, showing the continuous and living evidence of the past in the inmost vital substance of the present.[15]

If anything might at first complicate our appreciation of "Powhatan's Daughter," it is this explanation of it. However, in this passage Crane does make explicit certain attitudes implicit in "For the Marriage of Faustus and Helen" and "Voyages," and by con-

15. *Letters*, p. 305.

sidering this statement in light of the pattern we have been tracing, it is possible to understand Crane's meaning here. His stated aim in these poems is to possess imaginatively the body of the continent; by identifying this body as the woman Pocahontas, he underscores the erotic nature of his exploration. As in "For the Marriage of Faustus and Helen" and "Voyages," his desire diffuses itself through the landscape and he moves through a natural landscape which is sexually charged. But by identifying the woman here not only with geography but with history and myth, he endows her with powers so vast that she becomes not merely a woman to be possessed but a superhuman spirit which threatens at every second to possess and overwhelm him. She is the feminine principle, the symbol of fertility and vitality and creativity, with whose mystery the poet longs to unite himself; but she is also aggressive, dominant, demanding, the seducer and not the seduced. The tribute she demands is the annihilation of her lover; he cannot be her master, but as her submissive suitor he possesses through his own death the vision of bliss and perfection which is her bounty to bestow.

Like all Crane's women figures, Pocahontas is a complex and contradictory image. She appears to him first in a dream as a seducer whose promise of a blissful union is delightful but unrealized, perhaps delightful because unrealizable. She is called a woman but her seduction involves only hand-holding and kissing, and what Crane seems to be describing in this first poem is a homosexual union. But she assumes various identities as a woman too: she appears in succeeding poems as the cruel mother, the wanton woman, the virgin bride, the temptress, and finally the possessive and rejected mother. In each role she is inaccessible yet somehow alluring, and the poet's desire for her is always agonizing. Only in his pursuit of her is he energized because only by union with her will he possess the bliss which she embodies and for which he longs. And this bliss involves in Crane's imagination suffering and death because he ultimately envisions it as a state of ecstasy in which he is totally consumed. The basic rhythm of this dream we have seen in "For the Marriage of Faustus and Helen" and "Voyages," and it arises from Crane's private experience of love and creativity as states of ecstasy. Certainly working through this dream are homosexual associations of love and death, the longing and dread of the mother, the fear of the aggressive woman. Yet he also transfers to the feminine principle here certain positive associations: she is the desired object, she alone can give him that purity of joy he imagined as sexual consummation, only through her is his lust purified into harmony and bliss. "Powhatan's Daughter" is love poetry of a spectacular kind. It was Crane's special gift to write magnificent love poetry and to communicate through poetry the beauty and power of a passion which was in his life almost always tormenting and ugly.

In addition, he always associates in his poetry this state of love as possession with a similar state of possession which involves creativity. To be truly creative was, for Crane, to be totally possessed by beauty. In a letter to Gorham Munson he says, "At times, dear Gorham, I feel an enormous power in me—that seems almost supernatural."[16] The power in him that seemed almost supernatural overwhelmed him in his flashes of inspiration. In actuality, he attempted to induce this state frequently through alcohol, but in his poetry this state is often expressed in sexual fantasies. His pursuit of the earth goddess is for that happiness he called ecstatic, which found its only perfect form in poetry.

It still remains, however, to consider the relevance of this private dream to American history. In what sense is Crane's Pocahontas an American version of the ancient Teutonic myth of Hertha, and how do these five poems express an "organic panorama, showing the continuous and living evidence of the past in the inmost vital substance of the present"? To elevate the historical Pocahontas to mythological status is poetically possible. Although her origins were not divine and although she never inspired a cult of worshippers, some Americans, certain Virginians, trace their biological descent from her, and in Crane's poems she represents as an Indian princess the complex associations of guilt and desire normally at-

16. *Ibid.*, p. 91.

tributed to divine ancestors. In her fertility the poet sees the pro-
creative urge of the universe. To return to her is to return to the
beginnings, to the moment of creativity, in which the world and
the poet were born. The poet's consuming desire for the Indian
princess carries guilt-ridden longings for the mother figure, but
only through a mystical union with her can he achieve the rebirth
he desires and the possession of a new identity. Pocahontas represents for Crane the primitive beginnings of America, a time before
the coming of the white man with his repressive order, a time
when the fertility of the earth was exalted and the fertility of
women was a source of joy. This point is made clear by the epigraph
to "Powhatan's Daughter," an abridged passage from William
Strachey's *History of Travaile into Virginia Britannica: "—Poca-
huntus, a well-featured but wanton yong girle . . . of the age of
eleven or twelve years, get the boyes forth with her into the market
place, and make them wheele, falling on their hands, turning their
heels upwards, whom she would followe, and wheele so herself,
naked as she was, all the fort over."* [17] Although Strachey's wanton
girl is far from an image of Mother Earth, her playfulness and seductiveness recall a primitive delight in fleshly pleasure from which
modern man has recoiled to his great loss. It is this image of the
alluring young girl, of the woman as temptress, that starts the poet's
dreaming in "Powhatan's Daughter," and although she is transformed in the course of his fantasy into various manifestations of
the female, it is her continuing seductive tug on his imagination
that calls forth his poems. The historical Pocahontas was only a
point of departure for Crane's associative imagination; in these five

17. It is interesting to note that William Carlos Williams had used this passage
from Strachey in *In the American Grain* (1925) as evidence of the terror that
such sexual wantonness inspired in the Puritan mind. See "The May-Pole at Merry
Mount," in *In the American Grain* (New York: New Directions, 1956), pp. 75–80.
Crane was enthusiastic about this book, although he claimed to have put off reading
it until his own ideas about *The Bridge* were clear in his mind. See *Letters*, pp.
277–278. Actually Crane took this passage neither from Strachey nor from
Williams's book but from Kay Boyle's review of Williams's book in the Apr. 1927
issue of *transition*. Boyle had abridged a passage quoted by Williams from Strachey,
and it is this abridged version that Crane uses. See Weber, *Hart Crane*, pp. 324–325.

poems he succeeds in realizing the mythic possibilities of her role. She exerts on the poet's mind the same kind of power exerted by the fertile women of myth.[18]

In his comments to Otto Kahn, Crane's choice of words to describe his intentions for this section (an "organic panorama, showing the continuous and living evidence of the past in the inmost vital substance of the present") recalls T. S. Eliot's famous statement about the mythological method. And Crane's own method is perhaps best explained in contrast to that of Eliot. Eliot wrote in a review of James Joyce's *Ulysses*, "In using the myth, in manipulating a continuous paralllel between contemporaneity and antiquity, Mr. Joyce is pursuing a method which others must pursue after him. . . . It is simply a way of controlling, of ordering, of giving a shape and significance to the immense panorama of futility and anarchy which is contemporary history."[19] We know that Crane read *The Dial* and that he was tremendously enthusiastic about *Ulysses*, and so it is not too much to assume that he also read Eliot's review and that perhaps he took his critical vocabulary from it. The similarity and difference in the words used by Eliot and Crane are first of all an interesting commentary on their relationship. Crane felt the tremendous power of Eliot's influence, and yet he felt too that Eliot was his opposite and that *The Bridge* would be the counter-testimony to *The Waste Land*. Crane's "organic panorama" is diametrically opposed to Eliot's "immense panorama of futility and anarchy." For Eliot, as for Joyce, myth provided a means of ordering an otherwise chaotic mass of materials, but for Crane myth implied no narrative order but rather a power of vision. To state it baldly, Eliot knew his classical myths and Crane

18. In the spring of 1926 Crane was reading Waldo Frank's *Virgin Spain* and D. H. Lawrence's *The Plumed Serpent;* these inspired him not only with the epic possibilities of his theme but, in the case of Lawrence's book, with some of the imagery of this section, e.g., the serpent and the eagle which he connects with Pocahontas. See *Letters,* pp. 235–236.

19. T. S. Eliot, "Ulysses, Order, and Myth," *The Dial,* LXXV (Nov. 1923), 480–483.

did not. When Crane talks about a mythological nature symbol, he is referring not to an actual myth or even to a mythic figure but to an image of his consciousness which, if he could express it, would be infused with a power that he sensed was mythic. The Pocahontas of his poem could then exert the same hold on the modern mind as the fertility goddess had on the practitioners of fertility rites. Crane does not search out parallels between the twentieth century and antiquity to demonstrate the terrible discontinuity with the past; in fact, he did not feel as Eliot did that the present was totally discontinuous with the past. Crane felt that there was "living evidence" of the past in the present and that the poet could discover it there, perhaps hidden but still available. For the poet, it was accessible in his dreams. There was a world infused with power and mystery and beauty, a world as vital to this twentieth-century poet as the mythic world had been to the myth-makers. Crane had little knowledge of the history of myth or religion, but he did have an intuitive understanding of the importance of primitive rituals and cults not because he had studied them but because in his consciousness he felt the powerful rhythmic forces they reveal. In the sense that dreams are personalized myths, "Powhatan's Daughter" is a formulation of one poet's dream, but in its magnificence it transcends the privacy of Crane's personal fantasy and becomes symbolically meaningful.[20]

Crane's conscious intentions to gather up various strands of American folklore in this section (to include Pocahontas, Rip Van Winkle, the Mississippi steamboat captains, black minstrels, and the Indian chief) are often misleading. Simply by naming names, he does not elevate his poem from a private expression to a public one. The real power of the poem arises from the turmoil at the secret depths of the poet's consciousness, a turmoil which he symbolizes through various historical figures in his poem. It is in his

---

20. For a more complete discussion of the connection between myths and dreams, see Joseph Campbell, *The Hero with a Thousand Faces* (New York: World, 1956), pp. 3–25.

personal desire for possession that he best expresses the meaning of America—in its fecundity and vastness it has from the beginning evoked the dream of possession. The cartwheeling Pocahontas perfectly symbolizes the seductiveness of the American continent, which has always tormented its explorers, actual and imaginary.[21]

In emphasizing the universal and literary significance of this pattern, I do not wish to minimize the secrecy of Crane's poems. "Powhatan's Daughter" is intensely private in its associations. It is not a simple story; it has almost no narrative continuity. As a dream, its images are often blurred or fragmentary, and they are layered with meanings both private and public which often pull against each other. His desire to suggest the intricacy of his dream leads frequently to jammed lines and scenes. The inclusiveness of his references is another source of confusion. The language experiments in the poem, the desire to saturate his words with meanings, to combine them in extralogical orders, to create through the magic of words a new understanding of the world, all combine to make "Powhatan's Daughter" a brilliantly compact but difficult group of poems. Yet in the intensity of its verse, which slackens only in the last poem, it is the great expression in twentieth-century poetry of a vision beyond *The Waste Land*, a vision of the world still inspired by love and, through love, beauty and vitality. The power of the poem will become clear in following the dreamer who appears first as modern man in the city harbor, uncertain about the body of Pocahontas that lies beside him in his sleep, through his dream in "The Dance" where he is ecstatically certain about "rainbows currying each pulsant bone," to the final section in which he emerges from his dream.

21. Crane shares with Williams this dream of possession. William's *In the American Grain* also personifies the landscape as a seductive woman who lures De Soto, Raleigh, Daniel Boone. For Williams, as for Crane, the fullest response to the land is the desire to possess it as a man desires to possess a woman, and the worst violation of the land was the Puritan's denial of its attractions. Williams develops this theme fully in *Paterson*. And both Williams and Crane owe a literary debt to Whitman, who addresses the "voluptuous cool-breath'd earth" as "Prodigal" and urges her to "Smile, for your lover comes."

"The Harbor Dawn"

The first poem of the series opens onto the dreamer's winter sleep:

> Insistently through sleep—a tide of voices—
> They meet you listening midway in your dream,
> The long, tired sounds, fog-insulated noises:
> Gongs in white surplices, beshrouded wails,
> Far strum of fog horns . . . signals dispersed in veils.

In the border state between sleep and consciousness, he remains suspended and insulated from the city world whose noise is expressed in funereal images and is later described as the siren's song of death. To wake up to the morning world is not only to wake up to "the darkling harbor" of death but to the "Cool feathery fold" of winter. The poet retreats from the cold world that encloses his "wavering slumber" to his lover's embrace:

> And you beside me, blessèd now while sirens
> Sing to us, stealthily weave us into day—
> Serenely now, before day claims our eyes
> Your cool arms murmurously about me lay.
>
> While myriad snowy hands are clustering at the panes—
> *your hands within my hands are deeds;*
> *my tongue upon your throat—singing*
> *arms close; eyes wide, undoubtful*
> *dark*
> *drink the dawn—*
> *a forest shudders in your hair!*

Despite the coolness of her arms, this blessed figure arouses his passion and his song. Unlike the snowy hands of the world, her hands caress him, and the caresses promise to unfold to him a new day, a new vision. In his dream the poet imagines that the lover who embraces him is the embodiment of the continent, its dawn and forested hair. But as the morning brightens the city, the speaker in confusion asks, "*Who is the woman with us in the dawn?* . . .

whose is the flesh our feet have moved upon?" Like all dreams, this one remains arrestingly clear and totally vague. The hands and tongue and arms and hair are intimately specific, promising in their singing and pleasurable in their shuddering; but the nature of the encounter is puzzling. Although in all respects this blessed figure is preferable to the actual dawn with which her presence coincides, this woman, as she is called, is confusing to the poet. Her singing is sweeter than the stealthy sirens' song; her "*eyes wide, undoubtful*," are clearer than the "bright window-eyes aglitter" of "Cyclopean towers across Manhattan waters"; but her identity remains unknown. In a sense, the poet is justly confused by his first encounter with the earth woman whose presence in the guise of Pocahontas inspired the early Virginians with amazement and unbelief. But unlike Strachey's wanton Pocahontas, this figure's actions are uncertain. The gloss notes and Crane's explanation in the letter to Kahn mentioned above add to the interpretative difficulty. The gloss notes begin the poem, "*400 years and more . . . or is it from the soundless shore of sleep that time*" and later on, they continue, "*recalls you to your love, there in a waking dream to merge your seed.*" And Crane's explanation to Kahn amplifies these notes: "The love-motif (in italics) carries along a symbolism of the life and ages of man (here the sowing of the seed) which is further developed in each of the subsequent sections of 'Powhatan's Daughter,' though it is never particularly stressed. In 2 ('Van Winkle') it is Childhood; in 3 it is Youth; in 4, Manhood; in 5 it is Age. This motif is interwoven and tends to be implicit in the imagery rather than anywhere stressed."[22] But there is no indication in the poem and especially in the italicized passage within the poem that there has been a merger of seed. If any seed has passed between the two figures, it is the seed of song from the blessed figure to the poet. She is the fertile one, and, as such, she assumes the masculine role of sowing seeds. Their encounter, however, has been only a handclasp sealing a bargain, although the tongue and arms raise this contact to an erotic level. Yet even on that level the contact has been a

22. *Letters*, p. 306.

promise, not a merger. And it is that promise that launches the poet on his voyage.

Crane's outline of these five poems from birth to age in his letter to Kahn provides another source of difficulty, especially when it is considered against his identification of Pocahontas as a fertility goddess. The fertility cycle from decay to rebirth does not naturally coincide with the initiation process from birth to manhood. It is only possible to make sense of Crane's freewheeling way with mythology if we keep clearly in mind that he was not using the mythological method in the same way that Eliot used it. Mythological reference provided for him no means of order; rather, it served to broaden his meaning, to enrich his associations. In referring to Pocahontas as Hertha, Crane seems to be simply investing the native girl with a significance she has not historically but in his consciousness. For Eliot, the term and the referent are fixed points, and his meaning derives from the tension between these points. For Crane, neither term nor referent is a fixed point, and his meaning is clear only as it plays against other terms in the poem. Crane is not playing Eliot's game without knowing the rules; he is using mythological references (in this instance outside the poem) in a very traditional way, extending his own meaning by significant allusions. As the poems progress, it becomes clear that there are two patterns at work here. The winter harbor dawn does give way in the course of "Powhatan's Daughter" to the springtime of the fourth poem, "The Dance," and the summer of the fifth poem, "Indiana." And so the movement is from decay to rebirth. At the same time the poet moves through his own cycle of experiences, sifting through his childhood and eventually emerging through his dreams into manhood. And the poet's coming of age is intertwined with the changes of the seasons. Only through him is the winter world transformed into springtime.

"Van Winkle"

It is significant that Crane chose for the title of his second poem the name of Irving's fabled sleeper because, although the poem seems to take place in the day-to-day world of reality, its real action occurs as the troubled dream of the poet's childhood. Like Rip Van Winkle, who appears in this poem with a certain amount of appropriate poetic license in Sleepy Hollow, the poet wanders back to the vaguely familiar realm of his childhood and examines it with puzzlement. The blessed figure who slept beside him in the harbor dawn is here both his guide and the person he seeks. As such, she represents not a person but an atmosphere, the atmosphere of dreaming and of the enclosure provided by dreams. Van Winkle's name is a play on the word "wink," a suggestion which is taken up in Pocahontas's smile in the gloss note: *"Streets spread past store and factory—sped by sunlight and her smile...."* And Pocahontas's smile is metamorphosed in the course of the poet's dream into the ominous and threatening "Sabbatical, unconscious smile" of his mother.

The poem opens with a panoramic view of the continent:

> Macadam, gun-grey as the tunny's belt,
> Leaps from Far Rockaway to Golden Gate:
> Listen! the miles a hurdy-gurdy grinds—
> Down gold arpeggios mile on mile unwinds.

This panorama provides a great contrast to the body of the continent in female guise that the poet had imagined intimately embracing in "The Harbor Dawn." As in "Voyages III," where on a similar quest he used also the Blakean figure of winding and unwinding, the poet's unwinding in this poem leads him not only across the continent but back in time to the schoolbook stories of Pizarro, Cortes, Priscilla and Captain Smith, and Rip Van Winkle, and from these musings back to his own frightening boyhood memories of nature:

> The grind-organ says ... Remember, remember
> The cinder pile at the end of the backyard
> Where we stoned the family of young
> Garter snakes under ... And the monoplanes

> We launched—with paper wings and twisted
> Rubber bands . . . Recall—recall
>
>   the rapid tongues
> That flittered from under the ash heap day
> After day whenever your stick discovered
> Some sunning inch of unsuspecting fibre—
> It flashed back at your thrust, as clean as fire.

The snake is to become in the fourth poem a symbol of time intimately connected with Pocahontas; but here, as it is associated with the lost time of his youth, it carries threatening overtones. It is something evil to be stoned to death, and yet it seems indestructible as at every thrust it flashes back at its attacker. The "rapid tongues" of the snake are a demonic image of his own tongue upon the throat of the blessed earth figure in "The Harbor Dawn." Also, as a phallic symbol, the snake persists to reveal the poet's fear of his sexual identity. His youthful backyard is no paradise of lost innocence, and as he sifts through his memories, the scene darkens:

> So memory, that strikes a rhyme out of a box,
> Or splits a random smell of flowers through glass—
> Is it the whip stripped from the lilac tree
> One day in spring my father took to me,
> Or is it the Sabbatical, unconscious smile
> My mother almost brought me once from church
> And once only, as I recall—?
>
> It flickered through the snow screen, blindly
> It forsook her at the doorway, it was gone
> Before I had left the window. It
> Did not return with the kiss in the hall.

The snake's tongue flittering shades into the mother's smile flickering, both equally frightening to the young boy and a disturbing contrast to Pocahontas's smile. The lilac tree has been stripped to a whip by his father, as if all nature conspired to attack him, and his dream of spring and youth is one of torment and suffering.

If this is, as Crane said, a poem of childhood, it is not a poem that expresses a desire to return to the tranquil state of infancy. If anything, its revelations have been an attempt to exorcise the fears that work cripplingly upon his imagination. To strike a rhyme out of a box and split the smell of flowers—in other words, to free himself by the violent effort of poetry—has been the poet's desire. Only by releasing himself from the cruelty of his real parents can he embrace his true mother earth. Yet this female earth, the body of the continent, is girded with macadam, and as he presses close to it, he finds not the warm flesh of the woman he is seeking but the hardness of Rockaway and Golden Gate. Still, the end of "Van Winkle" finds the poet urging Rip to hurry along on his journey because it is getting late. "Have you got your '*Times*'—?" the poet asks at the end of the poem, and the play on the word "times" underscores the multiple meanings of the poem. "Van Winkle" is a remembrance of times past, of the conquistadores and early settlers of the new continent, of the pastoral retreat of Irving's Dutch villages and villagers overcome by progress, and also of the poet's own childhood fears, which contain neither the adventure nor the calm of the continent's beginnings. By this juxtaposition of national and personal history, the poet contrasts the two and expresses his own ambivalent attitude toward them. That he phrases his comment about the times in a question is important because his reverie has not been entirely revealing to him. He hurries along in search of a more certain identity, a closer contact with the continent.

"The River"

The movement of "The River" follows the pattern of the fighter pilot in Part III of "For the Marriage of Faustus and Helen" and the lover in "Voyages III": the poet merges with the element associated with the female figure. In "For the Marriage of Faustus and Helen" it involved an assault on the sky realm of Helen, and in "Voyages III" the poet descended into the sea. Here the poet moves not only across the continent but "under wires that span the

mountain stream" and "Under a world of whistles, wires and
steam," finally to be submerged in the Mississippi River in a longing for a union with the earth goddess. Although this movement is
toward quiescence, the voyage as in the earlier poems is at first
frenzied. As the poem opens, the speaker is on the Twentieth
Century Limited, moving away from the confusion of commercial
America, the "telegraphic night" of patent names and signboards
which have defaced the body of the continent and thus of the earth
goddess. The poet joins a trio of "Hobo-trekkers" who, the gloss
notes tell us, *"have touched her, knowing her without name."* It
is curious that in the most intense point of his voyaging this lone
poet always goes with fellow-travelers, the "Capped arbiter of
beauty" in "For the Marriage of Faustus and Helen" and the cavorting sea in "Voyages." Here he associates himself with the tramps
who "know a body under the wide rain." "They lurk across
her, knowing her yonder breast / Snow-silvered, sumac-stained or
smoky blue—." The white, red, and blue of these nature images
associate Pocahontas not only with the weather and vegetation but
with the American flag in a kind of gratuitous patriotism. But the
movement across this body is westward toward the setting sun and
into a night journey, and it is the night dream that holds the imagination of the poet:

> —As I have trod the rumorous midnights, too,
>
> And past the circuit of the lamp's thin flame
> (O Nights that brought me to her body bare!)
> Have dreamed beyond the print that bound her name.
> Trains sounding the long blizzards out—I heard
> Wail into distances I knew were hers.
> Papooses crying on the wind's long mane
> Screamed redskin dynasties that fled the brain,
> —Dead echoes! But I knew her body there,
> Time like a serpent down her shoulder, dark,
> And space, an eaglet's wing, laid on her hair.

This is a nightmare confrontation with the body of the continent
appearing as a Medusa-like figure who elicits screams and wails.

She has turned men not into stone but into dead echoes. To un-bind her name, to know her, is to unleash her destructive fury upon the world, not, as the poet had earlier imagined, to fructify the world. In this dream, as sound is diffused through space and historical time coalesces and disperses, the terror of the dark figure overpowers the poet, and yet the dark is also protective of the poet, who is attracted to this horrifying image. "I knew her," he says without fear. In the specificity of detail of the last two lines (the serpentine movement, for instance, which suggests sexual know-ledge as well as a grotesque beauty), this direct confrontation with the body of Pocahontas renders the abstractions of time and space intimate if no less terrifying. The dark woman absorbs again in the vagueness of his dream the expanse of time and space with which the poet wrestles throughout *The Bridge*. Like the "dark confessions" of the female sea, the dark shoulder of this earth goddess and the immediacy of his contact with her flesh remind the poet of his quest. The woman that he claims to know is actually the presence that eludes him. The "crying on the wind's long mane" is her call, refracted through time and space, to which the poet responds imaginatively.[23] The wind of poetic inspiration car-ries hints of her existence to him, and he is energized to continue his pursuit. The female figure has put him in touch with the mythic realm which lies buried under the modern world:

> Under the Ozarks, domed by Iron Mountain,
> The old gods of the rain lie wrapped in pools
> Where eyeless fish curvet a sunken fountain
> And re-descend with corn from querulous crows.

Here again is the image of binding and wrapping which the poet must unloose if he is to confront the full power of this mythic

23. Paul reads this passage as an experience of the poet's youth. The female is the mother whose "wails" Crane knew from his childhood memory of parental quarrels. The crying of the child is linked with the screaming of the redskin dynasties, "the terror of whose warfare, or extermination, provides an image of both the child's hysteria and imagination of sexuality." The "dead echoes" recall the past "when, to be comforted, the screaming child had perhaps been 'brought' to its mother's bed." See Paul's discussion, *Hart's Bridge*, pp. 212–213.

region. The fertility symbols of rain and fish and corn belong to old and sunken gods who demand their propitiation if they are to rise again to new life.

Then the scene shifts to the modern age, and the poet accompanies the Pullman breakfasters who also glide into dusk and night as the train merges with the Mississippi River. The spoliation of the train ("timber torn / By iron, iron—always the iron dealt cleavage!") suggests the masculine world of conquest even as the train's motion is recast into a ritual "dance of wheel on wheel." Against the rigidity of the train's timetable is the eternal power of the river, where

> Maybe the breeze will lift the River's musk
> —As though the waters breathed that you might know.

The lifting breeze, the inspiriting wind, seems but a faint reminder of another time, but the tug of the river is actually irresistibly strong even in this modern age. The poet reminds the trainmen that "you, too, feed the River timelessly. / And few evade full measure of their fate." Once again the movement is downward:

> Down, down—born pioneers in time's despite,
> Grimed tributaries to an ancient flow—
> They win no frontier by their wayward plight,
> But drift in stillness, as from Jordan's brow.

Moving into the river, the poet and the Pullman travelers win no conquest. They are absorbed into stillness where "even stone / Is not more hushed by gravity." The train's conquest of time and space is nullified as "The River, spreading, flows—and spends your dream." Crane's use of a favorite word, "spends," recalls its sexual implications in "Legend" and "For the Marriage of Faustus and Helen," Part III. Here, "lost within this tideless spell," he does not win the "bright logic" by his self-expenditure. Rather, he repeats the myth of his fathers (he says, "You are your father's father"), the myth of rape, of the conquest of the continent, and he suffers their fate: to "win no frontier" but to be spent, exhausted, and overcome by the very force he longs to conquer.

In the river the travelers seem to abandon the body of the continent only to discover it again in the slime and mud of its bed:

> Damp tonnage and alluvial march of days—
> Nights turbid, vascular with silted shale
> And roots surrendered down of moraine clays:
> The Mississippi drinks the farthest dale.
>
> O quarrying passion, undertowed sunlight!
> The basalt surface drags a jungle grace
> Ochreous and lynx-barred in lengthening might;
> Patience! and you shall reach the biding place!

Here is the real confrontation with the elemental force under the water in the darkest retreat, where the shale is pulsing with life (throbbing in a later stanza), and while the pioneer is lost in this "tideless spell," he is curiously caught up in its "quarrying passion." The poet's identification of himself with the flow of the river and the muddiness of the river bed indicates a desire to submit, to be possessed, to be released from the terror and tensions that have built up in these poems. The body of the continent is revealed here in all the grace and might of its great river. Described as vascular and passionate, the river is the sustaining and life-giving mother. And through submission to this force, the poet is prepared for a new life as the river itself breaks into the open ocean:

> And flows within itself, heaps itself free.
> All fades but one thin skyline 'round . . . Ahead
> No embrace opens but the stinging sea;
> The River lifts itself from its long bed,
>
> Poised wholly on its dream, a mustard glow
> Tortured with history, its one will—flow!
> —The Passion spreads in wide tongues, choked and slow,
> Meeting the Gulf, hosannas silently below.

The beauty of this passage is in the harmony of movement and stasis. The rhythmic flowing, heaping, and lifting of the river against the tortured, choked, and slow tide suggest brilliantly the grace as well as the tortuousness of this great forceful urge. And since the river's flowing includes the poet, the poised moment between movement and stillness accurately details the psychic state of the poet; he wishes to lift himself free, yet longs to remain submerged. The desire to be forever secure and the desire to be released, the irresistible undulation and the tremendous effort of moving, hold the poet in a moment of ecstatic stasis, perfectly imaged in these stanzas in the river's rhythm.[24] The river, like the poet, lifts itself from its bed, yet remains poised in its dream. "Tortured with history," the poet himself does not wish to enter the flux of time. Yet, in the flow, his passion becomes the Passion, his ritual death is toward a new life.

As part of the exploration of the body of the continent, "The River" seems to express paradoxically a wish to escape from the land and its history. But the poet says, as he enters the flow of the river, "The River, spreading, flows—and spends your dream." Examined as a dream, the movement into the river reveals the poet's death wish, the desire to submit himself, to be overpowered, and thus to be relieved of his search. The serpent-time, wrapped around the Medusa-like figure of the land, uncoils itself in the vast serpentine movement of the river, and thus the horrible serpent stretches out and loses its grip upon the poet's imagination. The wails and screams that had attended the serpent-bound land are transmuted into hosannas in this final beatific scene. The natural landscape in "The Harbor Dawn," "Van Winkle," and the first part of "The River" has been described as first a winter world of "pallid air," then a frightening springtime in which lilac trees become whips, and finally a dry and desiccated world "WITHOUT STONES OR / WIRES OR EVEN RUNning BROOKS." It is a world where the old gods await their propitiation, where nature itself lies in a deathlike state. Flowing into the "quarrying passion" of the river, the poet flows into the vast creative and life-giving force; it is an escape from the death grip of the land into the lustral waters.

24. This moment is reminiscent of the ending of "Voyages II," which describes the same desire to remain afloat and to be bound, to continue in a moment of ecstatic stasis. Time figures there as it does in "The River."

Crane's outline of "Powhatan's Daughter" lists "The River" as the poem of youth, and although this statement seems at first irrelevant, the dream sequence in the poem points to the youth's first terrifying confrontation with the female figure in the guise of the Medusa-like image and his recoiling from that meeting into a merger with a protective figure. The backward movement here is psychically accurate as the youth seeks to flee from what he knows he must face. He longs to "spend" his dream, to escape it, to purify himself of it, and in the magnetic flow of the river to surrender his terror. And in this retreat the poet is prepared for his new identity as the consort of the earth goddess. Merger with the water here, as in "Voyages III," produces a "single change"; it is a death which "Presumes no carnage." And from it he emerges renewed and energized in the next poem, the climax of "Powhatan's Daughter."

"The Dance"

In his unending search for Pocahontas the poet finds himself ashore once more in a new and strange land ruled by powerful forces. The entire landscape takes on the symbolic form of a ritual dance between a willful woman and her escort. In the opening four stanzas of the poem the poet witnesses the pageant of his own desire in the glacier woman's cavorting with the winter king. As he watches, he is overpowered with uncertainty about the dance he seems to see, and the poem begins in questions:

> The swift red flesh, a winter king—
> Who squired the glacier woman down the sky?
> She ran the neighing canyons all the spring;
> She spouted arms; she rose with maize—to die.
>
> And in the autumn drouth, whose burnished hands
> With mineral wariness found out the stone
> Where prayers, forgotten, streamed the mesa sands?
> He holds the twilight's dim, perpetual throne.

Here is a variant vegetation rite in which the winter gods are sacrificed and the high priest magically brings water out of stone to fertilize the land; but the poet is filled with confusion by this ritual. Pocahontas, as the dancer, assumes once more the tantalizing qualities of the young wanton. She seems to outpace all partners in her frenzied descent and magical ascent, and her dance in its fury unleashes the poet's fears about his potency. Who is it, he asks, who could squire such a woman? Was it the winter king and could it be the poet? This wild ritual revolves around the woman. The man, although royal, assumes a decidedly secondary role. The poet concludes:

> There was a bed of leaves, and broken play;
> There was a veil upon you, Pocahontas, bride—
> O Princess whose brown lap was virgin May;
> And bridal flanks and eyes hid tawny pride.

There, in that mythic time, was enacted not the pattern of two figures dancing in consort but "broken play." The earth goddess in her bed of leaves has received no lover capable of possessing her; her running, spouting, rising, dying have been solo performances. She remains still a virgin bride, desirable in her purity but proud in her assertiveness. She has lifted her veil for no man, yet she is eternally appealing. Although she is described as the bride and virgin, her brown lap and flanks reveal her sensuosity. Crane has said that here he is on mythical soil at last, and one critic has read this passage as "the vision of a mythic world in which the gods are identified with the forces of nature."[25] It must be pointed out, however, that in this vision the poet transfers to the mythic world his own uncertainties. The ritual dance, as the poet sees it, is almost a solo; the woman as the glacier and the maize seems to subsume all nature into herself. Even in those mythic days the winter king in no way controls her movements. And it is this woman, this tormenting mixture of virginity and sensuosity, that the poet imagines as the Indian princess of his desire. He longs to do what from the poet's view it is clear the winter king never succeeded in doing, and that is to possess her totally. This Pocahontas embodies the creative principle, but she has few of the qualities normally asso-

25. Dembo, *Hart Crane's "Sanskrit Charge,"* p. 74.

ciated with the woman—submissiveness, peace, harmony. Yet the poet is irresistibly drawn toward her, and the next six stanzas describe his agonizing ascent to her.

He first imagines her as a moon goddess, as he sees her "hair's keen crescent running" in the evening of his search. For reasons that remain obscure, he starts after her in a canoe. But he cannot reach her. "What laughing chains the water wove and threw!" he exclaims in his frustration. Here, as in "Voyages II," water is imagined as laughing, perhaps approving, perhaps mocking his love. Propelled toward her yet drifting in the water, his efforts are rendered tormentingly ineffective and he, "watching, saw that fleet young crescent die." Pocahontas is then transformed into a star "swinging" and "Cupped in the larches of the mountain pass." All nature seems to taunt him as he climbs toward the goddess whose radiance is caught in the natural scene yet remains always out of his reach. He leaves his canoe and climbs into the mountains; as he does so, he sees Pocahontas in the waterfalls, where her "Feet nozzled wat'ry webs of upper flows." Still, he cannot stop in his obsessive climb, and upward he moves toward her:

> O Appalachian Spring! I gained the ledge;
> Steep, inaccessible smile that eastward bends
> And northward reaches in that violet wedge
> Of Adirondacks!—wisped of azure wands.

Climbing to the ledge's heights, he finds that Pocahontas is behind him in the steep depths from which he has come, and yet she is also beyond him in the magic of her smile in the sky. Running, swinging, fleet she is, like the glacier woman of the poem's opening, and the poet cannot overtake her; she bends toward him but he knows her "inaccessible." Completely encircled by her, yet unable to reach her, the poet feels himself in "some boding shade." Just as the scene has cleared into the eastward smile of dawn, it loses its luminosity in "Smoke swirling through the yellow chestnut glade."

The storm that grew in a "thunder-bud" announces the Indian

dance, which in its fury resembles not only the cyclone but the glacier woman's dance; but here the sole performer is the man. The poet's upward rush, the natural scene that has been constantly in motion, the goddess herself in all her changes of identity, all are whirled into one rhythm by the storm. The furious cyclone releases all the pent-up frustration in the poet as it "—Siphoned the black pool from the heart's hot root!" Although all nature participates, this is a solo dance of the Indian prince, Maquokeeta, and the poet who becomes one with him, performed as tribute to Pocahontas, the woman who grieves.

This man who dances is closely identified with the Medusa-like figure the poet had encountered in his dream in "The River." He has eagle feathers down his back, and he is called a snake, and his ceremonial dance inspires yelling as it brings everything swooping down with it. Of the female figure the poet had boasted, "I knew her body"; here the contact is more direct, as Crane says, "Know Maquokeeta, greeting." As the rhythmic fury of the dance intensifies, the poet becomes one with Maquokeeta and acknowledges the dance as his own: "I, too, was liege," he says. The snake-bird image here also recalls D. H. Lawrence's plumed serpent, and the ritual dance is the dance of consummation and restoration. Time that had coiled around the female figure in "The River" releases its grip upon the dancer who lives before and beyond it in the magical movement of the dance:

> Dance, Maquokeeta! snake that lives before,
> That casts his pelt, and lives beyond! Sprout, horn!
> Spark, tooth! Medicine-man, relent, restore—
> Lie to us,—dance us back the tribal morn!

The serpent-time becomes a symbol of immortality as it is renewed by its own destruction. Like the snake which is transformed to new life by shedding its old skin, the Indian is transformed by the magical change of the dance which is counter-historical. The "lie" is the central truth of his dance in which the Indian casts off the burden of history and restores the "tribal morn" of a new day.

Time is conquered in the sacred circle of the dance. The poet
moves to participate in this metamorphosis. He says:

> Spears and assemblies: black drums thrusting on—
> O yelling battlements,—I, too, was liege
> To rainbows currying each pulsant bone:
> Surpassed the circumstance, danced out the siege!

The imagery of the war dance underscores the violence of the
transformation. Earlier, as the poet approached the dance, he said,
"its rhythm drew, / —Siphoned the black pool from the heart's
hot root!" His psychic and sexual turmoil is intensified here by
association with the war drums of Indian history. But the siege
is danced out and the circumstance of time surpassed in the circumference of the dance.

In this magical dance the man performs both a militant and a
sexual ritual. Characterized by "saber hair," "red fangs," "splay
tongues," "horn," "tooth," and "spears," the Indian embodies the
warrior's fury. But he dances also for the woman he desires and
who demands such tribute. The fire that consumes the dancer in
the next stanza is erotic, and it releases the vital and magical forces
of fire and water upon the earth:

> And buzzard-circleted, screamed from the stake;
> I could not pick the arrows from my side.
> Wrapped in that fire, I saw more escorts wake—
> Flickering, sprint up the hill groins like a tide.
>
> I heard the hush of lava wrestling your arms,
> And stag teeth foam about the raven's throat;
> Flame cataracts of heaven in seething swarms
> Fed down your anklets to the sunset's moat.

Although the dancer is consumed by his own passion, wrapped
in fire, his act has released vital forces in the world. He is bound
to the stake, but the world around him is unbound by his sacrificial
death. "Flickering," "wrestling," "seething" powers are unleashed
in space that appears as an erotic presence. The world is imaged
in its groins and arms and anklets as a woman possessed, her

insatiable desires answered by swarms of escorts. Once again the Indian is compared to the "serpent, Time itself," who is transformed by his own destruction. The poet says, "I saw thy change begun! / And saw thee dive to kiss that destiny." The Indian has kissed not his bride but the destiny of death. Yet in that kiss he is released and dwells "At last with all that's consummate and free." His dance of death fertilizes the earth goddess who lives before and beyond a "bride immortal in the maize!"

His dance promises "infinite seasons" for his immortal bride who is, if the corn goddess, also the virgin. Unlike the winter king who had escorted the glacier woman, the Indian prince here, as the sole dancer, assumes the dominant role. Here the purpose of his ceremonial dance is not to possess or control the woman but to liberate her:

> High unto Labrador the sun strikes free
> Her speechless dream of snow, and stirred again,
> She is the torrent and the singing tree;
> And she is virgin to the last of men . . .

She is the frigid snow queen, the virgin, who must be warmed by man's passion, revived by his life-giving powers endlessly. The poet, inspired to song, identifies with the Indian's restorative powers in the next stanza as the seasonal winds combine with the inspiriting winds of poetry to transform the virgin into a sensual, fecund woman:

> West, west and south! winds over Cumberland
> And winds across the llano grass resume
> Her hair's warm sibilance. Her breasts are fanned
> O stream by slope and vineyard—into bloom!

In the ritual of the dance the Indian evokes the magical powers that govern fertility. Through his sacrifice they "resume" their activity. And in the same way poetry is an evocation of vital forces, a recreation of the world, a restoration of fecundity.

For once, in Crane's poetry, the agent of transformation is the male and the change is wrought upon the passive female. However, at the very moment of renewal the poet is overwhelmed by the miracle in which he has poetically participated, and he is moved to awesome questions:

> And when the caribou slant down for salt
> Do arrows thirst and leap? Do antlers shine
> Alert, star-triggered in the listening vault
> Of dusk?—And are her perfect brows to thine?

The questions recall the earlier questions about the winter king and the glacier woman, and, in fact, the caribou and reindeer remind us of their winter world which will return in the cycle of seasons and demand again the sacrificial dance. The metamorphosis so miraculously achieved in the dance is, the poet realizes now, eternally to be achieved in time through the magic of art. The "listening vault" is the void that must be filled with poetry, the female world that must be responsive to the energies and rhythms of the male dancer. But the questions assert the possibility of such a transformation, such a response, as Lewis has noted.[26] The poem ends on a note of affirmation and prayer:

> We danced, O Brave, we danced beyond their farms,
> In cobalt desert closures made our vows . . .
> Now is the strong prayer folded in thine arms,
> The serpent with the eagle in the boughs.

In this final imagery the poet calls forth a series of references not simply to Pocahontas and Maquokeeta, who have both been associated with the serpent-time and eagle-space, but to the ritual they have performed. The serpent suggests sexuality, phallicism, and also the connection between guilt and sex. As a creature that casts its skin (imaged also as a lizard and associated with "Time itself"), the serpent represents immortality and renewal, the purification of the dance of lust and passion. In the "boughs" it is connected with the tree of life. The eagle, associated with flight, is also an

26. Lewis, *Poetry of Hart Crane*, p. 316.

image of sexual drives. As it soars, however, it suggests space and the sky realm of the gods, the ideal brought down to rest with the real, the serpent, in the newly fructified real world.

In highly individualized language "The Dance" re-enacts the ritual of sacrifice and transformation which has become familiar in Crane's poetry by now. Tormented by his unassuageable lust and rage, the poet is driven into a seizure in which he is totally possessed by his inner conflict. He dances out his siege and emerges purified. Here the Indian prince with whom he associates himself is annihilated, yet only through his destruction is the world re-vivified. As in "For the Marriage of Faustus and Helen" and "Voyages," destruction is the certain means of renewal.

Crane described this poem in terms of the conflict between the two races which he saw reconciled through Pocahontas, the body of the continent.[27] There is certainly conflict here, but it seems to be only peripherally racial. The white poet does not supplant the "swift red flesh" but rather merges with the Indian in his pursuit of the woman. The winter king and the Indian prince experience the poet's fury. They too chase the wild woman of their dreams, their sexual and desirable opposite but also the ideal for which they all anguish in the secret depths of their hearts. The conflicting emotions this woman inspires flame equally in the red and white man and extend even to nature, where the cyclone perfectly images the inner storm of passion. Only by consuming himself in his ritual dance is this conflict released. The trials of the poet are brought to a magnificent climax in this performance, and he is rewarded with a beatific vision of the object of his desires. The woman is transformed into a singing tree, and the winds that blow through this final passage are the life-giving winds that fan the world into bloom.[28]

27. *Letters*, p. 307.
28. The affirmation and careful qualification of Crane's vision here are discussed by James McMichael, "Hart Crane," *Southern Review*, VIII (Spring 1972), 290–309.

"Indiana"

The woman has been the dominating figure in "Powhatan's Daughter." Appearing first as the blessed figure of "The Harbor Dawn," she is but a brief glimpse of the goddess he seeks. In "Van Winkle" she becomes a guide to the voyaging poet; she speeds him on his way and takes him by the hand. But the real women he meets in his journey share little of the divine guide's beneficence: Priscilla is the ideal girl, too young and innocent to be a real guide, and his mother is a demonic image of the female principle. The woman in "The River" appears as a monster, although her bare body attracts him until he merges with it in the dark waters of the river. In "The Dance" she again seduces him, tantalizes him, as she appears inaccessible. Only by ritualizing his lust can he pay her homage and consummate his passion for her.

It is no surprise, then, that she turns up as the old woman in "Indiana," where, as the gloss notes tell us, he reads *"her in a mother's farewell gaze."* She has been guide, seductress, bride, divinity, and now she appears in her final role as the pioneer mother whose first son is leaving the farm to go to sea. Her appeal is to return to the land, but more than that it is the mother's crippling appeal to her son. This poem has been regarded by most critics as trite and sentimental, and it is a great decline poetically from the earlier poems of "Powhatan's Daughter," but in a sense, the tone here is appropriate. Here is a woman who mourns her dead husband and the son who is forsaking her, and in her plaintive plea she symbolizes the pitiful, if demon, mother. Aged and infertile herself, she is still skilled in all the tactics of emasculation. She recalls to her son the pain of his birth, and she upbraids him with his father's faithfulness. As if she knew that that would not keep him, she tries another approach, warns him that she and his father were once "Prodigal" too. Vainly recalling her own "dream called Eldorado," she says it was "but gilded promise" and yielded "barren tears."

Larry, her son, is all that atones for the cruelty of her life, and in one frenzied effort to bind him to her, she puts him above her new husband and the Indiana farm and makes her plea quite direct:

> I'm standing still, I'm old, I'm half of stone!
>   Oh, hold me in those eyes' engaging blue;
> There's where the stubborn years gleam and atone,—
>   Where gold is true!

But the son does not turn back. He has, like many sons, like Crane himself in fact, been fatally close to her, and he longs to escape her possessiveness. Her demands alone will probably make him "a ranger to the end." The appropriateness of this poem has been questioned. It is a matter of some bafflement that Crane tacked this rather weak poem to the end of the most powerful series he had ever written. After "The Dance" any poem would be an anticlimax, but this one seems particularly dull. In the letter to Kahn, Crane confessed that this section was unfinished (in fact, it was put together just before the entire work went to the printers), but his explanation of it is revealing. He says, "It will be the monologue of an Indiana farmer; time, about 1860. He has failed in the gold-rush and is returned to till the soil. His monologue is a farewell to his son, who is leaving for a life on the sea. It is a lyrical summary of the period of conquest, and his wife, the mother who died on the way back from the gold-rush, is alluded to in a way which implies her succession to the nature-symbolism of Pocahontas."[29] In the writing the father was superseded by the mother, and the son's departure from his mother is a more appropriate conclusion to these five poems in which the son has enacted his own deliverance. Her lament is for the lost promises of her youth, the gold of her westward trek, and, as such, it blends with the wailing of women from time immemorial who have bemoaned the failure of fertility and the dearth of the land. Her son has escaped this fate through his own search. He is forever free from the sterility which his mother henceforth represents for him. Crane does make some attempt here to connect the white mother with the Indian woman; they pass on the homeward trail, and the white woman holds

29. *Letters*, p. 307.

up her baby to show the Indian woman. In the smile that passes between them, the women connect their fate, but, insofar as their common bond is the son, the fate of the white woman is quite different from her Indian ancestor. The white son abandons his mother and he does so largely because he has known truly the seduction of the Indian woman, or what the Indian woman represents. The poem concludes with the coming of age of the white man, which gains meaning only as it forms a part of the longer work.

Taken together, "For the Marriage of Faustus and Helen," "Voyages," and "Powhatan's Daughter" are the best poems Crane ever wrote. His creative talent achieved its most illumined moments in these love poems where he expresses a vision of the world so revolutionary in American poetry and so deeply embedded in his own consciousness that to formulate it at all required an intensity of language, an explosion of images, a fusion of meanings, that would have been impossible for a lesser poet. Crane is working here at the outermost reaches of communication, and in his achievement he redefines the meaning of love. He had in American poetry no real model to follow, although he drew selectively on the agonized romanticism of Poe's love poetry and on the mysticism and auto-eroticism in the poetry of Walt Whitman. But he aimed for fuller effects than Poe and a more intense realization of his subject than Whitman had achieved. The death of a beautiful woman was no more his subject than was Whitman's amativeness. Where Poe fades into aestheticism and Whitman into diffuseness, Crane maintains the integrity of his art and the purity of his vision. In English poetry he is closest to John Keats, whose "La Belle Dame sans Merci" contains the germ of Crane's attitude toward love, and Algernon Swinburne, who elaborates on the tainted beauty of the inaccessible woman.[30] He was also, as his letters attest, greatly moved by John Donne's poetry, which he saw as "musky, brooding, speculative vintage, at once sensual and spiritual, and singing rather

30. See Mario Praz's discussion of this fatal woman in *The Romantic Agony* (New York: World, 1956), pp. 187–286.

the beauty of experience than innocence."[31] But the beauty of
Donne's experience as well as the intellectuality of his appeal had
almost nothing in common with the experience Crane wished to
create in his love poetry, and although Donne's use of language
was an education for him, Donne's love poems could not point the
way for Crane. Among his contemporaries there were no great
poets of love. The Eliot whom Crane knew and revered was the
poet of the "Preludes" and *The Waste Land,* works which are
distinguished by the eloquence with which they express the inability to know love. The cruelty of women was a source of attraction for Crane, not a matter of ironic detachment as it was for
Eliot. Although it is not clear that he knew enough French to be
essentially influenced by him, Crane is closest in his vision to
Rimbaud and behind him Baudelaire.[32] In the intoxication of his
search and the purity which he longed to create through the alche-
my of poetry, he resembles Rimbaud. Like Baudelaire, he looked
upon art as mediation by genius of the correspondences between
the visible and the invisible. But Crane wrote in a language which
veered off toward easily paraphrasable meanings and for a poetry-
reading audience which had always placed lucidity above luminosity. Poetry in English had resisted the extremes of the French
symbolists; insofar as the Decadents had pursued them, they had
exhausted their impulse in affectation. Crane's genius lies in the
distillation of divergent sensations into a new vision of the illuminations of love. He escapes affectation by the honesty of his efforts,

31. *Letters,* p. 68.

32. See Wallace Fowlie's discussion of the parallels between Crane and Rimbaud
in his *Love in Literature,* pp. 128–138, in which he traces the history of modern
symbolism as the history of the secularization of medieval Christian man. Fowlie
says, "Between the 'narrative' of love and the 'celebration' of love arising from
some projection of God's created beauty, both of which represent a kind of peace
or triumphant unity, lies the poem which is closer to being love because it condenses passion into an image. The experience of its composition, of its very construction, is love—and therefore the poem doesn't have to talk 'about' love; and
it can't celebrate love because it has found no peace" (p. 128). Although my own
interpretation of Crane does not coincide with Fowlie's emphasis on the Grail
cycle, he does have illuminating things to say about the shared vision of Rimbaud
and Crane.

but that very honesty forces his poems to the boundaries of expression. It is easy to misread them, to mistake one strain in his poetry for the total pattern and to distort his meaning in one direction or the other. He draws upon the language of Christian mysticism; for example, the "imaged Word" of "Voyages VI" suggests the Christian vision of God. His reference to "Mythical brows" in "The Dance" brings into his poetry associations from the fertility rites of antiquity. Naming the figures in his poems Helen and Pocahontas evokes the legends of these elusive women. In all that he said outside his poetry and in the identifications of geographical locations in his poems, he seems to emphasize a national and cultural significance that meshes not only with the universal but also with the highly personal aspects of his theme. He has also been called a poet of the Absolute. As the power in his poetry threatens at every moment to render the world immaterial, he seems to be an idealist longing for escape from reality. But he cannot be both Christian and pagan, nationalistic and absolutist. In his dynamism he is at the furthest remove from the passivity of Christian mysticism. His mythic proclivities pull against the cultural and nationalist tendencies that would locate his poems geographically and historically. These tensions are there, but all these references and associations must be understood as subsumed in his dreams by a power that transcends them. He draws upon every available means of expressing his dream, and only by submitting to the power of that dream is it possible to describe its unique brilliance. To read Crane against any one of his predecessors, against Whitman, Eliot, or Rimbaud, for example, does not do entire justice to the special and unique qualities of his own effort. He is truly solitary in his vision.

I have described the pattern in "For the Marriage of Faustus and Helen," "Voyages," and "Powhatan's Daughter" as the dream of possession. Perhaps now it is possible to define this term more conclusively. It is a dream in several senses. First of all, the initial action of the poems takes place in a state between sleeping and waking in which the poet experiences a much desired but fleeting sense of harmony which is at once unreal and gratifyingly promissory.

The poems then arise from a state beneath consciousness which at the same time corresponds to the poet's intense and most conscious desires. As they unfold, the poems remain close to a somnolent moment, dipping into further reaches of the unconsciousness in the deathlike submission of "The River" or veiling with darkness visions of both ecstasy and horror as in "Voyages III" or soaring to such intensity that consciousness is transmuted to a state of whiteness as in Part I of "For the Marriage of Faustus and Helen." Although the dreams of his poetry imply for Crane no loss of control, no unmediated stream of consciousness, the fact that in these dreams certain patterns recur with obsessive regularity suggests that the magical incantation of his artistry calls forth again and again certain elements from the deepest recesses of his consciousness. Conscious artist that he is, he still cannot escape the revelations of his dreams. The hands, arms, hair, rainbows, smile, snow, trees, flowers, and water that appear over and over in his poems are elements that only assume their deepest meaning as dream images.

These three poems also resemble dreams in the compulsion of their movement. Although they have no narrative thread, they are sustained by a sense of urgency which is as inevitable as it is unexplained by the logic of the poet's activity. The siege must be danced out not for any purposeful end but in response to the psychic energy that impels the dancer. In a sense, the poet in the poem is possessed; he cannot extricate himself from the compulsions that force him on. He cannot ward off the horror any more than he can refuse the ecstasy. Thus the urgency of the dream's movement is part of the dream's meaning. In each poem the speaker longs to possess a beloved object, to hold, to know, to bind himself to this figure most frequently described in feminine terms. Yet, paradoxically, he is possessed by her; his search is energized by her presence, and he cannot control the dynamism of her inspiration. His activism is a state of heightened passivity. He is from the very start possessed by the ecstasy that he seeks. His voyagings are neither to nor from any object but through a state which reveals to his searching eye the beauty and the horror of its grip upon him. His frantic grappling with the demons that hound him, his tortured submission to the beneficent angelic powers that overwhelm him, form one pattern in these poems. Possessed, he longs to possess. Seduced, he longs for seduction. Aroused, he desires arousal. Overcome, he seeks submission. The agony of his desire is one with the passion of its fulfillment. The force that drives him is objectified as something outside the poet, as the poet himself seems to be outside his dream, recording and experiencing it at the same time; yet hovering always within the dream and the dreamer is the awful and beautiful realization that the objectified force is himself. His dream of possession is that purity of self-recognition in which the contraries of his sensations are perfectly reconciled by love. Love imagined as possession starts in these three poems from the double desire to possess someone else sensually and to be possessed by a supersensual power. When Helen first appears to the poet in his dream, she appears as the woman who arouses in him a sensual response and in the same instant as a spirit empowered with the "Reflective conversion of all things." The sensuosity of the lover's appeal in "Voyages" is refracted in the "wide spindrift gaze toward paradise." And the embrace of the "blessed figure" in "Powhatan's Daughter" transports the poet at the very peak of his sensual pleasure to a new day. Physical possession is converted almost instantly into visionary power. At the moment that the loved object materializes in the poet's dream, she reduces the world to immateriality, and she herself becomes not separate from the poet but one with him. Love is a power greater than the woman who inspires it and the man who responds to her. It is the harmony that dissolves all opposites: the opposites of man and woman, lover and beloved, the poet and the world, pain and ecstasy, the possessor and the possessed, the physical and the imaginative. Love is the state of immanence for Crane, and in the resonance of his song he expresses its splendor.

In this expression he is unique among the poets of his time. For all the sexual frankness of the poets of the 1920s, they suffer from a certain emotional reticence. Sex without passion is Eliot's subject.

Although Cummings celebrates sex, he veers away from passion. Ezra Pound's early love poetry turns to the exalting effects of love in such a way as to abstract it into a force. In the clinical skill of William Carlos Williams's early poems, sensual pleasure is detailed without reference to extravagant emotional responses. The gaudiness of Wallace Stevens's beginning poems once again conceals his emotional control. Among these poets Hart Crane must take his place as the single greatest love poet of his generation. He returned to English poetry the intricately structured world of feeling that had been absent from it since the exhaustion of the Romantic impulse. In expressing his private dream through language newly minted in intensified configurations, he expresses for his time the universal power of love. That the inspiration of his love poetry was his own homosexual experience influenced obviously his choice of images, his particular insistence on hands and arms, his apprehension of the female figure as the divine grotesque and the engulfing mother; but in his power to transmute this experience into poetry, he speaks to all conditions of men. He understood the mystery of passion, and in the torment and bliss of his poetry, he makes known a love that is the only human entrance into the ideal. Love is the violence that destroys the world and the beatific power that creates it anew.

chapter four: The World in Flight

Flight is such a dominant sensation in Crane's consciousness that it is impossible to avoid mention of it in any discussion of his work. His poems of violence are poems of passage in which he moves through purgatorial fires, flees from ravines, breaks out of towers, and escapes all constrictions. Compulsive pursuit alternates with ecstatic transport in his poems of possession. The obsessive nature of flight in his poetry suggests its origin in sexuality. Crane was driven by powers that arose from the recesses of his consciousness to run, flee, pursue. But, more that that, flight is in Crane's poetry a means of knowledge, an experience of totality. If he was driven to flee, he also saw flight as a new dimension, a world in itself in which demonic forces are released and given expressive form. Flight is not only the compulsive movement of his dreams, it is itself the "dream of act," as he called it in "Cape Hatteras." It is the symbolic action which so changes man's perspective that he sees a totally new world. Flight revolutionizes man's relationship to time and space so thoroughly that he enters into a new conscious- ness of it. It becomes an important visionary experience in a world where the perspective of the observer everywhere determines what is being observed.

The theme of voyage and flight is age-old in literature, and Crane's use of it is an extension of the Romantic conception of the voyage as a willful projection of feeling. But, like Whitman before him, Crane's is a symbolistic voyage, concerned less with the exploration of emotion than with exploration as a means of existence. As Charles Feidelson has pointed out, Whitman's object "is not so much to impose a new form on the world as to adopt a new stance in which the world takes on new shapes."[1] As Crane's consciousness absorbs the accelerated motion of the machine age, it transforms its furious speed into a vision of dynamism. In "Passage to India" Whitman's imagination soars far beyond the three great engineering feats of his day. The great achievements of the present (the completion of the Suez Canal, the linking of east and west by the railroad, the laying of the Atlantic cable) receive only brief mention in Whitman's poem; it spins "farther, farther" into thin air. In *The Bridge,* on the other hand, Crane's imagination is riveted to modern means of transportation until their heavy weight of steel dissolves and they become pure symbols of flight. They do provide a focus for him, and his poetic effort is bent on envisioning in them the dynamism that he imagined poetically as inspiring the universe. While Walt Whitman takes to the open road afoot, Crane sees the same route as superseded by travel on bridges, trains, airplanes, subways. He seeks to spiritualize these forces and to reconcile their movement with the movement of the universe. To do this, he often has to redirect their flight imaginatively, complete the broken arc of their movement, destroy the image to create the symbol of movement. But his gaze fastens first on the speed of mechanical conveyances.

What is being formed in the vision which arises from the poet's apprehension of modern routes of transportation is a vast circular movement which corresponds to the new truths of Einsteinian physics, but it also corresponds to the poet-voyager's perception of the world as animated by a cosmic dance in which in the highest

---

1. Charles Feidelson, Jr., *Symbolism and American Literature* (Chicago: University of Chicago Press, 1953), p. 27.

flights of his imagination he can participate.[2] In the bridge's "one arc synoptic," the train's "dance of wheel on wheel," the plane's demonic "marauding circles," and the subway's "tunnels that rewind themselves," the poet catches in *The Bridge* a glimpse of the "star-glistered salver of infinity, / The circle, blind crucible of endless space." Although Crane evokes the new verities of the machine age, his poetic intention is to connect them to the old truths of the natural world imagined in the circling rhythm of its life as a symbol of supernatural perfection. Crane's poems of flight work through a spiral of correspondence from the machine to nature to the cosmos in a pattern that recalls the poem that serves as an epigraph to Ralph Waldo Emerson's *Nature*:

> A subtle chain of countless rings
> The next unto the farthest brings;
> The eye reads omens where it goes,
> And speaks all languages the rose;
> And, striving to be man, the worm
> Mounts through all the spires of form.

Whereas Emerson had been content to trace the subtle chain through nature and man, Crane extends it to include the machine. Observing in his dream the movement of mechanized transportation, the poet idealizes it as the projection of his own supreme desire to express the dynamic harmony at the center of his vision. To see in particular objects the universal form or Idea is the poet's way in Crane's imagination and connects him with the whole tradition of idealism which stems from Plato.[3]

2. Jean Guiguet has commented on the richness of references to circles and gyrations in Crane's poems and points out that "si Hart Crane envisage la civilisation mécanique sous le signe du cercle, il projette aussi cette même image sur le cosmos. . . ." See Jean Guiguet, *L'univers poétique de Hart Crane* (Paris: M. J. Minard, 1965), pp. 72–75. For a discussion of Crane's use of Einsteinian physics, see Hyatt Howe Waggoner, *The Heel of Elohim* (Norman: University of Oklahoma Press, 1950), pp. 171–192.

3. Joseph J. Arpad discusses Crane's Platonism and dissociates it from Romantic mysticism in "Hart Crane's Platonic Myth: The Brooklyn Bridge," *American Literature*, XXXIX (Mar. 1967), 75–86. Arpad is especially good in exposing Crane's synoptic insight into the bridge's ultimate reality.

The mechanism of the machine has been traditionally opposed in poetry to the organic rhythm of man and nature, but Crane sees in these two systems no opposition. In his imagination they move along "companion ways." What he admires in nature is exactly what he admires in the machine: dynamic power. In the man-made conveyances of the machine age Crane envisions the workings of the same movement that vitalizes the dynamic universe. While earlier poets had turned away in disgust from mechanical images, Crane focuses upon them, strips them to bare movement, and thus attempts to reconcile them to the harmonic movement of the spheres.

The bridge, train, airplane, and subway are means of transport as well as transportation in Crane's poem. Their fury, a word which Crane summons up again and again to describe them, is a correlative of his own "possessed" state. As they spiral in his imagination, they are fused with his own sense of psychic transport until they become the pure form of circular movement. In their movement the solidarity of the world is dispersed, and a new fluid perception of time and space arises. Modes of transportation are the dominant scheme of imagery in *The Bridge*, and by examining the patterns they form, it is possible to see how Crane transmuted the motion of his world into a poetic dream of harmony. The mechanical conveyances in his poetry move toward no terminal; they speed toward no resting place. Instead, they are absorbed into the cosmos. The bridge is subsumed into the sky above it and the earth below; the train fades into the river. Thus the world of the machine is reattached to the dynamism of nature, which itself reflects a kind of harmonic motion. Critics have generally overlooked this movement in *The Bridge*. In focusing chiefly on the blinding, deafening, deadening qualities of Crane's technology, most critics have concluded that Crane had a negative attitude toward the machine.[4]

4. R. W. B. Lewis says, "But in Crane's view, the eyes and the ears—those interchangeable instruments of vision—had been quite put out and spoiled for the modern American and even, temporarily, for the poet, and precisely by the smoke and the steam and the hissing of the age of iron." See Lewis, *Poetry of Hart Crane*, p. 234. And again in referring to Whitman's *Democratic Vistas*, Lewis says, "This

The view has been that it is the machine and the world it spawned which Crane reacts against and labors to transform through his supreme creative powers. His job is to make out of words an ideal world of order and meaning which is nowhere apparent in the real, modern, mechanized world.[5] To be sure, part of Crane's materials are drawn from his own awareness of man's machine-made capacity for destruction, devitalization, and disjunction. But the images of cyclonic and centerless power, machine-driven massacres, and the paralysis caused by steel and iron must be placed against the order of the technological bridge, the movement of modern means of transportation, the unity of Crane's imagined landscape in which the machine and nature can exist in an inspired equilibrium. *The Bridge* is a poem of flight, and the vehicles on which the poetic imagination rides are the bridge, the train, the airplane, even the subway of the twentieth-century industrial complex; they hold the poet no captive at all.

In *The Bridge* Crane diverges from the host of American writers,

---

was an essay Crane expressly admired, both for its savage indictment of American 'materialism' and 'industrialism' . . . and for its staunch belief that only poetry could rescue the country from the spiritual blindness and moral degradation that resulted from the elements indicted" (p. 243). Herbert Leibowitz concedes that the machine is important as an image in Crane's work, but he is hard pressed to find a positive industrial metaphor in the poems. See Leibowitz, *Hart Crane*, pp. 257–264. While Alan Trachtenberg has traced the development of the real bridge from fact to myth, his chapter on Hart Crane's poem is dominated by his thesis that in Crane's bridge the real bridge has become pure myth. Thus he does not emphasize the industrial metaphor. See Alan Trachtenberg, *Brooklyn Bridge: Fact and Symbol* (New York: Oxford University Press, 1965), pp. 143–165. The single critic who emphasizes Crane's genius in absorbing the machine is David Bulwer Luytens, *The Creative Encounter* (London: Secker and Warburg, 1960), pp. 98–127. His emphasis is slightly different from mine, but I agree almost entirely with his introductory statements: "It is in his ability to incorporate into poetry a whole sphere of contemporary experience—not often regarded as poetic—that his greatness lies. Hart Crane humanised the machine, and in this consists a power that bears witness to an encounter with the reality of modern life, which is truly existential" (p. 99).

5. Talking about the new American epic, of which Crane's was a prime example, Roy Harvey Pearce says that it is "one of ordering, not of order; of creation, not confirmation; of revealing, not memorializing." See Roy Harvey Pearce, *The Continuity of American Poetry* (Princeton, N.J.: Princeton University Press, 1961), p. 83.

classically described by Leo Marx, who subscribe to the symbolic value of the green landscape which the machine has somehow stripped of meaning. Marx contends that the literary history of the pastoral ideal in an increasingly industrial society has led to a "recurrent metaphor of contradiction."[6] This contradiction, Marx says,

> compels us to recognize that the aspirations once represented by the symbol of an ideal landscape have not, and probably cannot, be embodied in our traditional institutions. It means that an inspiriting vision of a humane community has been reduced to a token of individual survival. The outcome of *Walden, Moby-Dick,* and *Huckleberry Finn* is repeated in the typical modern version of the fable; in the end the American hero is either dead or totally alienated from society, alone and powerless, like the evicted shepherd of Virgil's eclogue. And if, at the same time, he pays a tribute to the image of a green landscape, it is likely to be ironic and bitter.[7]

But Crane's metaphor is one of assimilation, of accomodation. He seeks to establish a bridge of correspondence between the natural and the mechanical realms, and thus to express his consciousness of unity. Crane's frontal approach to the machine age is divested of all nostalgia, as well as the estrangement which that sentiment betokens. Perhaps Crane's success stems from the fact that his consciousness works from the counter-force of industry back to the force of nature, and so the movement is altogether in the opposite direction from the writers of the pastoral ideal.

Crane has also been accused of falling into the technological fallacy. In his book on the period Frederick J. Hoffman maintains that poets could write verse about the machine only by endowing it with the very qualities of emotion and value most conscientiously omitted from its construction or by speaking simply of its effect upon human experience.[8] Hoffman sees no poetically satisfactory

6. Leo Marx, *The Machine in the Garden* (New York: Oxford University Press, 1964), p. 364.
7. *Ibid.*
8. Frederick J. Hoffman, *The Twenties* (New York: Viking Press, 1955), p. 257.

way of dealing with the machine; its structure is too complex to be understood by nonspecialist poets, and any attempt to humanize or spiritualize the machine is invalidated by the incompatibility between technology and human value. Of course, Crane's use of the imagery of transportation verges on this fallacy; he does attempt to bridge the gap between technology and human value. But, in his emphasis on flight, Crane manages to pinpoint the convergence of man's aspirations and his technological inventions. Man cannot reach heaven in an airplane, but in the flight of the airplane, as in the flight of birds, man can apprehend a symbol of his inmost desires.

Crane's own view of the relationship between machinery and poetry pivots on what he called Gorham Munson's "very rich suggestions" about "the treatment of mechanical manifestations of today as subject for lyrical, dramatic, and even epic poetry."[9] Crane's friend Munson presented a cogent argument for bringing the "Machine into the scope of the human spirit,"[10] and his views, published in his work on Waldo Frank and no doubt hashed over in conversation with Crane, had confirmed Crane's own growing conviction that machinery had to be poeticized or poetry mechanized in an age where the two were bound to be fraternal geniuses.

Munson argued not only against the outright rejection of the machine by the "back-to-nature revoltes" but also against the acceptance of the machine simply as a necessary evil. In fact, Munson felt that the exclusively modern sensations of the machine were perhaps the most healthy and significant phenomena in American civilization; yet, he said, they "lie undigested in our spiritual anatomy like pebbles."[11] For one hundred years artists had devoted themselves entirely to the art of maladjustment, railing against the machine for upsetting the old equilibrium between man and nature. What was needed now, Munson said, was a poetry of adjustment

9. *Letters*, p. 125.
10. Gorham Munson, *Waldo Frank* (New York: Boni & Liveright, 1923), p. 24.
11. *Ibid.*, p. 23.

which would work out an entirely new harmony among man, nature, and the machine.

Munson saw in the work of the Europeans Marinetti and Tristan Tzara a start toward this new kind of poetry. The Futurist's view of speed as a new beauty and the Dadaist's desire to relate man positively to the machine were excellent approaches, but they were limited, Munson felt, by their refusal "to channel emotional profundities, to take up love and desire and religion into its form."[12] They had so far produced only a mechanized art of minor aesthetic thrills; still, they were to be encouraged, according to Munson.

But, Munson contended, and to this point Crane must have responded most enthusiastically, it was probably not Europe but the more mechanized America which would produce the poet of the machine age, the poet who could "string some constant harmony" out of the forces of modern life. It was the peculiar genius of America that had proliferated "skyscrapers, bridges, motion pictures, jazz music, vaudeville, electric light displays, advertising," and it was perhaps this genius which would through literature "put positive and glowing spiritual content into Machinery."[13]

These ideas were very much on Crane's mind when he was first thinking of *The Bridge*. They were for him certainly an important part of his great poem about America. In direct response to Munson's challenge, Crane wrote him, "Potentially I feel myself quite fit to become a suitable Pindar for the dawn of the machine age, so called."[14] He claimed already to have incorporated Munson's ideas in "For the Marriage of Faustus and Helen," and he promised they would figure even larger in *The Bridge*. Crane wrote further, "The field of possibilities literally glitters all around one with the perception and vocabulary to pick out significant details and digest them into something emotional."[15] To pick out significant details

12. *Ibid.*, p. 25.
13. *Ibid.*
14. *Letters*, p. 129.
15. *Ibid.*, p. 125.

from the mechanical manifestations of the day and transform them into something emotional was exactly Crane's program, as it was Munson's.

From the beginning Crane conceived of his bridge, for all its metaphorical rightness, as a mechanical image, "symbol of our constructive future, our unique identity, in which is included also our scientific hopes and achievements of the future."[16] And in very early drafts of the long poem he had already developed what was to become a characteristic pattern for dealing with the machine. By juxtaposing the machine and nature, the mechanical metaphor could be not only absorbed by the landscape but both tempered and vitalized by it, as we can see in the early fragment of what he called then the first verse of *The Bridge*:

> Macadam, gun grey as the tunny's pelt,
> Leaps from Far Rockaway to Golden Gate,
> For first it was the road, the road only
> We heeded in joint piracy and pushed.[17]

Although only the first two of the four lines are preserved in the final version and then not as the first verse but as part of "Van Winkle," this stanza is significant because it demonstrates how Crane's consciousness absorbed the sensations of industrial America in order to build his imaginative bridge. Also, the simile (later and better between macadam and the tunny's belt) illustrates how the machine could be improved by harmony with nature and how nature could accept man-made macadam as its own. What Crane is doing here and what he consistently does in *The Bridge* is to absorb the machine into the landscape. Although he had doubts about the possibility of investing his metaphors with symbolic value, he felt to the end of his life that the function of the poet in the machine age was, as he said in his much quoted but often misunderstood essay on modern poetry, to "absorb the machine, i.e. *acclimatize* it as naturally and casually as trees, cattle, galleons,

16. *Ibid.*, p. 124.
17. *Ibid.*, p. 123.

castles and all other human associations of the past."[18] To acclimatize the machine, to habituate it to a climate not native to it, to season
and inure it to the landscape, that is his method. And it is an honor-
able method in American culture, going back to the advocates of
industrialization who argued in the eighteenth century that the
New World environment could purify the industrial system.[19]

After working on the poem off and on for three years and still
before its final form had been realized, Crane toned down his
enthusiasm for machines and said simply that the poem was to be
"based on the conquest of space and knowledge."[20] How strongly
the metaphor of transportation figures in his concrete realization of
this conquest can be seen by the progress from an early summary
of the parts to the actual working out of the poems. In 1926 he
listed the sections as:

  I   Columbus—Conquest of space, chaos
  II Pokahantus [*sic*]—The natural body of America—fertility, etc.
  III Whitman—The Spiritual body of America . . .
  IV John Brown
      (Negro Porter on Calgary Express making up berths. . . .)
  V   Subway—The encroachment of machinery on humanity; a kind
      of purgatory in relation to the open sky of last section
  VI The Bridge—A sweeping dithyramb in which the Bridge be-
      comes the symbol of consciousness spanning time and space[21]

In this scheme (all parts of which except the John Brown section
he incorporated into the final poem) half the sections deal with
means of transportation, a significant part despite the fact that the
subway here is indicted in traditionally Romantic terms as an
encroachment on humanity. In the actual writing of these sections,
however, the subject took hold of his imagination and served as
a way to approach also the nonindustrial subjects of Pocahontas and
Whitman.

18. "Modern Poetry," *The Complete Poems*, pp. 261–262.
19. Leo Marx traces this idea from the Philadelphia merchant Tench Coxe in
The Machine in the Garden, p. 158.
20. *Letters*, p. 241.
21. *Ibid.*

Columbus is left appropriately untainted by technology except for his compass, but his section is superseded as an opening by an ode to the Brooklyn Bridge. That "magnificent structure," as Crane called it, took the lead in the conquest of space and chaos from Columbus, and Columbus's journey repeats in a sense the man-made curveship of the bridge. Pocahontas and Whitman, the natural and spiritual bodies of the nation, became in the writing inextricably bound up with the machine. The approach to the fertility goddess of America is through the city harbor and coast-to-coast railroad, an unlikely route through which Crane leads us nonetheless not only into nature but back in time to the primitivism of "the tribal morn." The ode to Whitman becomes as much an ode to the spiritual possibilities of the airplane as to the poet, and Whitman himself is hailed as the poet who spiritualized the machine: "Our Meistersinger, thou set breath to steel." So the bridge, the train, the subway, and the airplane become the conveyances which carry the poet on his imaginative journey into America. Crane does not treat these modes of transportation with equal enthusiasm. The bridge is incomparably acclaimed. The train, the subway, the airplane, are all involved in the spoliation of the landscape, but as images of flight they are each in different ways acceptable vehicles of conveyance for the poet, who must use them not only practically but imaginatively. In the final version of *The Bridge*, of course, there are not six but fifteen poems, of which six deal directly with transportation. In addition, two poems deal in large part with the machine-produced city and highways.

The Bridge, as Crane wrote Kahn, "starts in the present and 'progresses backwards.'"[22] His inspired vision of America rises very much out of his consciousness of the present. What Crane had to start with was neither a myth nor much knowledge of history but "cerebral excitements," and a title, an expansive image, a real bridge. He develops his theme through certain symbols of transportation which enter his imagination not as objective fact but as

22. *Ibid.,* p. 307.

dream images of powerful movement. He has what he regarded as the supreme qualification of the poet in the machine age, "an extraordinary capacity for surrender, at least temporarily, to the sensations of urban life," as well as "sufficient spontaneity and gusto to convert this experience into positive terms."[23] In his surrender he imagines the chaotic movement of the modern world as reconciled in one vast spiraling coil. To make manifest to the modern world his intuitive apprehension of harmony, the poet has first to reconcile the machine's vast potential of power and force with the primeval power of nature. The new harmony which Munson sought among man, nature, and the machine becomes in Crane's imaginative grasp a harmony of circular movement.

I

The flight of the seagull is the opening vision of *The Bridge*. In its "inviolate curve," its circling, the poet sees the natural reflection of the bridge which the bird pivots. "Proem: To Brooklyn Bridge" is a dreamlike meditation on the bridge, engineering fact and scenic symbol, which becomes in the poet's vision the pure movement of flight. The poet addresses the bridge:

> And Thee, across the harbor, silver-paced
> As though the sun took step of thee, yet left
> Some motion ever unspent in thy stride,—
> Implicitly thy freedom staying thee!

The splendor of this man-made structure is the supreme naturalness of its artifice. The laws of its construction are confirmed by the laws of nature. The circling sun above it and the rippling waters under it absorb it into their movement and remove it from the unnatural world of the suicidal bedlamite who tilts on its parapets and from the denaturalized life of the commercial city. Its flight is to the clouds, and its "cables breathe the North Atlantic still"; the

23. "Modern Poetry," *The Complete Poems*, p. 262.

bridge appears to the poet as inspired by the powers of nature. The curve of its structure embraces modern man; it is an "Accolade" and "Vibrant reprieve and pardon" for all the havoc that man has, using the same materials, created. Again the poet addresses the bridge:

> O harp and altar, of the fury fused,
> (How could mere toil align thy choiring strings!)
> Terrific threshold of the prophet's pledge,
> Prayer of pariah and the lover's cry,—

How could "mere toil," simple mathematics, technical know-how, engineering skill, build something which seems to break the bounds of rationality, to partake of realms beyond science, to be at once a work of art and a sacred place, the poet asks. Science is imagined here as working through its arch-enemy, primordial fury, to contruct a bridge of steel which will transcend its own method and materials. The century-old fear of poets that the machine would grind man to its own grist is belied in this poet's apprehension of the Brooklyn Bridge. Through technology, man has arrived at the threshold of a new consciousness. He has lifted himself beyond his petty systems to create not only a harp on which he can celebrate artfully his new awareness but the altar at which he can worship.

As the poet's thoughts veer upward and far beyond the bridge, his eyes follow the traffic lights along the bridge which coalesce with the stars to "condense eternity." "And we have seen night lifted in thine arms," the poet says. The harmony between the bridge and nature dispels the utter darkness of the world and gives man not only a vision of wholeness in its harmonic movement but an "Unfractioned idiom" by which to express this vision. Yet "Only in darkness is thy shadow clear," the poet says, as if to remind us that this has been a dream. In the final stanza of "Proem" the bridge's harmonious circling is again extolled:

> O Sleepless as the river under thee,
> Vaulting the sea, the prairies' dreaming sod,

> Unto us lowliest sometime sweep, descend
> And of the curveship lend a myth to God.

The gulls, the circles of stars, the round ocean are one with the curveship of the bridge. Its form reveals the image of wholeness in the modern world.

Crane is no latter-day Newtonian, aligning man-made machines with God's larger design. The forces in nature which the bridge shares are not the precise and accurate movements of a mere mechanism but rather the circling, moving, breathing, sighing, sleepless, dreaming qualities of a dynamic life force. Crane's poetic insistence is on the circle, and his method is to build circle on circle (the gull's curve on the curve of the harp on the stars and finally the bridge itself) in a kind of spiral whirling upward. The bridge blends with the natural world, but it also blends with the supernatural and serves as an intercessor between man, its creator, and these worlds. Crane's bridge is no mere linear connection between two shores.

From "Proem" the long poem progresses backward to the voyage of Columbus, where man first apprehended "This turning rondure whole, this crescent ring." In the twentieth century man and his technological inventions appear to be at the center of the circling natural scene; in the fifteenth century they were only beginning to emerge as significant forces on the "teeming span" of the universe. The whirling sea and the "eddying breath" which appear benedictory to the bridge at every turn threaten Columbus's flight. Yet Columbus's vision of the universe is a perception of circling stars and a circular world that marks him as the true predecessor of the modern poet-voyager. His apostrophe to the universe might have been spoken by his twentieth-century counterpart:

> Of all that amplitude that time explores,
> A needle in the sight, suspended north,—
> Yielding by inference and discard, faith
> And true appointment from the hidden shoal:
> This disposition that thy night relates
> From Moon to Saturn in one sapphire wheel:

> The orbic wake of thy once whirling feet,
> Elohim, still I hear thy sounding heel!

Like the poet who sees the meaning of the bridge's circling only in darkness, Columbus's knowledge is also a revelation of the night, a dream vision of the eternal wheel that spins the vastness of space.

II

The poet's flight continues through the harbor dawn in the leap from Far Rockaway to Golden Gate and finally to the train of "The River."[24] The train that roars into the nighttime wilderness of America and carries the poet with it is on the same track as the locomotive that came whizzing and shrieking through Concord, Massachusetts, in 1844, to upset Hawthorne's peaceful reveries; it is a descendant of the iron horse whose ear-rending neighs pierced the silence of Walden Pond; it is naturally of the same species as the snakelike machine that intrudes upon the unaxed campsite in "The Bear." But the extent to which Crane's Twentieth Century Limited differs from these other trains is marked and suggests how Crane had absorbed the sensations of twentieth-century industrialized America.

In Crane's consciousness there exists a certain sensorial correspondence between nature and the machine. He does not contrast the noisy, whizzing train with a pastoral world of calm and silence; rather, the train's frenzied speed has its counterpart in nature as the poet hears "Trains sounding the long blizzards out." The eye is not blinded by the ugliness of the machine any more than it is blinded by the real ugliness of nature; the elements themselves are not all sunshine and clear water. The grimiest train resembles the Mississippi River, described accurately as "Damp tonnage and

24. In the opening lines of "Van Winkle" macadam "Leaps from Far Rockaway to Golden Gate," from the shores of Long Island to the gateway to the Orient. It is too bad for our purposes that the Golden Gate Bridge was not built until after Crane's death; what an affirmation of the machine age this particular juxtaposition would make—from the rocks of the landscape to the golden bridge.

alluvial march of days— / Nights turbid, vascular with silted shale."
The mechanical and seemingly unnatural force of the machine
finds its natural model in the ruthless flow of the river, which drags
everything with it to its biding place as, in a curious combination
of mechanical and organic metaphors, the river's "freighted floors
/ Throb past the City." Crane does write of the "iron dealt cleavage" of the train, the destruction of nature by the machine. But it
is also a reminder of the natural origin of the train, the iron taken
from "Iron Mountain," the iron-dealt cleavage of the mines which
has become the train. Now "iron strides the dew— / Straddles the
hill, a dance of wheel on wheel," and so the circle is closed as the
iron returns to nature in a dance, a foretelling of as well as a contrast to the mythic dance of the Indian in the next section of *The
Bridge* and another form of the harmonious "sapphire wheel" of
Elohim from the earlier Columbus section. Crane here echoes
Whitman's address in "To a Locomotive in Winter":

> Type of the modern—emblem of motion and power—pulse of the
> continent,
> For once come serve the Muse and merge in verse, even as here I
> see thee,
> With storm and buffeting gusts of wind and falling snow,
> By day thy warning ringing bell to sound its notes,
> By night thy silent signal lamps to swing.

The remarkable fact about this section of *The Bridge* is that this
particular train, the plushest conveyance of the glittering 1920s,
leads the reader not away from nature into the great world of civilization but directly into the interior of the country and back in time
to the "primal world of the Indian."[25] The train in all its splendor
does in fact fade into the landscape, and in one of the long poem's
several metamorphoses it becomes the Mississippi River.

The tramps whom the Twentieth Century Limited deposits
along the banks of the Mississippi have been regarded as anti-

25. *Letters*, p. 307.

industrial figures, "pastoral Charlie Chaplins."[26] These childlike figures, uncorrupted by civilization, have a direct, sensual, and intuitive response to the land, which the Indian and the pioneer shared and which industrial man must recapture "Under a world of whistles, wires and steam." It is true that these hoboes have the "elemental gist," remember certain nature favors like "watermelon days" and the best place for "early trouting," and have touched "something like a key perhaps" in the continent. They can count time not measured by the "Keen instruments, strung to a vast precision" of scientific America; they are in tune with the freer movements of nature and measure "The river's minute by the far brook's year." In a sense, then, they are quite the opposite of the "EXPRESS" that "makes time like / SCIENCE" and the world that exists in a "telegraphic night." But these "humpty-dumpty clods," as Crane also describes them, are not the only people in modern America who know at first hand the time and movement of the land. They share their awareness with two figures straight out of the machine age, the steamboat pilot and the Negro train porter, *"Memphis Johnny, Steamboat Bill, Missouri Joe."* The pilot and the porter as they merge into one person, an "ancient clown," lead the modern pioneer, the "Pullman breakfasters," to the special knowledge that nature bestows. Man must move as far as he can on his modern contrivances to conquer space and time, and then he must harmonize his flight with the same powerful primitive force of nature which the steamboat captains as well as Columbus knew. Modern man must flee in a sense in the opposite direction from Columbus, away from the skill and control of "Sheriff, Brakeman and Authority" to the intimate knowledge which Columbus had from the beginning of the "ancient flow," the "quarrying passion," the "jungle grace," "this tideless spell" of nature, rampant, free, and wild. The new "liquid theme" of flight will be a version of Columbus's *Te Deum,* the Negro spiritual *Deep River,* in which is celebrated man's flight from slavery to freedom, from death to life, from this world to the next. And in this case the deep

26. Lewis, *Poetry of Hart Crane,* p. 300.

river carries man from the confusion of the present back through the steamboat era into the world of myth, where in "The Dance" that follows he comes to possess a sense of the primal movement of life.

III

The poet travels afoot or by canoe for two poems after "The River" until "Cutty Sark," where he is deposited again in the harbor, this time in the company of a sailor whose rummy reminiscences of sea life recall to the poet visions of the clipper ship, that glorious "white machine" whose circular voyage had in an earlier day cleared the Orient and brought back the mysteries of Cathay. The drunken sailor is a wanderer, bewildered by "Murmurs of Leviathan," of the awesome spirit of the deep. But still, he says, "life's a geyser," and although, in leaving the bar, he barely misses being killed by a truck, he lunges symbolically as the voyager he is into the dawn. The "long tack" of the clipper ships rounds off Crane's version of the history-making epochs of America; he returns in the next section to the point from which he started and to a new era of discovery made possible by the airplane, a conveyance which has created, much like the clipper ship in its day, a new world.

"Cape Hatteras," Section IV of *The Bridge*, is the symbolic center of the long work, Crane said, and his meaning is made clear in the centripetal force of its chief symbol, the airplane. The airplane travels in "oilrinsed circles of blind ecstasy," "down gravitation's / vortex," from circumstances of violent speed into the very center of turbulence where the poet finds in the eye of this man-made storm the pivot of its movement. The flight of the airplane, like the span of the bridge and the movement of the train, is circular; it does not lead from one point to another but moves in spirals inward to the still point at the center of all motion. However, unlike the bridge, the airplane moves toward its own destruction; its pivot and still point are its crash "into mashed and shapeless debris." Only the poet escapes the destruction and moves "upward from the dead." Here again is Crane's typical plot—the destruction that portends creativity—but now it is strained to its limits. The destroyed are deservedly destroyed; the resurrection must be achieved by imaginative, not mechanical, means.

The poem itself is circular in its development; it moves from "Combustion at the astral core" to "Easters of speeding light," tracing over and over again the "marauding circles" of the airplane against the perfect movement of the circling stars and attempting always to spin one spiral into another. The poem's length (it contains some 240 lines and is the longest single poem in *The Bridge*) has been attacked as excessive, and its language has been disparaged as overstatement. Yet the length is justified by the complexity of forces Crane is trying to harmonize here, and its language, although sometimes giddy, is in its intensity appropriate to the new insights it proclaims.

"Cape Hatteras," projected as an ode to Whitman and the spiritual body of the continent, begins with a treatment of the airplane and the perspectives of flight it provides. In this newest form of transportation man seems to have invented a revolutionary machine which can propel him to that end foretold by Walt Whitman in the stanza from "Passage to India" from which Crane took the epigraph for his poem:

> Reckoning ahead O soul, when thou, the time achiev'd
> The seas all cross'd, weather'd the capes, the voyage done,
> Surrounded, copest, frontest God, yieldest, the aim attain'd,
> As fill'd with friendship, love complete, the Elder Brother found,
> The Younger melts in fondness in his arms.

Like Whitman, Crane sees the aim of all voyaging attained in the beatific vision of God's global universe reflected in human terms of love and harmony. That the airplane has actually brought no such vision to man is played against its vast potential to do so. In the airplane the seas can all be crossed, the capes weathered, the voyage done; but the poet's aim is not attained in this way. The airplane is the agent of war, not friendship; of doom, not

love; of destruction, not harmony. Although, like the evolution-
ary and geological changes that open the poem, the airplane
is a new stage in the "change / Of energy," it has not provided man
with an affirmative view of the universe.

As the seafaring age gives way to the new era of airplanes, the
poet is hopeful that he will arrive at a new awareness of the cosmos,
but his hopes are immediately shattered. He says:

> What whisperings of far watches on the main
> Relapsing into silence, while time clears
> Our lenses, lifts a focus, resurrects
> A periscope to glimpse what joys or pain
> Our eyes can share or answer—then deflects
> Us, shunting to a labyrinth submersed
> Where each sees only his dim past reversed . . .
>
> But that star-glistered salver of infinity,
> The circle, blind crucible of endless space,
> Is sluiced by motion,—subjugated never.
> Adam and Adam's answer in the forest
> Left Hesperus mirrored in the lucid pool.
> Now the eagle dominates our days, is jurist
> Of the ambiguous cloud. We know the strident rule
> Of wings imperious . . . Space, instantaneous,
> Flickers a moment, consumes us in its smile.

In these lines vision clears and clouds, focuses and blurs, as in a
dream. The poet senses the possibility of a liberating perspective,
the glimpse of endless space, and his own inability to see. His eyes
cannot "share or answer"; they cannot register the vastness of space.
Caught in time's labyrinth, man cannot view infinity. The "strident
rule" of warplanes is powerless against the vastness of space. Lifted
and submersed, resurrected and shunted, enlightened and blinded,
man is overwhelmed by the infinitude of space that consumes him
and yet gives him at the same time a flickering sense of the circling
harmony of the spheres. In his vision

> Dream cancels dream in this new realm of fact
> From which we wake into the dream of act;

> Seeing himself an atom in a shroud—
> Man hears himself an engine in a cloud!

The dream of flight and the dream of infinite space cancel each other in the scientific age of the airplane. Man can never subjugate the skies, although his airborne power inspires in him that hope of focusing on infinity. Space is "jurist / Of the ambiguous cloud," not man, and if through the airplane man has released himself from the death grip of the confining earth, he then is consumed by space. He wakes only into a new dream, a new fantasy in which the act of flight must be reconciled with a new perspective of the world, and that perspective harmonized with the vision of infinity.[27] The spiraling airplane, the circling stars, and the poet's eyes that would envision the harmony between these forms are the central images of this poem.

The fear aroused by the vastness of space leads the poet to invoke the spirit of Walt Whitman, the "Saunterer on free ways still ahead," and inquire of him "if infinity / Be still the same as when you walked the beach." The poet is also seeking Whitman's help

27. L. S. Dembo has commented on the parallels between Crane's poem and Verticalism, a doctrine set forth by Eugene Jolas in 1932 from ideas that Jolas might have discussed with Crane when they met in 1929. Verticalism stressed "the creative urge towards a liturgical renascence by reconstructing the myth of the voyage, migration, flight, and particularly ascent, in all its romantic-mystic manifestations." Jolas writes that Verticalism "sought the 'marvellous of the skies' in the poetry of aeronautical flight, in the conquest of the law of gravitation, and in an aspiration towards aerial perspectives. It also developed the poetry of cosmic or sidereal flight, tried to sing of the stellar spaces, and accentuated the vision of the 'third eye.' In the poetry of mystic flight it sought a transcendental reality. This new poetry of ascent wanted to express its vision in a language that would make possible a hymnic vocabulary." Jolas felt that modern man was in the shadow of a "primeval *fear*, a rationalist *possession*," part of a general "daemonism" brought on by a mechanistic way of thinking. The poet must "*exorcise* this *possession* through the mantic word," according to Jolas. By writing of the aeronautical experience of a demonic technological world, Crane exorcises the fear. The appearance of doom in "Cape Hatteras" elicits a terror that yields to jubilation, and thus the poem expresses its "romantic-mystic" meaning. See L. S. Dembo, "Hart Crane's 'Verticalist' Poem," *American Literature*, XL (Mar. 1968), 77–81. Although I see the perspective as vertigral (Jolas actually changed the name of his doctrine to Vertigralism) rather than vertical, the parallel is illuminating.

in finding a free way out of "this breed of towers," again imaged as a labyrinth, the "prison crypt / Of canyoned traffic," because, as he admits, he has not even attained Whitman's "empire" of the open road. The modern poet is doubly trapped by the city that encloses him and the infinity of space that consumes him. "The nasal whine of power whips a new universe," he says, and in this new universe the poet must find his way not only in the linear perspective of the open road but in the sidereal perspective of circular space.

As if in parody of the poet's desires, he first sees this new universe as a closed circuit where

> Power's script—wound, bobbin-bound, refined—
> Is stropped to the slap of belts on booming spools, spurred
> Into the bulging bouillon, harnessed jelly of the stars.

The poet must rewrite power's script if he is to break out of the closed system of the mechanical world. The stanza continues in the poet's question:

> Towards what? The forked crash of split thunder parts
> Our hearing momentwise; but fast in whirling armatures,
> As bright as frogs' eyes, giggling in the girth
> Of steely gizzards—axle-bound, confined
> In coiled precision, bunched in mutual glee
> The bearings glint,—O murmurless and shined
> In oilrinsed circles of blind ecstasy!

The verbal excesses here are a parody of elevated poetic style; the language perfectly expresses the parodic movement of the machine, coiling, whirling toward nothing. The machine's glee and giggling are demonic renditions of the "smile" of space; glinting and shining, the machine gives us no light. Its coiled precision is a burlesque of the perfect circle. Yet even in this new universe of machinery the poet, bound and confined, knows that

> Stars prick the eyes with sharp ammoniac proverbs,
> New verities, new inklings in the velvet hummed
> Of dynamos.

If the mechanical world has blinded and deafened him, "moment-wise," the poet senses in his dream the still greater power of infinite brightness to blind his weak sight. The vision of infinity glimpsed in the stars still overpowers him:

> Stars scribble on our eyes the frosty sagas,
> The gleaming cantos of unvanquished space . . .

Not power's script but the "prophetic script" of the stars is what the poet desires to read. With "eyes raised in pride," mechanical man has tried to decipher this script but has failed to read its prophecy. It is supreme. In despoiling the sky with warplanes, man repeats Adam's error in despoiling the earth, and

> Hell's belt springs wider into heaven's plumed side.
> O bright circumferences, heights employed to fly
> War's fiery kennel masked in downy offings,—
> This tournament of space, the threshed and chiselled height,
> Is baited by marauding circles, bludgeon flail
> Of rancorous grenades whose screaming petals carve us
> Wounds that we wrap with theorems sharp as hail!

Bright circumferences are turned into marauding circles; the only flowers are the flowers of war in this newly fallen universe. "Surely no eye that Sunward Escadrille can cover," the poet exclaims as he surveys another foray into the sky where the fighter plane's "rapid helix" zooms into the clouds. The poet calls in vain to the "Corsair of the typhoon." "Thine eyes bicarbonated white by speed, O Skygak." The pilot is blinded by power; his "stilly eyes partake / What alcohol of space." But the poet sees clearly and calls out again:

> Remember, Falcon-Ace,
> Thou hast there in thy wrist a Sanskrit charge
> To conjugate infinity's dim marge—
> Anew . . . !

The circle of endless space is subjugated never, but the airplane has opened new perspectives of flight that will allow man to conjugate infinity, to join his own aspirations to the newly realized world, to unite his hopes once again with the observable universe. The stars circle, the planets spin in harmony, but the fighter pilot speeds only to destruction:

Now eagle-bright, now
                     quarry-hid, twist-
                              -ing, sink with
Enormous repercussive list-
                 -ings down
Giddily spiralled
                  gauntlets, upturned, unlooping
In guerrilla sleights, trapped in combustion gyr-
Ing, dance the curdled depth
                       down whizzing
Zodiacs, dashed
              (now nearing fast the Cape!)
                   down gravitation's
                     vortex into crashed
. . . dispersion . . . into mashed and shapeless debris . . .

Like the bobbins and spools of the power house, the spirals and loops of the airplane are parodic twistings of the circles of the heavens. There has been no conquest of the laws of gravity in this space age. Once again man's Promethean impulse has led to destruction. Overcome by his own power, the pilot has not danced in harmony with the universe; he has instead performed only the dance of death. At this point again the poet recalls that "The stars have grooved our eyes with old persuasions." Lifting his eyes to the stars, man has imagined in their mystery the secret of infinity. Ascending toward them in his airplane, modern man has "splintered space"; but the stars remain eternally unconjugated, as they are unsubjugated. The old persuasions of "love and hatred, birth,—surcease of nations," the old mystery of the universe, of life and death, remain for the poet to reveal even in this new universe of space. Walt Whitman is again brought into the poem; now the poet knows that infinity is still the same as in Whitman's pre-space age, and he can more readily read Whitman's message. At these "junctions, elegiac, there, of speed / With vast eternity," the poet is inspired by Whitman's "pure impulse inbred / To answer deepest soundings!" "Ascensions of thee hover in me now," Crane says to Whitman, who has known the heights of man's eternal aspiration and the depths of his need. Not only Whitman's vision of the open road, his pact of brotherhood, but his knowledge of war have inspired the modern poet who has known the dark underside of man's nature, the "Ghoul-mound of man's perversity," as well as his aspirations. Thomas Vogler suggests that Crane distinguishes between Whitman's confidence in industry and the machine and Whitman's acceptance of "Time absolutely," which he hopes will overcome the misuse of the machine in time. Whitman's acceptance of the machine as an immediate good cannot serve the modern poet, but Crane hopes that he still can be sustained by Whitman's affirmation of "Time absolutely." However, Vogler suggests, it is impossible to ignore the fact that one aspect of Whitman's dream has failed Crane and that the second may fail him too.[28]

But it is neither Whitman's deepest soundings nor his visionary ascensions that make their way into Crane's poem at this point. It is Whitman's power "to wield the rebound seed," Whitman's celebration of life and fecundity despite death, that Crane celebrates. From the "flight of ravens" and "condor zones," the poet with Whitman in his mind is "shivered back to earth," and the song that Whitman inspires in him is a song of springtime, a beautiful pastoral moment in which Crane sees the earth blossomed in his imagination with cowslip (another word for the shooting star), shad-blow, Potomac lilies, violets, Pontiac rose, Klondike edelweiss. The bounty of the season is "speechful" to the poet, who hears "thunder's eloquence" "Set trumpets breathing in each clump and grass tuft." This burgeoning landscape calls forth from the poet an impassioned address affirming Whitman's vision, his celebration of the machine:

28. Vogler, *Preludes to Vision*, pp. 173–176.

Our Meistersinger, thou set breath in steel;
And it was thou who on the boldest heel
Stood up and flung the span on even wing
Of that great Bridge, our Myth, whereof I sing!

Crane exclaims, "Years of the Modern!" and simultaneously asks, "Propulsions toward what capes?" Here Crane reminds us of his struggle with doubt about the machine age, as Paul suggests, but he moves immediately to a confirmation of Whitman's vision of new life:[29]

O, something green,
Beyond all sesames of science was thy choice
Wherewith to bind us throbbing with one voice,
New integers of Roman, Viking, Celt—
Thou, Vedic Caesar, to the greensward knelt!

It is the fecundity of the earth, the ancient fertility rites, that Whitman celebrates and for which he is finally memorialized by Crane. However, as the culmination of this long poem about the airplane, the meaning of this homage is not entirely clear. After the shattering destruction wrought by the airplane, the poet is "shivered back to earth" in what appears to be a reversal of the "technological sublime" expressed in the epigraph from "Passage to India" and in the earlier stanzas of "Cape Hatteras." The "Sanskrit charge / To conjugate infinity's dim marge / Anew" seems to be dismissed in this stanza as Crane returns to the green earth to worship nature. Whitman's pantheism fits into Crane's poem rather uneasily. It is not confirmed by the airplane's flight as Crane has traced it, nor is it consonant with the interlude of pastoral calm and beauty which appears in the poem after the dispersion of the airplane and which the poet claims was inspired by his first reading of Whitman's poems. However, in these final stanzas Crane moves back and forth between the Whitman who has spiritualized the machine and the Whitman who worships nature. The next stanza of "Cape Hatter-

29. Paul, *Hart's Bridge,* p. 241.

as" returns to the theme of voyaging and attempts to join Whitman's aspirations to the modern perspective:

> And now, as launched in abysmal cupolas of space,
> Toward endless terminals, Easters of speeding light—
> Vast engines outward veering with seraphic grace
> On clarion cylinders pass out of sight
> To course that span of consciousness thou'st named
> The Open Road—thy vision is reclaimed!
> What heritage thou'st signalled to our hands!

The leap from the greensward to abysmal cupolas of space is a vast one. The vision of the open road, extended to endless space, is reclaimed at this point only by the poet who transmutes against all recorded facts the "agonized quittance" of the airplanes into "seraphic grace." The airplane passes out of sight, and only in its passing can the poet reclaim his vision, transpose the roar of its engines into the trumpet call of poetic utterance. Only by dissolving the machine does the poet redeem his consciousness of infinity. Once again, in Crane's poetry, we witness the process of destruction and recreation; the world must be destroyed so that it can be created anew by the poet. Above the shapeless debris of the airplane, "Above the Cape's ghoul-mound," the poet, the "joyous seer," envisions a new dispensation in the "rainbow's arch," the "aureole" around Whitman's head. The promise of the rainbow, the anointment of the poet, have almost nothing to do with the space age; they reflect the eternal mystery of the universe and the sacred calling of the poet-prophet, which are quite independent of any scientific advance. In other words, the entire ending of "Cape Hatteras" after the destruction of the airplane is a repudiation of all the possibilities of flight in the modern age. Only the poet has "passed the Barrier that none escapes— / But knows it leastwise as death-strife." The upsurge of the poet's hymn, his own poetic springtime, follows the natural season and incorporates into itself the imaginative redemption of the scientific age, its "Easters of speeding light." The stars that figured so prominently in the first two-thirds of "Cape Hatteras" are abandoned for earthly images:

the open road, the rainbow, and the "pasture-shine" of Whitman.
The eyes that have been lifted throughout the earlier parts of the
poem toward space and the stars that circle space become in the end

> Eyes tranquil with the blaze
> Of love's own diametric gaze, of love's amaze!

Despite the excess of their triple rhyme, these lines express the endurance of poetic vision and specifically of Whitman's vision of
brotherly love at the center of things. In "Voyages III" love is
called a voyage, and here the word assumes that meaning again.
The poet's voyage, the poet's love of the world that is a voyage into
consciousness, persists in these years of the modern. Against all
destruction it survives, and with it survives the mystery of the universe, the wonder and remoteness of the spheres which, in the
highest reaches of his imagination, the poet glimpses. The "bright
circumference" of space is embodied in the poet's "diametric gaze."
"Combustion at the astral core," which in the opening lines of the
poem accompanied certain geological changes, has become transformed into the poet's blazing vision of centrality.

IV

Four poems separate "Cape Hatteras" from "The Tunnel," but in
these poems between the hymn to the airplane and the dirge of the
subway the movement is steadily one of descent. The first of these
poems is entitled "Southern Cross," and references to the con-
stellation abound in the poet's address to a woman whom he simultaneously idealizes and parodies. But the poet's imagination travels
earthward in "National Winter Garden," "Virginia," and finally
"Quaker Hill," which ends in the injunction to descend, descend.
The poem of the subway, "The Tunnel," opens with an epigraph
from Blake which strikes the sure direction of this journey; from
the Columbus section on, it has been "To Find the Western path
/ Right thro' the Gates of Wrath."

As Lewis has pointed out, this is a traditional epic phase corresponding to the visit to the underworld in the eleventh book of *The Odyssey*, the sixth book of the *Aeneid*, and the *Inferno*.[30] But it is a direction clearly indicated in earlier sections of *The Bridge*. The sweep of the bridge *descends* in "Proem"; Columbus moves "under tempest-lash"; the whole movement of "The River" is down and "Under a world of whistles" as well as "under the wide rain," "Down, down—born pioneers in time's despite" the passengers move, and "Down two more turns the Mississippi pours." The Indian chief is made to "dive to kiss that destiny" in "The Dance." Jim in "Indiana" moves "Down the dim turnpike to the river's edge," and the clipper ships in "Cutty Sark" "ran their eastings down." In "Cape Hatteras" the earth is "surcharged / With sweetness below derricks," and the warplanes "dance the curdled depth /down whizzing / Zodiacs."

The movement downward has throughout the long poem pointed paradoxically both to chaos and to a world of peace and power in repose which is a reflection of ideal harmony. Descent is connected in these poems with defeat and destruction, but it is also true that from destruction a new life, a new ascent, is made possible. The bridge must descend to man; the river descends to the sea where it finds its outlet; the airplane crashes and thus destroys its own destructive capacity. The actual way down into the tunnel leads to a death in life and a power never in repose but pointlessly moving. Still, the way of the poet is to descend: "The subway yawns the quickest promise home." Crane is not talking prudentially here; rather, the "home" he seeks is the haven of the poet where vision is renewed. In taking this final descent, Crane follows the path that Blake traces in "Morning" "thro' the Gates of Wrath" to "see the break of day." Dembo sees the subway as an ideal image because it provides "an almost complete correspondence between the literal action of the hero and the symbolic implications of a Dantean journey," and it serves as "a microcosm of modern urban

30. Lewis, *Poetry of Hart Crane*, p. 334.

life that the poet had to transcend in his final test of faith."[31] However, the point to be noted here is that the subway does not lead the poet astray; it takes him straight to "the River that is East" and the hopeful haven he seeks. In "The Tunnel" he forsakes the open road of Walt Whitman and finds the direction of his own day carved deep in the earth by modern technology. The path is as tortuous as it is torturous, but it winds homeward. If in this downward plunge the poet sees the absolute opposite of the "sweetness" and "destiny" he had sought, his descent leads him finally to the threshold of a beatific vision.

The worst thing about this journey through the modern underworld is the unnatural quality of the route. While the bridge could be envisioned as part of a natural harmony and the train rushes into the Mississippi River and even the airplane's flight is somehow connected to the rainbow's arch, the technological creation of the subway finds no form in nature to imitate. It is at best "rivered under streets," but the correspondence is limited: the "monotone / of motion" underground shares nothing of the force of the river's flow. Like the airplane, the subway's circular patterns are aimless spirals. The images pile up: the "Circle burning bright," the "glass doors gyring," "tunnels that re-wind themselves," "The car / Wheels off," "Newspapers wing, revolve, and wing," the "oily tympanum of waters," "the coil of ticking towers." Even the fire that burns in this modern purgatory is no natural flame; "Thunder is galvothermic here below," the poet says, and the elements seem in this new combination bent only on destruction.

This unnatural world is inhabited chiefly by inhuman people. Crane's early statement that this section was to show the encroachment of machinery on humanity is worked out here. In this technological tunnel of horrors mankind has been completely overwhelmed by the machine. Life, thoroughly mechanized, seems only a process for achieving results for the "fandaddle daddy" who wants his change from the prostitute, the girl who is interested

31. Dembo, *Hart Crane's "Sanskrit Charge,"* p. 120.

only in the money and the time, the executive who wants service in his office, and the wop washerwoman who cleans the corridors and goes home. The "interborough fissures of the mind" of modern man have been deeply cut by the machine. These automatic people seem eternally damned.

Flight seems impossible in "The Tunnel," where the subway "hurries along to a dead stop." Like Poe, whom the poet sees "swinging from the swollen straps," the poet is also "caught like pennies beneath soot and steam." He is trapped by the Daemon's "demurring and eventful yawn! / Whose hideous laughter is a bellows mirth / Or the muffled slaughter of a day in birth." It is impossible to escape the death-grasp of this demonic force who holds the poet helpless and in agony. He is totally passive here, suspended in space, waiting for the "Daemon" "cruelly" "To spoon us out more liquid than the dim / Locution of the eldest star." In the birthing imagery ("the conscience navelled" "Umbilical to call") the poet depicts the subway as a maternal force that resists the separation of birth while he himself suffers the desire to be released. The dynamism of the machine, affirmed in earlier sections, is stilled here, "Condensed" in a moment of hideous stasis.

Still, "beneath soot and steam" the poet is "Impassioned with some song we fail to keep." There is the "Word that will not die" even in the machine age. The melody of the spheres comes back to him as he is reborn and emerges from the subway to feel "the slope, / The sod and billow breaking,—lifting ground." Once again it is a harmony with the land itself that exerts its spiritualizing power on man and his machine-made discord. The poet's consciousness of the machine in "The Tunnel" becomes "Kiss of our agony," the natural and purifying fire in which the demon is finally purged. The subway has carried him from the modern hades into, if not light, at least the place of hope, where

> Kiss of our agony Thou gatherest,
> O Hand of Fire
>   gatherest—

V

In "Atlantis," the final section of *The Bridge*, the poet returns to a meditation on the bridge. His flight has been circular; he comes back to the point from which he started. In rounding out his voyage, he puts himself in harmony with the circular movement of all voyaging in the world imaginatively perceived. Brooklyn Bridge is his Atlantis, not the terminus of voyaging but the focus of all aspirations of flight.[32] His movement has not been toward some end; it has been rather an attempt to harmonize the motion of the machine world, imaginatively apprehended, with the vast circling movement of the universe, the symbol of order and perfection. The arching bridge, the transversing train, the spiraling airplane, the coiling subway, all move in circles in the poet's imagination, and only by reconciling the apparent chaos of their movement with the ideal motion they imperfectly reflect in his mind does the poet redeem the world and sing his song.

The epigraph to this section from Plato suggests Crane's purpose in other terms: "*Music is then the knowledge of that which relates to love in harmony and system.*" Since musical imagery is abundantly associated with the bridge in "Atlantis" and since the bridge has already been called a harp in "Proem," it is possible to appreciate the multiple harmonies Crane is attempting to express in the relationships between the poet's song and the bridge. The flight of the poet's imagination, the song he sings, is one with the bridge's "arching strands of song." The poet meditates on the real bridge until it becomes in the luminosity of his vision a perfect circle and, in the resonance of his song, a musical harmony. To translate his vision of wholeness, the poet calls upon all the strands of imagery in the long poem; the bridge is not only a song but a word, a flower, "Deity's glittering Pledge." These elements, the vast

---

32. Atlantis, Plato's legendary Utopia, was associated at one time with any land for which one had an attachment; here it stands for the desire to flee toward the unknown, to make it known, to understand the world as harmonious. See Weber's discussion of "Atlantis" in *Hart Crane*, pp. 375–378.

correspondences which foliate in this poem, are fused in an ecstatic paean to wholeness and to the harmony which the poet apprehends.

As the real bridge appears in the poem, it is seen as bright, new, fresh, and young, as if in the poet's imagination technology had been purified. It is "*fresh* chemistry" that sings a new canticle "To wrapt *inception* and beatitude" (my italics), as if the modern technological world had created a new beginning, a new paradise. In this revision science is united, as it had been in "Proem," with all the passion and fury and irrationality from which in the modern mind it has become dissociated. The bridge is a "white seizure," a product not of rational laws but evolved in some momentary fit. Yet it is absolutely dependable: it is "the circular, indubitable frieze / Of heaven's meditation." And although "Sibylline voices flicker" in it, it is the "peal of secular light," of worldly and, in the old-fashioned view, of scientific light. Thus the bridge, the supreme product of technology, is brought into the realm of an ideal harmony.

The bridge receives its special sanctity not from its granite and steel nor even from the laws of its construction but from its hallowed place in the harmony of nature. It stands as "Deity's glittering Pledge" not because man has made it but because man has gleaned in its creation the order of the universe. More powerfully than in "Proem," the bridge here is attached to the earth and sea below it and sky above it, and this harmony with nature makes it the perfect bridge between earth and heaven. Its "flight of strings" are "Taut miles of shuttling moonlight syncopate." It is "The loft of vision, palladium helm of stars." And in its form "the suns / And synergy of waters ever fuse." It is "River-throated" and "conclamant with ripe fields." And, searching to express its utter beauty and perfect form, the poet calls this steel structure "whitest Flower." The bridge is not only in balance with nature; it becomes a flower of nature, and as such it shares symbolically the beauty and perfection of nature.

In beholding the bridge, the poet himself experiences a moment of integration, a reflection of the wholeness he perceives. His song is one of sight and sound synaesthetically fused as "Eyes stammer" and the bridge is revealed as a "Swift peal of secular light."[33]

The poet's vision veers upward and upward as he follows the "arching path," the "One arc synoptic" of the bridge. His aim is to:

> link
> What cipher-script of time no traveller reads
> But who, through smoking pyres of love and death,
> Searches the timeless laugh of mythic spears.

As he does so, makes the link, reads the script, assumes the perspective of timeless voyaging, the poem is infused with light:

> Tall Vision-of-the-Voyage, tensely spare—
> Bridge, lifting night to cycloramic crest
> Of deepest day—O Choir, translating time
> Into what multitudinous Verb the suns
> And synergy of waters ever fuse, recast
> In myriad syllables,—Psalm of Cathay!
> O Love, thy white, pervasive Paradigm . . . !

The vision of the voyage is cycloramic, a vast circling system envisioned briefly in the arch of the bridge, which in its harmony shows man the way to conjugate infinity. The system and harmony of the bridge relate their message as the poem continues:

> O Thou steeled Cognizance whose leap commits
> The agile precincts of the lark's return;
> Within whose lariat sweep encinctured sing
> In single chrysalis the many twain,—
> Of stars Thou art the stitch and stallion glow
> And like an organ, Thou, with sound of doom—
> Sight, sound and flesh Thou leadest from time's realm
> As love strikes clear direction for the helm.

The clear direction is the circle of the bridge which leads from time to eternity as its movement corresponds to the circling stars.

33. For a complete discussion of Crane's use of synaesthesia in "Atlantis," see Leibowitz, *Hart Crane*, pp. 137–143.

In the orbit of the bridge, opposites are reconciled in a vast whirling movement, and the machine world is revealed as continuous with the circling cosmos. The center of Crane's poem is the vision of the universe as a cosmic circling dance in which all flight is reconciled and man's voyaging as well as the systems he constructs for transport are united with the dynamism of the cosmos. In an earlier version of "Atlantis" this vision was expressed as

> that radiant field that rings
> The Universe:—I'd have us hold one consonance
> Kinetic to its poised and deathless dance.[34]

In still another very early version of the poem, written in 1923, the vision of totality is again expressed in the circular movement of the spheres:

> And, steady as the gaze incorporate
> Of flesh affords, we turn, surmounting all
> With keenest transcience to that sear arch-head,—
> Expansive center, purest moment and electron
> That guards like eyes that must always look down
> In reconcilement of our chains and ecstasy
> That crashes manifoldly on us as we hear
> The looms, the wheels, the whistles in concord
> Tethered and welded as the hills of dawn
> Whose feet are shuttles, silvery with speed
> To tread and weave our answering world,—
> Recreate and resonantly risen in this dome.[35]

The expansive center and the radiance that rings the universe are the two references of "Atlantis," as indeed of the entire movement in *The Bridge*. As the poet's eye moves upward from the circular bridge to the "circular, indubitable frieze / Of heaven's meditation," his vision moves

34. Weber, *Hart Crane*, p. 425. For various versons of the finale of *The Bridge*, see Weber, *Hart Crane*, Appendix C: "The Development of 'Atlantis,'" pp. 425–440. The worksheets reveal that Crane several times revised this passage which eventually became stanza four but which was at the very heart of his earliest conception of the poem.

35. *Ibid.*, p. 427.

> Always through spiring cordage, pyramids
> Of silver sequel, Deity's young name
> Kinetic of white choiring wings . . . ascends.

The vertical images—the bars, "twin monoliths," "humming spars," "mythic spears," "pyramids"—give way as his imagination speeds along them to "planet-sequined heights." Flight, imagined as vertical movement from one point to another, is replaced in Crane's poem by a new conception of flight as endless spiraling not toward some end but into a new dimension. The "palladium helm of stars," this cyclorama is a totally new awareness of the universe given to the poet by "Migrations that must needs void memory." He translates his release from time, his sense of totality, into floral imagery, as he had done in "Voyages," in an attempt to express his ineffable experience, his new direction:

> Unspeakable Thou Bridge to Thee, O Love.
> Thy pardon for this history, whitest Flower,
> O Answerer of all,—Anemone,—
> Now while thy petals spend the suns about us, hold—
> (O Thou whose radiance doth inherit me)
> Atlantis,—hold thy floating singer late!

At the very moment that the poet feels his experience is inexpressible, he feels that he has the answer to all. It is a moment of imaginative plenitude in which the poet's apprehension is weighted with a consciousness that words can but dimly express. His voyage has been love, as in "Voyages III," where love is ecstasy, a moment of transport beyond this world. At this instant the bridge becomes for him a vision of radiance in which he experiences a sense of being simultaneously released and consumed. Suspended in space, he feels still sustained by light. The bridge is dissolved by the brilliance of his vision and transformed into the pure and delicate anemone whose whiteness and circling petals hold his imagination. At this moment he is released from time, pardoned for this history, but also released from gravity into a weightlessness, a consciousness in which he floats blissfully.

The final stanza returns to the aerial perspective:

> So to thine Everpresence, beyond time,
> Like spears ensanguined of one tolling star
> That bleeds infinity—the orphic strings,
> Sidereal phalanxes, leap and converge:
> —One Song, one Bridge of Fire! Is it Cathay,
> Now pity steeps the grass and rainbows ring
> The serpent with the eagle in the leaves . . . ?
> Whispers antiphonal in azure swing.

The circling stars, the converging sidereal phalanxes, have formed the pattern of his song; his song and the bridge are one with the antiphony of the sky. In the rainbow's ring he sees the sign of unity for which he has longed. He asks, "Is it Cathay?" And in the question he repeats the aspiration of all voyagers to find the mysterious and ideal end of journeying, to know with certainty the realm he has reached. But, in the question, he also affirms the questing spirit that knows no certain end. As he hears "Whispers antiphonal in azure swing," he ends his song with the sense that man's desire for flight will always be a response to his awareness of infinity.

Crane said many things about his intentions in *The Bridge*, but perhaps none is so pertinent at this point as his comment to Kahn that it was "an epic of the modern consciousness."[36] In returning again and again throughout the separate poems that make up *The Bridge* to modes of transportation, to a contemplation of movement, Crane focuses on the central experience of the modern consciousness. Not only the mechanical conveyances of applied science but the new conception of pure science that space is movement have so changed man's relationship to the universe that he has a totally new consciousness of it. In expressing this new consciousness, the poet celebrates not movement from one point to another but movement itself. There is no fixed point of reference in Crane's world. The universe becomes a vast cyclorama, and the poet's

36. *Letters,* p. 308.

sensibility absorbs it through its own gyring perspective. The poet does not impose order on the world; instead, he evokes in his poem an autonomous world of powerful movement. In this poem the solidity of the world and the fixity of the perceiving mind are dissolved. The new consciousness finds expressive form in the circle, which appears over and over in *The Bridge* as a magical realm of dynamism and vitality. The world is energized and sanctified by its circular movement.

Illusion, apparition, is important here. In his apostrophes to the Brooklyn Bridge, the fighter pilot, and his description of the train and subway, Crane is not standing back from these objects and addressing them. Nor is he attempting to tell us how they look. Nor is he warning us against the demonism of the machine. They impinge upon his sensibility as "panoramic sleights," dream images which leap and spiral and dance and coil. The dead weight of iron and steel gives way in his imagination to weightlessness; the laws of gravity are defied. The "new realm of fact," the deadened machine age, is dispersed by a vital dream of movement. Brooklyn Bridge is not a bridge but a vault, a spiring form, a synoptic arc in the poet's imagination, and in his dream it encircles a realm of magical powers. The mechanical force of the train becomes, however briefly, a circular dance in the poet's dream. The airplanes also "dance the curdled depth / down whizzing / Zodiacs," and the movement becomes "circles of blind ecstasy" in the poet's consciousness. Even the subway, moving to the accompaniment of "phonographs of hades in the brain," is experienced as a rewinding tunnel. The movement of the train, the airplane, and the subway is not celebrated in the same way as the bridge; the dance they enact is in some cases a demonic rendition of the circles of the spheres.[37] Yet in this dance, this vast circular motion, the poet feels himself swimming, floating, sinking, sliding, flowing. His sensation is of flight, of weightlessness, of speed, of magical performance, of a

37. Paul has commented on the complementary arcs of "The Tunnel" and "Atlantis," which together make a circle. See his graph in *Hart's Bridge*, p. 262, n. 230.

universal rhythm. He senses space as a chasm, the abyss, "zenith havens," "the last peripheries of light"; but in this realm of infinite space he senses also the force of sacred powers, a force that holds him, suspends him in a hallowed realm. The "new realm of fact" in which modern man lives is a minimal world in which power is bobbin-bound, mystery is subjugated. But as the dynamic speed and fury of this world are absorbed by the poet's consciousness, they assume a new significance. In the poet's dream world power is unbound and mystery released from rationalistic control, and in this loosening power and mystery assert their old hold on the imagination.

The experience of modern man is the experience of the technological world, not the experience of nature or of God. The modern mind, subjected to the machine, looks upon its world as a waste land, a dead garden. But this view of the world does not answer man's eternal longing for meaning, his desire to understand what he senses still to be the mystery of experience, nor does it really serve as an accurate response to the complexity of modern life. Crane faced this fact squarely, and his poetry is written out of a need to formulate another view. He said that "mere romantic speculation on the power and beauty of machinery keeps it at a continual remove; it can not act creatively in our lives until, like the unconscious nervous responses of our bodies, its connotations emanate from within—forming as spontaneous a terminology of poetic reference as the bucolic world of pasture, plow, and barn."[38] In *The Bridge* he demonstrates how his unconscious nervous responses have absorbed the machine, and how he has converted it into positive terms.

38. "Modern Poetry," *The Complete Poems*, p. 262.

chapter five: The World in Stasis

The sensation of flight and movement dominates Crane's consciousness and finds various forms in his poetry; yet he was not unaware
of the opposite sensation, stasis. The sense of standing still, of being
rooted in space, emerges from time to time in his poems. It is the
experience of the opening of "For the Marriage of Faustus and
Helen" where the poet feels himself "Divided" and "stacked," and
of the speaker in "Voyages V" who is "Infrangible and lonely,"
and of the mother in "Indiana" who sees herself as "half of stone."
But such states are only momentary in the process of these poems;
they give way almost immediately to movement and fluidity.
However, Crane did write a series of poems in which stasis is the
central experience. These poems compose a curious grouping in
Crane's work. They were written, if not as a group, at least during
a relatively short period of time and stand quite apart in subject
and technique from almost everything else that he wrote. In fact,
as a series they are an enigma. Attempts to explain them by their
subject or by their date of composition must deal with certain
paradoxical facts. Still, it will be worthwhile to review the circumstance of their composition simply because they occupy such a
unique place in Crane's imaginative world.

These poems, all but one of which were intended for inclusion in a projected third volume of lyric poetry, were inspired by an extended stay in the summer of 1926 at the Crane family house on Isle of Pines. They have as their subjects tropical flora and fauna or the island landscape, as a list of their titles will indicate: "The Mango Tree," "Repose of Rivers," "O Carib Isle!," "Key West," "Island Quarry," "Royal Palm," and "The Air Plant." One other poem, "The Idiot," while not naturalistic, deals with Crane's experience on the island. Their subject alone, then, sets them apart from Crane's other poems. To be sure, he had written about rivers before and there are certain references to tropical vegetation in "Voyages," but the emphasis on tropical trees and plant and animal life is new. Crane's letters from the island attest to the fact that he was overwhelmed by the environment of the tropics. He told his friend Wilbur Underwood that "the mind is completely befogged by the heat and besides there is a strange challenge and combat in the air—offered by 'Nature' so monstrously alive in the tropics which drains the psychic energies."[1]

It is the mind's assault by nature that finds expression in these poems. Yet the brutality of the natural surroundings cannot adequately account for the unique quality of these poems. Crane had felt the psychic drain of urban life as well, but still he could convert poetically the technological bridge into a flower. However, when he came to envision in his imagination a tropical plant, it remained ineluctably a plant, and he became its static observer. The paradox is that when Crane uses natural images to express his creative response to the world, he chooses images of fluidity: the undulating sea of "Voyages" or the fleeting figure of the earth woman in "Powhatan's Daughter" or the circling stars in "Cape Hatteras." But when he focuses on the natural scene itself, he sees and describes it as static. In a sense, of course, the stasis of these island poems derives not from the actual scene, which must have been teeming with life and movement, but from the poet's consciousness. That Crane chose as subjects for his poems from the fecundity of the tropics the quarry,

1. *Letters*, p. 264.

the fruitless palm tree, the sterile air plant, suggests the extent to which his consciousness restructured the landscape. However, the play between the poet's consciousness and the scene is severely limited in these poems. When in "Voyages II" the poet recalls "these poinsettia meadows of her tides," he evokes a series of imaginative associations about the sea which do not depend on any visually accurate view of the sea. His vision is freely creative. By contrast, the "Flat prison slabs there at the marble quarry" in "Island Quarry" exist as a visual image, although the term "prison" reverberates with certain associational meanings, and the distinctness of this image resists any imaginative reconstruction. The meaning of the poem depends upon the visual acuteness of the image and is at the same time limited by it.

If the stasis of these island poems derives from the poet's consciousness, it is perhaps possible to understand them as expressions of an imaginative paralysis, and, in fact, this has been the most frequent explanation of these poems.[2] Crane was at a low point when he arrived at Isle of Pines. He had received a grant from Otto Kahn to work on *The Bridge*, and all during the winter and early spring of 1926 he had been reading and drawing up plans for the structure of the long work; but he had not actually written very much. Transplanting himself from the hectic and disruptive atmosphere in Patterson, New York, where he had been attempting to work on *The Bridge*, to the isolation of his Caribbean retreat, Crane was at first exhilarated by the contrast. The luxuriance of the tropics overpowered him. Soon he settled into a period of contentment in a life where nothing ever seemed to happen and finally into a kind of stupor brought on by the island heat and

2. Weber underscores the turmoil and depression of the early weeks on the island. Crane was worried about the publication of *White Buildings*, which had met with some complications. In addition, he suffered some doubts about the validity of *The Bridge* and in fact about his poetic existence. See Weber, *Hart Crane*, pp. 279–287. Lewis essentially agrees with Weber, and his reading of "Repose of Rivers" as an auto-elegiac poem is based on these biographical details. See Lewis, *Poetry of Hart Crane*, pp. 211–215. Lewis also reads "O Carib Isle!," "Royal Palm," and "The Air Plant" as variations on the theme of vision and visionary utterance. See pp. 395-402.

his own creative block. It is from this stupor that he roused himself to write "The Mango Tree," "O Carib Isle!," and "Repose of Rivers." And then in one month he experienced a period of unparalleled poetic activity in which he put the finishing touches to "Atlantis" and "Ave Maria," wrote "Proem," "The Dance," "Cutty Sark," "Three Songs," "The Tunnel," and started "The Harbor Dawn" and perhaps "The River."[3] During and after this time he wrote more island poems. So it is perhaps possible to regard the three poems that Crane wrote before he recommenced work on *The Bridge* as reflections of his creative stasis, but that view leaves unexplained the other poems in the island group which are equally poems of stasis and which were written during and after this period of intense productivity. Only if his work on *The Bridge* is regarded as the primary activity of his mature writing years and the other poems he wrote almost simultaneously are relegated to a secondary status is it possible to explain the island poems as expressions of creative paralysis. In that view, Crane must be seen as expending his major effort on the poems in *The Bridge* and expressing his exhaustion from this work in the island poems. Such an interpretation is seriously misleading. There is no reason to believe that a poet who had just written some of the best poems of his career should write another series of poems to detail his sense of creative paralysis. Also, if "Atlantis," "Ave Maria," "Proem," and "The Dance" are rightly considered the best poems in *The Bridge*, it is necessary to assume that the magnificent creative power which produced these poems manifested itself also in some of the island poems written during the same period. These island poems must then be judged as works not only of Crane's maturity but of his finest talent.

To say all this does not get round the obvious fact that these island poems fit uneasily into any view of Crane's career. They have been so easily divided from *The Bridge* in analyses of the poet's work because they are quite different from it. Crane himself is not very helpful in placing them. He seemed to have no sense that they were distinguished in any way from anything he had

3. See Lewis, *Poetry of Hart Crane*, p. 219.

produced before. In fact, he conceived of some of these poems as a part of *The Bridge*; for example, at one point he planned on including "The Mango Tree" after "Three Songs" in the long work.[4] He also suggested that one magazine might publish "O Carib Isle!" with "Cutty Sark" and "The Harbor Dawn" as a trio with a general emphasis on the marine.[5] One of these poems, "Repose of Rivers," was published in *White Buildings*, although he considered at one time that "Repose of Rivers," "The Mango Tree," and "O Carib Isle!" should form a poetic group despite the fact that they have little in common except a general tropical setting. However, Crane's suggestions for ordering the poems might be regarded simply as attempts to get them published in one form or another. Since they remained, except for "Repose of Rivers," uncollected at the time of his death, it is impossible to determine exactly what organization Crane would have given them.[6]

If it is impossible to establish Crane's organizing principle for these poems, it is possible to describe them as a group and to indicate how they differ from Crane's other poems. It is the sensation of stasis that distinguishes them. For a poet like Crane, who imagined knowing as voyaging, stasis is a terrifying state, and the overriding emotion of these poems is one of terror. It is a terror that comes from a sense of standing absolutely still in a world that appears from that perspective marmorealized. In this position there can be no interchange between the imagination and the world and so no knowledge of that world. There is a deep impulse in Crane's consciousness to destroy the world, to burn it, raze it, break it, in order to create a symbolic world of purity. But the island landscape will not give way to the destructive force of the poet's imagination. It remains in its obduracy unpossessed by

4. *Letters,* p. 272.

5. *Ibid.,* p. 283.

6. Brom Weber has arranged them according to Crane's tentative table of contents for "Key West: An Island Sheaf" in *The Complete Poems and Selected Letters and Prose of Hart Crane,* and Weber's organization must take precedence over the order of their first appearance in Waldo Frank's edition of *The Complete Poems of Hart Crane* (New York: Doubleday, 1958).

the poet, whose imagination simply clashes against it. If destruction is the first act of creation, as Crane believed, there can be no creation in such a situation; realizing this, the poet is driven in desperation to desire his own destruction. Unable to absorb the world, he seeks to be absorbed by it, to go "on into marble" or to render his "ghost / Sieved upward." His longing to merge with the landscape arises from his terrifying realization that he cannot merge with it, that it remains irresistibly apart from him. These poems have been called death-ridden, and they do express an intense desire for obliteration; but what the poet seeks to obliterate is the sense of otherness that overwhelms him. He seeks his own annihilation because only through that destruction will he break the deadlock between himself and the landscape that confronts him. To destroy himself is to create himself anew. To move into the landscape is to move from his static position and, in moving, to possess the landscape imaginatively.

These poems are poems of location. In no other poems does Crane give us such a sense of place. He tells us not only where he is but what season it is and even what time of day it is. Yet it is this very sense of location that is the cause of his disorientation. To be rooted and stationary forces this poet to lose his bearings entirely. He knows where he is, and, knowing that, he knows nothing. He can detail in confusion what he sees, but over and over again the details are added to each other only to prove that he sees nothing. In the visual acuteness of these poems the poet describes a horrible loss of sight. Although the poems rely heavily on naturalistic details, they are not naturalistic; that is, they do not suggest in any way that the actual scene is in itself meaningful. On the contrary, the poems abound in desperate pleas to the "Commissioner," "the blue's comedian host," the "Angelic Dynamo," the power behind the scene whose presence is so remote from the poet, trapped as he is in the real world. These pleas are reminiscent of the many petitions that run through Crane's poetry: of the lover's desire in "Voyages II" for an answer to "The seal's wide spindrift gaze toward paradise," of the poet's hope

in "Proem" that the bridge would "lend a myth to God," of
Columbus in "Ave Maria" who sees "Thy purpose—still one shore
beyond desire!" However, in these great flights of the imagination
toward vision, there is always the hope and the fervent belief that
God or the power that inspires the universe will manifest itself
in the symbols apprehended by the poet. In the island poems that
assurance is removed. What the poet sees is a world devoid of
symbols and so unredeemable. He sees only a world of details
which resists his restructuring and thus his preparation for the
influx of spirit. So he asks not for an affirmation of his vision but
for its denial. What he sees cannot be verified by any "Commissioner" because what he sees is not meaningful to him; therefore
he appeals beyond the scene to a power that will obliterate him,
and thus release him from the scene's hold upon him.

Stuck in a world of objects, the poet feels the heavy weight not
only of his position but of the world as it appears to him in that
position. He tries in "Island Quarry" to lift the world imaginatively, to float it in his vision; but it resists his efforts, and it is this
resistance that torments him. He see himself "annealed," "slagged"
in a world of hardened form. To describe the landscape, Crane
uses linear images, images of trees, of spiked marble and tentacled
plants. This linear perspective is also new in Crane's poetry. In
"For the Marriage of Faustus and Helen," "Voyages," and "Powhatan's Daughter" the natural world surges through the poet's
consciousness in circular movements, bending and winding and
whirling. The natural world in these poems is also associated
with a feminine figure, with Helen and the feminine sea and
Pocahontas. But nature in the island poems is imagined as steadfast, upright. The power to which the poet appeals in the poem
is masculine, the "Captain," the "host." If the poet longs to possess
the feminine figure that shifts and glides through the erotic landscape of his other poems, in the island poems he expresses his
agonizing awareness that the world in its fixity cannot be possessed.
In "Possessions" the "fixed stone of lust" is burned and razed until
it becomes "bright stones wherein our smiling plays." In the island

poems the poet cannot work that miracle; there is no "pure possession" and the "stone of lust" remains fixed.[7]

The stasis of these island poems appears all the more remarkable
when they are placed against the poems in *The Bridge*, composed
during the same period. The curving, circling, whirling rush of
movement in "Proem," "The Dance," and even "The Tunnel"
forms a formidable contrast to the fixity of such poems as "O
Carib Isle!," "The Air Plant," and "Key West." The vast dynamos
of mechanical power as well as the "synergy" of the natural elements soar through the poet's consciousness in patterns of flight
and movement while the actual landscape, "so monstrously alive,"
appears deathly still to him. Some time after his island stay Crane
wrote, "Even with the torturing heat of my sojourn in Cuba I
was able to work faster than before or since then, in America. The
'foreign-ness' of my surroundings stimulated me to the realization of natively American materials and viewpoints in myself not
hitherto suspected, and in one month I was able to do more work
than I had done in three previous years."[8] Perhaps this comment
does provide a clue to the island poems. It is the "foreign-ness," not
simply the strangeness of the tropical setting to this American poet
but the sense that nature is irresolutely separate from him, that
finds expression in these poems. Perhaps Crane was able to work
faster, to formulate the American materials that had been churning
in his head for so long without any pattern, precisely because he

7. Butterfield makes a brief comment on this point in discussing "Island Quarry."
He says, "This (homo)sexual symbolism and the need to resolve life's contradic-
tions we have seen before in Crane's poetry: but generally it has been the maternal
and consuming sea in which he has sought refuge from emotional fury. This firm,
mature resolution (or at least the desire for it) is something new. There is here
the unfamiliar strength of a man determined to be toughened by experience and
not defeated by it. The pity is that 'Island Quarry' remains conspicuously different
from other Crane poems. Elsewhere it was the sea, symbolic and actual, not stone,
that nourished his imagination." See R. W. Butterfield, *The Broken Arc* (Edin-
burgh: Oliver & Boyd, 1969), p. 217. Butterfield, however, sees a similarity between
"Island Quarry" and "Possessions." I do not share his conclusion that "Possessions"
has a stoical ending, and so my understanding of the symbolic function of the
stone imagery differs from his.

8. *Letters*, p. 309.

had at last located the dead center of his existence. The sense of stasis and the sense of flight form a creative tension in his work of this period, and this tension may account for Crane's intense productivity.

The first poem Crane wrote on the island is "The Mango Tree," "a little unconscious calligramme," he called it.[9] Convinced that the mango tree was the original apple tree of Eden, Crane gives the poem the shape of a tree as if it were to stand objectively for his location in paradise. "It's all like Christmas," the poet says at the beginning, and as the eye reads down the shape, the tree is heaped with images of light until, in its gaudy decoration, it comes to resemble a trimmed Christmas tree. In its "silking of shadows," its "golden boughs," its leaves that "spatter dawn / from emerald cloud-sprockets," its "ripe apple-lanterns" and "recondite lightnings / irised," the tree becomes a "Sun-heap" where "dusk is close." Yet this brightness has been yoked and plucked and wrenched, and even as the poet commemorates its light, people are arriving with baskets to pick its fruits, and "Fat final prophets with / lean bandits crouch" under it. The poem is a visual and verbal trick; words pile on words senselessly. Although the tree blushes, sprouts, and spatters, it remains a static image, there to be observed from its crown to its roots, even to be plucked, but to be ultimately unyielding.

Had Crane included this poem in *The Bridge*, as he planned, it would have replaced "Quaker Hill," a section long judged weak. The tropical setting of "The Mango Tree" would have been out of place in that North American work, and the ellipsis of the poem would have added little to the coherence of the longer work. However, this poem is a much more interesting elaboration than "Quaker Hill" of the epigraph from Isadora Duncan chosen for the section: "*I see only the ideal. But no ideals have ever been fully successful on this earth.*" In "Quaker Hill" the subject again is the misuse of paradise, but there is no sense in that poem, as there is in "The Mango Tree," of the natural luxuriance of paradise.

9. *Ibid.*, p. 254.

"Quaker Hill" is simply cynical, and although there is a certain amount of cynicism in "The Mango Tree" ("When you sprouted Paradise a discard of chewing- / gum took place"), the cynicism works against a kind of lushness in the tree. The ideal, imaged in the "golden boughs" of the mango tree, has been wrenched by "old hypno- / tisms," "First-plucked before and since the Flood." Although its "ripe apple-lanterns gush history," the mango is now only a tree, whose fruits are to be picked quickly and enjoyed. Its history is meaningless to the crowds that eat its fruit. The poet, like the fruit pickers, has plucked and wrenched the tree from its setting and transplanted it into words, and there it remains solidly a tree. Despite the old hypnotisms and the fat prophets and history itself, the tree does not yield its meaning to the poet.

"The Mango Tree" was to be grouped with "Repose of Rivers" and "O Carib Isle!" under the title "Grand Cayman," presumably because the two later poems were inspired by a harrowing trip to Grand Cayman taken in the early summer of 1926. The trip was made in part for pleasure but chiefly in the hope that it would stimulate Crane's flagging powers to finish *The Bridge*. Instead, it produced "Repose of Rivers," which Lewis has interpreted as "an eloquent statement about the failure of creativity."[10] It is important, however, to distinguish accurately the source of this failure. "Repose of Rivers" is about repose, but not the irksome repose of creative energy. The poet is rendered frantic in this poem not by his own dormant powers but by the repose of rivers; its stillness recalls him to an earlier scene which sets off a series of disquieting memories. Unlike the "repose of rivers," his memories, long dormant but now awakened, offer him no repose.

The actual trip to Grand Cayman, as Crane described it to Waldo Frank, forms quite a contrast to the poem it inspired. Crane says:

And the much bruited Grand Cayman was some torment, I can survive to tell you. Flat and steaming under black clouds of mosquitoes, and not a square inch of screening on the island. I had to

10. Lewis, *Poetry of Hart Crane*, p. 211.

keep smudge fires burning incessantly in my room while I lunged back and forth, smiting myself all over like one in rigor mortis and smoke gouging salt penance from my eyes. The insects were enormous; Isle of Pines species can't compare in size or number. After nine days and nights of that I staggered onto the schooner—and here I am—with a sunburn positively Ethiopian.[11]

Victimized by the ravages of nature in real life, the poet transposes this experience in "Repose of Rivers." In the poem the physical torment of the actual experience is transformed into the mental torment of the memories the scene inspires. The natural scene, despite its "sarabande" and "seething," remains fairly constant and tranquil. The "slow sound" of willows, the "steady leveling of the marshes," the cypresses that "shared the noon's / Tyranny," even the "mammoth turtles" that "Yielded, while sun-silt rippled them," all are contrasted in their slowness and lethargy to the speaker's harried movement through the varied landscapes of his memory.

That the poet has not before remembered the events that the scene recalls is not surprising. They are memories of torments that drew him "into hades almost." In recalling them, he says, "How much I would have bartered!" And his admission here suggests that he would have gladly exchanged them for more sustained experiences. They are memories of darkness, of places where cypresses hid the light, of "black gorges." The activity there has been brief, secret, and perhaps guilty, and in every sense not peaceful or happy. The poet does not participate, even in memory, in the repose of the landscape.

The poet's memory also figures in another way in "Repose of Rivers." Stemming as the poem does from his immediate experience, it is remarkably full of images Crane had used in his earlier poetry. The image of the willows that appears in the opening, middle, and closing of this poem is used in the final stanza of "Voyages VI":

> The imaged Word, it is, that holds
> Hushed willows anchored in its glow.

11. *Letters,* p. 258.

> It is the unbetrayable reply
> Whose accent no farewell can know.

Typically the symbol of sorrow, the willows become for Crane in "Voyages VI" a private symbol of tranquillity and peace beyond sorrow. While the willow is hushed in the awesome scene of "Voyages VI," it is significantly connected with sound in "Repose of Rivers" and with a sound that serves to attract the poet's attention at points where it tends to veer away from the scene. As a symbol of tranquillity here, however, the willows serve to remind the poet of a repose that he cannot experience. The poem opens:

> The willows carried a slow sound,
> A sarabande the wind mowed on the mead.
> I could never remember
> That seething, steady leveling of the marshes
> Till age had brought me to the sea.

Returning in the middle of the poem to the willows, the poet says, "The pond I entered once and quickly fled— / I remember now its singing willow rim." And the final stanza brings the poet again to the willows: "I heard wind flaking sapphire, like this summer, / And willows could not hold more steady sound." The repetition of the willow image, with its slow sound, its singing, reminds the poet of his separation from the natural scene. He has forgotten the willow's sound and has fled from its singing. The "steady sound" of his own music that the poet hears in the end is not the sound of the willows; it arises only after he has passed beyond the land and been cut off from it. The wind he hears comes from the sea and is contrasted to the repose of rivers. In "Voyages VI" the "hushed willows" are held in the poet's "imaged Word"; here, however, they will not hold the poet's "steady sound." He must move beyond them to write his poem.

The sun, sea, wind, and sapphire as well as the gorge that appear to the poet in "Repose of Rivers" are also images Crane had used before. They figure in "Passage," another poem where the poet treats memory. "Passage," as its title indicates, is a poem of movement, and although the movement is frenetic, the poet feels himself "justified in transience, fleeing." In "Repose of Rivers," however, the movement is not justified; he is drawn into hades by his remembrance. One more borrowing from his early poetry is the city image in the penultimate stanza of "Repose of Rivers" which is repeated in changed form from "Possessions." The "city that I finally passed / With scalding unguents spread and smoking darts" in "Repose of Rivers" is the city the poet was "turning, turning on smoked forking spires, / The city's stubborn lives, desires" in "Possessions." In that poem, however, the burning is purgative, and the poet experiences a "pure possession." In contrast, the fire in "Repose of Rivers" is scalding and tormenting to the poet; he must finally (twice repeated) pass not through it but beyond it. "Repose of Rivers" is a poem of escape from the tormenting city and from the equally tormenting natural landscape. The wind that rises at the end is the sea wind that seems in its miraculous flaking to be a wind of deliverance from the poet's harried contact with nature. Coming as it does from the sea, it is both a natural wind and a wind that flakes, cuts into the landscape, in a way that fulfills the poet's inmost desires.

The island landscape had completely inundated Crane's consciousness by the time he wrote "O Carib Isle!," which is a poem of the present and not of memory. The lily, eucalyptus, poinciana, tarantula, fiddler crabs, and terrapin are new to Crane's poetry, yet their strangeness is baffling to him. Once again the poet pits himself against an unyielding natural scene. "O Carib Isle!" owes its power to its pictorial quality, and the still life that the poet details is one of life and death intricately intertwined. However, when the poet probes the picture he presents for its secrets, he receives no heaven-sent message, no sustaining reassurances of its meaning.

The torpor of the "hellish hot day" in which he wrote the poem pervades the atmosphere of "O Carib Isle!" The "white sand," the "coral beach," the "Brutal necklaces of shells around each grave / Squared off so carefully," compose an absolutely still landscape, and the poet feels himself enclosed and suffocating in "these nacreous frames of tropic death." All movement is stultified in this place; the "rattling" of the tarantula, the "Side-stilting" of the crabs, the "palsy" of the eucalyptus, all suggest that movement requires a ponderous effort in this scene. Still, the poet longs to fertilize the scene, to speak in "a stranger tongue" than nature the "Tree names, flower names" that blossom in his imagination. Yet as he strives to speak, the wind "knots itself in one great death— / Coils and withdraws." Unable to move or breathe, he appeals beyond the scene in desperation to know:

> But where is the Captain of this doubloon isle
> Without a turnstile? Who but catchword crabs
> Patrols the dry groins of the underbrush?
> What man, or What
> Is Commissioner of mildew throughout the ambushed senses?
> His Carib mathematics web the eyes' baked lenses!

The island is without a turnstile, an entrance for the poet's creative power. There are here only the "catchword crabs" and not the poet's words and names. He wants to count the brutal shells, but his poetic arithmetic is no match for Carib mathematics. In the next stanza he abandons his wish to enter and control the scene and seeks rather to be obliterated, and so absorbed into it:

> Under the poinciana, of a noon or afternoon
> Let fiery blossoms clot the light, render my ghost
> Sieved upward, white and black along the air
> Until it meets the blue's comedian host.

Unlike the huge terrapins that "thunder in their strain," their "clenched beaks coughing for the surge again," the poet who had longed for the surge of new names and syllables now succumbs to the overpowering force of the scene:

> Slagged of the hurricane—I, cast within its flow,
> Congeal by afternoons here, satin and vacant.

> You have given me the shell, Satan,—carbonic amulet
> Sere of the sun exploded in the sea.

The poet has not been able to count the "Brutal necklaces of shells around each grave"; he has not been able to restructure the careful squares of the scene. But he is given in the end the magical shell as a "carbonic amulet" to ward off death. In another version of the poem[12] the shell is designated as "the ember, / Carbolic, of the sun exploded in the sea"; it is a spark of the life-giving sun which the poet, slagged and congealed, nonetheless receives. He has not learned the secrets of nature by careful observation, by rational accounting. The details of the poem offer him no insight. When he longs to speak, to subdue, to put himself in touch with the "Commissioner," he fails. He is reduced to passivity by the scene, and his attitude is finally one of resignation: "Let fiery blossoms clot the light," "Let not the pilgrim see himself again." What he is given in the end (significantly not what he has taken or created, but what he has been given) is the mysterious amulet of "the sun exploded in the sea." The image of fire burning on the waters figures in "Voyages VI" and in the aftermath of Maquokeeta's dance and consummation in "The Dance" as an expression of heightened imaginative possession. Here the image is totally removed from the poet, as it is not in the other two poems. The poet, both in "Voyages" and "The Dance," is himself burning, and in this fire he is purified. Here the fire is outside the poet. The magic of the moment in "O Carib Isle!" is not a result of the poet's own powers; it is a magic given to him and strangely separate from him.

Critics have not failed to note the predominance of death and waste in this poem, but they have failed to emphasize the images of life intertwined with death. What is so frightening to the poet is that "death's brittle crypt" is the natural world, the noontime scene which stirs with a strange kind of life, with the tarantula, the crabs,

---

12. Weber quotes this version as the one published in *transition*. See Weber, *Hart Crane,* p. 280.

the terrapin. Tropical vegetation is intimately tied to the "feet of the dead," the "dry groins of the underbrush." The point that the poet makes at the beginning of the poem is that in this death-ridden scene life goes on:

> No, nothing here
> Below the palsy that one eucalyptus lifts
> In wrinkled shadows—mourns.

Only the poet mourns, and in his desire to "speak a name, fertile," he seeks really to "gainsay" death; yet only he fails. He speaks obviously a "stranger tongue," a word estranged from the voice of nature. Through his "eyes' baked lenses" he cannot see, and if he could, "blossoms clot the light." Shut off from human vision and from the revelations of nature (its life paradoxically prevents him from seeing the light), he appeals to a supernatural figure identified as the "Captain." In the end this commissioner is re-vealed as Satan.[13] Satan has given the poet an amulet to ward off the evils of death, and thus he has exempted the poet from his power and from the power of the natural world that he patrols. However, the amulet is a curious gift. It is given to the poet who has been overpowered by nature, and thus its magical powers have not worked upon him. He receives it at a point where it will do him no good. His ghost has been "Sieved upward" and he remains "satin and vacant"; paradoxically it is in his own annihilation that he receives the amulet that will prevent his death. Only by merging with the landscape, by destroying himself, is he given the power that will allow him to "speak a name, fertile." Like the "bright stones" in "Possessions," this amulet is the creative remains of de-

13. Lewis suggests that Crane borrowed this figure from William Blake's "The Gates of Paradise," where Satan is addressed contemptuously as "the Accuser who is the God of this World." In Blake's poem, Lewis says, "Lucifer's day is waning; the harsh pieties of latter-day Christianity are losing their power; the accusing deity—worshipped as Jesus and Jehovah but conceived as a kind of Manichean devil—is no more than the false dream of the spiritually lost pilgrim; and a morning of true revelation is at hand." See Lewis, *Poetry of Hart Crane*, pp. 398–399.

struction. In "Possessions," however, it is the world that is destroyed; here it is the poet.

The Grand Cayman trilogy contains three poems as different as Crane ever wrote, and yet they plot the imaginative journey that he made in a short span of time. "The Mango Tree" is an exercise in objectivity; the tree is wrenched from its natural surroundings to stand on the poet's page. There is an element of fun and nonsense in the poem, yet behind its cleverness hides a desire to see life in bright colors. "Repose of Rivers" is a step backward, a frantic effort to reorder his life and poetic memories against the pressure of a natural repose. "O Carib Isle!" grapples forcefully with the meaning of the immediate scene, yet in this clash the poet is reduced to passivity. In the clarity of its pictorial detail the poem expresses the terror that the static landscape inspired in the poet. Yet in all three of these poems the poet assumes a new relationship toward his materials. He observes them carefully. For example, "The Mango Tree" is about the tree in a way that "Proem" is not about Brooklyn Bridge. The sense in all three poems is of an actual world that remains tormentingly resistant to the poet's imagination, yet inspires him to write these poems.

"Key West" might be read in connection with these poems as yet one more attempt to describe the position at which Crane had arrived in the early months at Isle of Pines. Its images owe little to the island scene, but it is a poem of location in which the speaker expresses his sense of alienation at the same time that he posits some little hope for the golden quality of his verse-making powers. It is in many ways a latter-day "Recitative," the poem which provided the title of his first volume, *White Buildings*. Many of the elements of "Recitative" appear here; the "ape's face," "the shafts of steel," "Wrenched gold," the wind, are all incorporated in "Key West" with much the same flavor. But while the earlier poem is a poetic yearning for communication, if not communion, the speaker in "Key West" seems resigned to his solitary stance, his "single march / To heaven or hades." In fact, he deliberately separates himself from his audience, "these millions" who "reap a dead conclusion." He will not be drawn as they have been "towards a doubly mocked confusion / Of apish nightmares into steel-strung stone." He is sustained by "water, and a little wind," but he knows there is "no breath of friends and no more shore / Where gold has not been sold and conscience tinned." It is a melancholy statement in which the poet whose "white buildings" had answered day in the earlier poem finds himself in no meaningful relationship to nature; her "skies impartial" "do not disown me / Nor claim me, either, by Adam's spine—nor rib."

"Here has my salient faith annealed me" is the opening line of the poem, and it recalls "O Carib Isle!," where the poet sees himself "Congeal by afternoons here, satin and vacant." It is the word "Here" that must be attended to; these poems are Crane's most persistent effort to locate himself in place. And the place where he finds himself is a place of absolute stasis. He sees himself annealed against an impartial horizon. It is night, but the moon, the light of the Romantic imagination, has sunk. Although the poet imagines that "The oar plash and the meteorite's white arch / Concur with wrist and bicep," that there is some intimate relationship between man and the cosmos, he discovers only a "frugal noon," the glare of the midday sun that hardens and eviscerates his once bounding imagination. Still, against the "apish nightmares" of the technological world, this static natural scene offers its frugal consolations. In a sense, the poet has arrived at a dead end; there is "no more shore" toward which to voyage. In this place he must find himself; "here is water, and a little wind," and with these elements the poet is forced to content himself. In other poems Crane had imagined the poet as the supreme sufferer, burned and tortured by the world and in the process purified, his poems released from him by that violence. Here, in this place, he experiences quite different sensations: the fear that suffering will release no poetry and simultaneously the hope against hope that he need not "reap a dead conclusion" from this scene. Yet, as his perspective is fixed, it determines a world of fixity which threatens at every moment to overpower him.

Once again in "Island Quarry" the poet seeks to locate himself against the landscape. The possibilities, canceled out in "Key West" as "equally frugal," are here presented in realistic detail; the choice is between the "goat path quivering to the right" that leads "to tears and sleep" and the "dry road" that leads "into marble that does not weep." Unlike the Romantic saunterer whose retreats to nature provided some unexpected solace, the poet here seems to wrestle with an uncomforting landscape depicted in stark pictorial detail and to set it against his dream vision. The "Square sheets" and "Flat prison slabs" of the quarry compose a "fierce / Profile of marble." The poet is unsettled by the uprightness of the view:

> that fierce
> Profile of marble spiked with yonder
> Palms against the sunset's towering sea, and maybe
> Against mankind.

It is the straightness of the landscape that confronts him with a fear of his own insignificance. Spikes, palms, and towers—all rigid forms—are not the symbolic forms of the poet's imagination; they are the unyielding configurations of nature. The poet makes an effort to reconstruct the scene, to dissolve the fierceness of the profile. He says:

> It is at times—
>
> In dusk, as though this island lifted, floated
> In Indian baths.

With the aid of the blurring light of dusk, he tries to reduce the weightedness of the scene, to soften the obdurate visual picture of the marble, in short to lift nature imaginatively out of its terrifying concreteness. But at the very moment that the images lift and float and silver under the poet's creative powers, he seems to turn on his own reconstruction and resign himself to the original view. The poem concludes:

> —It is at times as though the eyes burned hard and glad
> And did not take the goat path quivering to the right,

> Wide of the mountain—thence to tears and sleep—
> But went on into marble that does not weep.

The hard, glad eyes of the poet suggest that his vision has been marmorealized; its powers of transfiguration are gone and it submits to the obstinate dominance of the quarry scene.

The poem turns on the repetition of the phrase "It is at times." This phrase itself suggests that what the poet wants to see, he sees only with great effort and only intermittently. Only in the dusk does he succeed in detaching the quarry scene from its rigidity. But this effort does not satisfy him, and in the final confrontation with the marble quarry the poet chooses to merge his vision, "hard and glad," with the hard world of stone. The marble, at first imagined as fiercely against mankind, becomes in the end the only refuge for the poet. He cannot evade the actual scene and escape to his imagination with its frugality of tears and sleep, so he fronts it directly and "does not weep." By going "on into marble," he moves at last, but he moves into absolute stasis.

The straight, square, spiked fierceness of the marble quarry is drawn in sharp relief against the turning and quivering of the road. Crane often surrenders to the forces of nature in his poems, but always to fluid, moving forces, to the wind, the sea, the rainbow. In "The River," "The Dance," and "Voyages," for example, he succumbs to the pulsating powers of the elements, which are largely passionate and feminine. And even in "Repose of Rivers" and "O Carib Isle!" he surrenders in the end to the sea and the sky. In "Island Quarry," however, the natural elements are not only immobile but lifeless; to the extent that they are sexual at all, they are masculine, spiked, and towering, and as such threatening to the poet. The poet cannot possess the landscape here. Instead, it threatens to overcome him until he undoes its threat not by merging with it in any fruitfully passionate embrace but by matching his own hardness with it.

"Island Quarry" and two other poems that follow, "Royal Palm" and "The Air Plant," are Crane's most naturalistic poems. Here he scrutinizes nature, draws terrifyingly clear pictures of what he sees, and then tries to infuse his observations with some meaning. This method is almost the reverse of his usual technique. The vegetation of Crane's poetry outside these island poems blooms almost entirely in his imagination. In "Island Quarry," however, he starts and stops with the distinctness of the landscape; in the end the exactitude of the picture prevails over the imaginative world of tears and sleep. The poet, "Walking the straight road toward thunder," never reaches that creative explosion which would destroy the obdurate world he sees.

"Royal Palm," like "Island Quarry," is a poetic amplification of another actual island experience. In the early summer Crane had done some gardening around his house at Isle of Pines, and he reported his efforts to his mother: "I have succeeded in eradicating the carcasses of several dead and dying orange trees in the front yard, putting young royal palms in their places. How I wish you had thought of planting some of these perfect delights when the place was being built; they are the one perfect sort of tree to have round a house, their ornamentation, stateliness and open-airiness can't be surpassed."[14] "Royal Palm," dedicated for this obvious and probably for a more ironic reason to his mother, Grace Hart Crane, is an attempt to describe the particular delights of the tree. It ends where it starts, with an inspired description of the top of the tree. The poet here resists the temptation to merge with the image he has created as he had done in "O Carib Isle!" and "Island Quarry"; here he remains completely outside the picture. He seeks no message from nature in this poem; thus the straining of the other island poems is absent from this apostrophe to the palm. However, the royal palm does share with the marble quarry a certain distance from the "tears and sleep" of men. While man's "deathward breath is sealed," the royal palm remains "Uneaten of the earth or aught earth holds." It is

> Forever fruitless, and beyond that yield
> Of sweat the jungle presses with hot love

14. *Letters*, p. 256.

And tendril till our deathward breath is sealed—
It grazes the horizons, launched above

Mortality—

It is, as man is certainly not, "Unshackled, casual of its azured height." If the palm does not share man's mortality in the poet's view, it is still very much alive in its "Green rustlings," "whispered light," "communings," "frondings sighing in aetherial folds." The magician-poet appears to be at work in this poem; even in "the noontide's blazed asperities" he still creates in his palm tree an illusion of coolness and serenity, and so he transforms imaginatively the actual world he surveys.

But the coolness and distance of this palm tree have another dimension. It is "Forever fruitless," in one sense only a naturalistically exact statement about the palm, but when combined with other notations of its shape (the tower, "the grey trunk, that's elephantine," the "fountain at salute"), this description forces upon the palm tree a curious phallicism in which the generative principle is denied. Above mortality, it is also beyond the "yield" of "hot love." It is undying, evergreen, but also uncreative, a symbol of stasis. Despite its "regal charities" of coolness in the midday heat, it is essentially uncharitable. The poet is offered no solace from his contact with the royal palm. It moves away from him. Perhaps, the poet concludes, "it soared suchwise through heaven too"; but, unlike the soaring and bending bridge, it moves straight upward and away from earth, mortality, the human being that observes it. While the poet could shape the technological image of the bridge to his own purposes, the natural world resisted his reforming efforts. If the forms the poet sees in nature point heavenward, they do not inspire in him any hope.[15]

15. That Crane chose to dedicate this poem to his mother is significant beyond the fact that he wanted to impress upon her the beauties of the royal palm. A letter that Crane wrote to his mother about the time that he composed a first draft of "Royal Palm" suggests that the connections between the fruitless and cool royal palm and his mother might be more than accidental. He writes: "Grace,—you naughty old thing! Why don't you write me a line or so: *stingy!* You'd think you had some choice secret or so—that you wouldn't part with for the world!—

In "The Air Plant" Crane offers for our inspection one more object of tropical vegetation, discovered by him, we may judge from the subtitle, "Grand Cayman," on his memorable trip. The lifeless epiphyte provides Crane with another static and uncreative image. The poem dwells in some detail on the nullity of this plant. It is rooted to the palm trunk, and in the jarring and lurching of its tentacles it symbolizes movement halted and impeded:

> This tuft that thrives on saline nothingness,
> Inverted octopus with heavenward arms
> Thrust parching from a palm-bole hard by the cove—
> A bird almost—of almost bird alarms,
>
> Is pulmonary to the wind that jars
> Its tentacles, horrific in their lurch.
> The lizard's throat, held bloated for a fly,
> Balloons but warily from this throbbing perch.
>
> The needles and hack-saws of cactus bleed
> A milk of earth when stricken off the stalk;
> But this,—defenseless, thornless, sheds no blood,
> Almost no shadow—but the air's thin talk.

Once again, as in the other island poems, the poet is intent on setting down in verse what he actually sees, not what he imagines or would like to see. When he tries to lift figuratively the tuft from its roots, it becomes a "bird almost," but not quite a bird; it resists anything but a naturalistic description. The poet endows it with life and lungs, but still the plant assumes no creative and vital rhythm. Like the lizard that perches on it, this plant is bloated by the wind; it inhales but it exhales no life. Even the cactus is more lifelike than this plant. The wind that jars it is simply "thin talk," not the inspiriting wind. Yet the poet's vision, assaulted as it is by this object which refuses to yield to its transfiguring powers, gives

---

while I sit here sweating out masterpiece after masterpiece!" See Unterecker, *Voyager,* p. 452. Grace's "secret," like the royal palm's secret, is unfathomable to the poet. Crane suffered both in his poetry and in his love affairs the "sweat" of love, while his mother, for all her hysteric outbursts, often appeared to her son as a cold and heartless person.

vent in the last stanza to aeolism. Having deflated the image, reduced it to nothingness and bloodlessness, the poet turns in the last
stanza to a wild inflation:

> Angelic Dynamo! Ventriloquist of the Blue!
> While beachward creeps the shark-swept Spanish Main
> By what conjunctions do the winds appoint
> Its apotheosis, at last—the hurricane!

These lines arise out of a certain poetic exasperation with the air
plant, its lifelessness and ugliness. There is a grudging recognition
in the first three stanzas that the air plant is a part of nature, that it
is exactly as it is described. Although the poet cannot infuse it with
life, cannot even find any figurative language to describe it and
must thus rely upon a straightforward description of it, he cannot
leave his poem at this naturalistic level. So in the final stanza he
turns from the plant to the sky and sea and appeals to the dynamism of these elements to do what his own creative power could
not do. His appeal is to the hurricane, the destructive winds, which
in other poems he described as totally death-dealing, and not to the
life-giving winds. The hurricane is the apotheosis of this lifeless
plant because, in its wake, as Crane wrote in another poem,
"Nought stayeth, nought now bideth / But's smithereened apart."
The dynamism of its destructive force is a more glorious version
of the nothingness which is the air plant. It is death inflated as the
air plant is death deflated.

Another poem which grew out of his stay on Isle of Pines is "The
Idiot," where Crane turns from the landscape to human nature to
record a similar kind of fruitlessness and lifelessness.[16] The idiot
boy, whom Crane used to pass on the road when he went into town
for mail, is given the same kind of realistic treatment as the landscape. He is described as tormented by taunting children who
dance around the boy in "such infernal circles," while the boy
himself stands still "stretched in ghastly shape." The boy has a

---

16. Crane described this boy to Waldo Frank. See *Letters*, p. 273. See also
"Lenses," a prose poem which comments on the boy.

kite string in one hand and a tin can in the other which he uses as a telescope "though he'd clamped midnight to noon sky!" The poet hurries by this cruel encounter without offering the idiot boy any help, and when he meets him again, he is tormented by his own heartlessness. In the last line of the poem Crane says, "My trespass vision shrinks to face his wrong," an admission which is quite uncharacteristic of Crane and seems to associate him with Hawthorne and Eliot in their concern that the artistic probing of the human heart had its cruel and cold aspects.

The idiot remains "alone, agape." But the "squint lanterns in his head" are no more unseeing than the poet's "trespass vision," which shrinks from any human contact. Actually, as a letter to Waldo Frank reports, he had made friends with this boy, whom he found "rendingly beautiful at times."[17] But his poem is darker than the actual experience. In real life the tin-can telescope had been open at both ends; in the poem there is only one "peeled end" which is clapped to his eye, leaving no exit to the world or human community. Once again Crane depicts a moment of stasis. The lone boy stands still and the poet observes him from a distance; there is no movement toward human contact between them, no movement of love to draw them together. Also, there is almost no poetic commentary, no figurative description in this portrayal. The poet has heard the boy's song "halt serene," and in that stoppage, that vacuum, he does not rush to answer it. Yet the poem is a touching recognition of the poet's own inadequacy in the face of profound human "wrong." In its realistic description and in its lack of commentary until the very last line, "The Idiot" stands as one more evidence of the distance between the world and the poet on the Isle of Pines. The idiot boy is a human variation of the sterility and stasis that Crane saw everywhere about him in the tropical environment.

It will spoil the symmetry of this argument to recall that Crane's island vacation also inspired three very dynamic pieces: two poems, "The Hurricane" and "Eternity," and a fragment, "The Return,"

17. *Letters*, p. 273.

about the hurricane which ripped through the island in the third week of October, just before he left to return to the United States. The want of breath, the windlessness, of the tropical summer is a dominant sensation in the other island poems. The invocation to the "Angelic Dynamo" in the concluding stanza of "The Air Plant" condenses in one quatrain Crane's agonizing desire for some release from the stupor of the brutal summer season, and his poetic prayer was magnificently answered in the actual advent of the hurricane. Yet, paradoxically, it was the hurricane that forced him to leave the island. The house was left almost uninhabitable by the storm, and in the aftermath of the hurricane and the celebration with American sailors who had been sent to the rescue of the storm-wracked island, Crane found himself suffering from a combination of hangover, sinus headache, and hay fever. His physical discomfort, the wrecked house, and his chronic financial difficulties caused him to return to Patterson, New York.[18] There in the blizzards of the winter he wrote the poems about the tropical cyclone. The experience of these poems is not that of emotion recollected in tranquillity; in fact, the hurricane poems are as breezy as their subject and push breathlessly from start to finish. In this sense they form a drastic contrast to the other island poems, many of which were perfected during the same winter of 1926–1927. However, the hurricane poems do share with the other island poems a certain objectivity. "Eternity," for example, is a fairly prosaic account of the actual happenings during the day and night of the storm. "The Hurricane" is another poem in which the speaker stands back from his subject and addresses the lord of the hurricane. Apostrophe, invocation, and the imperative sentence are recurrent in Crane's poetry from the beginning, and the rhapsodic vein, here elaborately poeticized, is a familiar one.[19] But in his early poems as well as in the great invocations of *The Bridge*, the distance between the speaker and the object or person he addresses

18. Unterecker, *Voyager,* pp. 456–457.

19. See Leibowitz's discussion of the early poems for more information, *Hart Crane,* pp. 171–172.

is shifting, and frequently the space between them closes as the poet absorbs or is absorbed by his subject. "The Hurricane," on the other hand, is, for all its verbal inflation, a poem of decorum in which the poet observes and addresses the destructive winds but is not destroyed by them.

With the exception of these works, however, the island poems are uniquely static and lifeless. It is surprising that while Crane's letters from Isle of Pines are full of references to mimosa, oleanders in full bloom, the fecundity of strange fruits and vegetables, he should choose to write poems about the dry groins of the underbrush, the parched air plant, flat slabs of marble, the fruitless palm tree. It is even more remarkable that the poet who could imagine the Brooklyn Bridge as an anemone and whose imaginary islands appeared as "poinsettia meadows" could dwell in such detail on the lifelessness of a scene that must have been burgeoning with animal life and luxuriant growth. Crane's retreat to nature forced upon him a sense of sterility, and it is a sterility that rises from the weightedness of the hardened forms of the natural world. Tranquillity proved terrifying to this restless and frenetic poet. To see the world congealed in forms not of his own making was for Crane to see a strange world.

"Dream" is one of Crane's favorite words, and dreams, sleep, or the time between sleeping and waking are the frequent states of much of his poetry. However, except for a brief mention of sleep in "Island Quarry," the Isle of Pines poems never refer to that state. These poems are almost entirely the experience of noonday, of a world that exists in its concreteness tormentingly outside the poet's reforming dream. Like a man awakening from a long slumber, the poet looks out at the natural world with an air of confusion and puzzlement, tries to locate himself by detailing what he surveys, yet in the location places himself in a deadlock. The concreteness of the world is irreducible. It is itself a kind of nightmare. The world is frightening in its obduracy, and it is this fright that calls forth from the poet frantic appeals to the "comedian host," the "Ventriloqiust of the Blue." But the masculine god who rules this world, unlike the feminine nature spirit of his other poems, is as removed from man as the hard lines of the landscape. The dilemma of the poet in these poems is what to make of this strange world and its remote deity. What Crane does in fact make are some powerful poems that express not the beauty of nature but its irresolute force. In this strange world, this world in which he feels himself imaginatively estranged, Crane locates himself at dead center. Yet, paradoxically, it is from this point that his poetic powers revived. He wrote to Waldo Frank on 24 July 1926, "I feel an absolute music in the air again, and some tremendous rondure floating somewhere—perhaps my little dedication ["To Brooklyn Bridge"] is going to swing me back to San Cristobal again." And later he said to Waldo Frank, "Isn't it true—hasn't it been true in your experience, that beyond the acceptance of fate as a tragic action—immediately every circumstance and incident in one's life flocks toward a positive center of action, control and beauty?" In this last comment he was talking not only of his reading of Spengler's *The Decline of the West*, which had caused him momentarily to distrust his conception of *The Bridge*, but also of " 'things' and circumstances that seem to have uniformly conspired in a strangely symbolical way toward the present speed" of his work.[20] One of these circumstances was the sense of stasis he expressed so magnificently in the island poems.

20. *Letters*, pp. 267, 274.

chapter six: The Impulse to Mastery

"Havana Rose," a prose poem that Crane wrote sometime during the year before he committed suicide, concludes with a paragraph that provides an insight into the poet's deepest desire: "And during the wait over dinner at La Diana the Doctor had said—who was American, also—'You cannot heed the negative—so might go on to undeserved doom . . . must therefore loose yourself within a pattern's mastery that you can conceive, that you can yield to—by which also you win and gain mastery and happiness which is your own from birth.'" The poem begins, "Let us strip the desk for action," and it was written probably in 1931 in Mexico where, after a round of frenzied activity and a long poetic silence, Crane had settled down to write again.[1] He takes up his poetic career exactly where he had left it, with the resolution not to "heed the negative" and its "undeserved doom." What he says at that moment that he must do is what he had always felt he had to do, and the conclusion of "Havana Rose" may serve as a general statement of his poetic purpose. The opposing desires to "loose" himself within a pattern and to master it, to conceive it and yield to it, to win back the hap-

1. For details of Crane's activities in Mexico during this period, see Unterecker, *Voyager,* pp. 658–677.

piness that is man's birthright, these desires arise from an impulse that is, however contradictory, affirmative. What it affirms is a sense of order and design in the universe that can be apprehended by the poet. The affirmation depends upon an intense awareness of the mystery of existence in which the poet is "loosed." The happiness that is the poet's from birth is the happiness of being born, and in that imaginative return to his own beginning the poet celebrates the creative force at the center of his world.

Affirmation in Crane's poetry is the result of a process of association, a process which may be illustrated by "Havana Rose." In the poem's opening Crane says, "That night in Vera Cruz—verily for me 'the True Cross'—let us remember the Doctor." He is talking here about a specific incident, his memory of the doctor and the doctor's counsel to him. But for him, the experience, even the name of the place where it occurred, is laden with significance beyond the immediate. Elizabeth Jennings says, "The point about Crane is that he catches the inexpressible by abruptly yet inevitably swerving, in his verse, from the adamant to the tentative."[2] In this poem Crane swerves from the concrete detail to its larger importance, an importance he finds embodied in the word itself. Crane had an extreme receptivity to the resonance of language. His imagination never missed even the slightest hint of the meanings hidden in words, and his use of words is characterized by an openness to their multiple meanings. By linking the name Vera Cruz with both its English translation and its original meaning, " 'the True Cross,' " Crane draws into his poem a series of associations that expand the significance of his actual meeting with the doctor. He sees in the doctor an example of someone who bears the cross of suffering and redemption for others. He says, "Somewhere in Vera Cruz—to bring—to take—to mix—to ransom—to deduct—*to cure.*" The movement of the line is outward, to an expansive association of meanings. The doctor had brought typhoid-infected rats to Mexico in order to perform an experiment there, but in Crane's poem the bringing, taking, mixing, of the doctor's experiment becomes a

2. Jennings, *Every Changing Shape*, p. 226.

ransom and a cure, words that remind us of the ransom and cure of " 'the True Cross.' " Then, as the poem moves on, the physician becomes a meta-physician, and his connection with the poet, another cross-bearer, is suggested. The poem develops this suggestion as it continues. The doctor was spurred, Crane says, "into something nigh those metaphysics that are typhoid plus and had engaged him once before to death's beyond and back again— antagonistic wills, into immunity." And although Crane claims, "Poets may not be doctors, but doctors are rare poets," he clearly sees the doctor's purpose as his own. Engaged to death's beyond and back again, the poet himself becomes a metaphysician whose science is cosmological. To master the pattern in which one is absorbed is to understand the mystery of existence, to achieve an immunity to death and negation that is the essence of religious experience.

The process of association and affirmation that leads Crane from the doctor's experiments to a pattern's mastery is evident throughout his poetry. Crane does not deny the actual experience, the concrete detail, nor does he select his images because they correspond to some spiritual state; rather, he takes the materials at hand and works through them until they reveal a meaning beyond the immediate. We have seen this process at work in other poems. The pattern of suffering and violence, drawn from his private anguish, is associated in "Lachrymae Christi" with the passion of Christ and the consummation of Dionysus, and from this association comes the affirmation, the "Unmangled target smile" that redeems the torment. By identification with the Indian sachem in "The Dance," Crane extends his poetic desire for possession to an awareness of "all that's consummate and free / There, where the first and last gods keep thy tent." Even in the symbols of the machine age Crane sees by a series of connections "Deity's young name / Kinetic of white choiring wings ... ascends." And in the torpor of the tropical summer he imagines the possibility of release by the "Angelic Dynamo! Ventriloquist of the Blue." Crane's poetic patterns develop through accretion. He starts with a specific image and gathers into that image an intensity of feeling and significance that weights it not to the concrete world but to the world of meaning and value beyond the concrete.

Crane's use of religious and liturgical language to express those moments of extreme intensity and openness in which he feels he has achieved a pattern's mastery is significant. He unyokes this language, as Jennings has pointed out, from the bondage of dogma; yet there is a sense in which it retains, if not its orthodox meaning, at least its pristine quality of awesomeness, rediscovered anew by the poet in his ecstasy.[3] The impulse to mastery in Crane's consciousness stems from a desire to achieve not only a poetic pattern but a pattern that would be confirmed as universal. His effort is to connect his private sensations of joy with a source accessible to all men. The relationship between man and God, between this world and the divine world, between the real and the ideal, is always being forged by the poet. Yet in all the patterns of his poetry there is an opening outward, a yearning toward that other realm beyond the private and the actual. Crane longed for an answer from the power beyond himself, but his poetry always ends in supplication. That his prayers are often framed in exclamations suggests the fervency of his desire and at the same time his conviction that he had alone closed the gap between himself and that greater meaning. Flickering within his most intense affirmations is always the unanswered hope for confirmation. In moments of poetic transport he felt that he had moved beyond the boundaries of self and had entered into communion with divine powers, yet he had no faith to support that assurance. He had only poetry, only words with which to express his awareness of the ineffable. The doctor's counsel in "Havana Rose" to "loose yourself within a pattern's mastery that you can conceive, that you can yield to," spoke directly to Crane's needs and to his greatest desire. Crane sought to conceive a pattern's mastery in his poetry and through that conception to "loose" himself, to enter into the Master pattern.

Crane is describing in the concluding passage of "Havana Rose"

3. *Ibid.*, p. 232.

the sense of mastery which overpowered him at times. He felt within himself moments of illumination, an impulse toward concentration, a sense of being mastered and master. This experience is close to what Ernst Cassirer calls the "mythico-religious attitude." In his discussion of the origin and nature of myth Cassirer distinguishes this attitude or way of thinking from theoretical thinking, which has as its aim "to deliver the contents of sensory or intuitive experience from the isolation in which they originally occur. . . . Theoretical thinking proceeds 'discursively,' in that it treats the immediate content only as a point of departure, from which it can run the whole gamut of impressions in various directions, until these impressions are fitted together into one unified conception, one closed system." In contrast, Cassirer says, mythical thinking "comes to rest in the immediate experience; the sensible present is so great that everything else dwindles before it." Under the spell of the mythico-religious attitude, the world is annihilated and the immediate content so completely fills the consciousness that nothing can exist beside and apart from it. Cassirer writes:

> The ego is spending all its energy on this single object, lives in it, loses itself in it. . . . This focusing of all forces on a single point is the prerequisite for all mythical thinking and mythical formulation. When, on the one hand, the entire self is given up to a single impression, is "possessed" by it and, on the other hand, there is the utmost tension between the subject and its object, the outer world; when external reality is not merely viewed and contemplated, but overcomes a man in sheer immediacy, with emotions of fear or hope, terror or wish fulfillment: then the spark jumps somehow across, the tension finds release, as the subjective excitement becomes objectified, and confronts the mind as a god or a daemon.

For a mind enthralled in this way, "all bridges between the concrete datum and the systematized totality of experience are broken; only the present reality, as mythic or linguistic conception stresses and shapes it, fills the entire subjective realm." Cassirer continues:

> There is nothing beside or beyond it whereby it could be measured or to which it could be compared; its mere presence is the sum of

all Being. At this point, the word which denotes that thought content is not a mere conventional symbol, but is merged with its object in an indissoluble unity. The conscious experience is not merely wedded to the word, but is consumed by it. Whatever has been fixed by a name, henceforth is not only real, but is Reality. The potential between "symbol" and "meaning" is resolved; in place of a more or less adequate "expression," we find a relation of identity, of complete congruence between "image" and "object," between the name and the thing.[4]

Without arguing for the validity of Cassirer's explanation of the origins of primitive myth, it is possible to understand the consciousness he describes as the one Crane knew in his own experience and expressed in his poetry.

Crane said, "It is as though a poem gave the reader as he left it a single, new *word*, never before spoken and impossible to actually enunciate, but self-evident as an active principle in the reader's consciousness henceforward."[5] The newness of Crane's poetic *word* depends entirely on what Cassirer calls the "indissoluble unity" of the symbol and the object. The word of Crane's poems cannot be compared to some reality beyond it; it is, for Crane, reality. Yet, since the poet has to use ordinary words, words already spoken and enunciated, he must use them in a new way, not as they refer to something beyond themselves in the outer world but as they objectify his own "subjective excitement." His effort must be directed toward dissolving the "closed system" of discursive thinking in order to apprehend the world in an entirely different way. What Crane sensed in his own consciousness as the "pattern's mastery" is this new apprehension of the world. What he sought to do in his poetry was to make that apprehension "an active principle in the reader's consciousness." The revolution of consciousness that had taken place in his own experience had also to occur through his poem for the reader. His poems do not make the reader think

---

4. Ernst Cassirer, *Language and Myth,* tr. Susanne K. Langer (New York: Harper and Brothers, 1946), pp. 32, 33, 58.

5. "General Aims and Theories," *The Complete Poems,* p. 221.

about an experience; they attempt rather to render that experience in its immediacy to the reader.

In this endeavor he was often misunderstood. Harriet Monroe, for one, objected to the obscurity of one of his poems, "At Melville's Tomb"; in his answer to her objections he makes his poetic program clear. He says, "Much fine poetry may be completely rationalistic in its use of symbols, but there is much great poetry of another order which will yield the reader very little when inspected under the limitation of such arbitrary concerns as are manifested in your judgment of the Melville poem, especially when you constitute such requirements of ordinary logical relationship between word and word as irreducible." He amplifies his position: "If the poet is to be held completely to the already evolved and exploited sequences of imagery and logic—what field of added consciousness and increased perception (the actual province of poetry, if not lullabies) can be expected when one has to relatively return to the alphabet every breath or so? In the minds of people who have sensitively read, seen and experienced a great deal, isn't there a terminology something like short-hand as compared to usual description and dialectics, which the artist ought to be right in trusting as a reasonable connective agent toward fresh concepts, more inclusive evaluations?" Here Crane is arguing for the possibility of his kind of poetry, a poetry that could simply not be made clear in Harriet Monroe's critical terms, which sought to associate the image with its reference. Crane was convinced that "images, themselves totally dissociated, when joined in the circuit of a particular emotion located with specific relation to both of them, conduce to great vividness and accuracy of statement in defining that emotion."[6] In dissociating his images, Crane sought an understanding of them not as expressing some concept outside themselves but as objectifying an inner consciousness. His aim was not to understand the world but to possess it in the "complete congruence" "between the name and the thing."

To apprehend the world in a new way is for Crane to speak in

6. "A Letter to Harriet Monroe," *The Complete Poems*, pp. 236, 237–238.

"a stranger tongue" and to write in "wider letters than the alphabet." In the last years of his life Crane, tormented and harried as he was by private stresses, still longed to express the "pattern's mastery." Although he wrote only a few poems after "Havana Rose" and perfected only one, he turned in these poems to that moment of intense concentration which is in Cassirer's terms "the sum of all Being." Most of the poems Crane wrote in Mexico suggest how often that moment eluded him, but they also suggest how ceaselessly he struggled to objectify his "subjective excitement." To the end, he felt that only in being "possessed" by the original creative power of the word could the poet speak at all. In his mind during his Mexican experience was the vague notion that he would write something about the Christian conquest of Mexico. Although this plan never materialized, he did write a group of poems which express simultaneously his desire to render a "single new *word*" and his awareness that that word remained hidden, lost. In these poems the "keen vision" of the Indian that "Spells what his tongue has had," the dream of the "too-keen cider," the desire to "Return the mirage on a coin," the longing for the "more enduring answer," all express the poet's search for the word and his sense of loss. He feels removed from the word, the answer, the keen apprehension, the moment of concentration. If the "closed system" of the world is dissolved in these poems, no other world is created. Finally, in "The Broken Tower," the only perfected poem of this period, the poet is again "possessed" by the sheer immediacy of experience and so recovers the music that is his word.

"The Sad Indian" presents a figure who is removed from the world of sound and time; he "does not know the new hum in the sky," nor does he know the new time. Although he counts "scarcely sun and moon," his "keen vision / Spells what his tongue has had." In his release from time, however, he exists not in a moment of intense concentration but in a strange vacuum. His vantage has been lost; he is an image of the poet's dream of disorientation. Yet this "gymnast of inertia" exerts a powerful tug on the poet's imagination:

and so he looms
Farther than his sun-shadow—farther than wings
—Their shadows even—now can't carry him.
He does not know the new hum in the sky
And—backwards—is it thus the eagles fly?

The memory of the sun's worship and of the eagle's transcendent power is all that exists in the "Sad heart" of the Indian. But his backward stance is a holy one. The backward-flying eagle in this poem expresses the action of the feathered serpent, Quetzalcoatl, who, defeated by the superior magic of the Aztecs, fled to the sea from whence he departed for his original home.[7] Thus flying backward suggests a return to divine origins, and perhaps here an escape from the "prison" imposed by the Christian conquest in the Mexico of the Indian, but also an escape from all forms that obscure the "keen vision." The sadness of the Indian had a particular appeal for Crane. He told Wilbur Underwood that the "nature of the Mexican Indians, as Lawrence said, isn't exactly 'sunny,' but he is more stirred by the moon, if you get what I mean, than any type I've ever known."[8]

In "Purgatorio" (he had been reading Dante in Mexico) Crane expresses his sense of isolation and confusion in a new land:

And are these stars—the high plateau—the scents
Of Eden—and the dangerous tree—are these
The landscape of confession—and if confession

7. Deena Posy Metzger has attempted to associate the myths of Quetzalcoatl, the Toltec god of civilization, and of the serpent and the eagle, with the myth of *The Bridge*. See "Hart Crane's *Bridge*: The Myth Active," *Arizona Quarterly*, XX (Spring 1964), 36–46. Her contention is that Crane knew of these myths from Padraic Colum, D. H. Lawrence, and William H. Prescott's *History of the Conquest of Mexico*.

8. *Letters*, p. 390. "The Sad Indian" may have been inspired by an illustration in Anita Brenner's *Idols behind Altars*, a book Crane mentioned he was reading during this period. See *Letters*, p. 372. Reproduced in this book is a pastel entitled "The Sad Indian," by Francisco Goitia, which is a modern interpretation of a famous pre-Spanish sculpture discovered in Mexico City. Miss Brenner also suggests that there is a street named "Street of the Sad Indian" to commemorate the story of the Indian who pined away because of grief after the conquest. See Anita Brenner, *Idols behind Altars* (New York: Payson & Clarke, 1929), p. 334.

> So absolution? Wake pines—but pines wake here.
> I dream the too-keen cider—the too-soft snow.
> Where are the bayonets that the scorpion may not grow[?]

Here again, side by side, are rendered the sense of release in the natural world of paradise before the fall, where sin does not exist, and the sense of constraint in the Christian world of ceremony with its confession and absolution for sin. In the final stanza the poet hears church bells and at the same time the hours they forget to chime, perhaps the days of pagan celebration, that he will also know:

> I am unraveled, umbilical anew[,]
> So ring the church bells here in Mexico—
> (They ring too obdurately here to need my call)
> And what hours they forget to chime I'll know,
> As one whose altitude at one time was not [. . .]

In the image of unwinding, a familiar image in Crane's lexicon, the poet formulates his psychic release; he has disengaged himself from one world, presumably his own land, mentioned at the beginning of the poem, and has reached a "high plateau," a new "altitude" of peace and harmony. He is also "umbilical anew," tied to another force. The bell rope and the umbilical cord bind him to a new system of music, the heavenly music of religious celebration.

In words that seem to be a reworking of passages from "Cape Hatteras," Crane turns in another Mexican poem, "Reliquary," to the creative power of the word and to the various and interrelated systems of belief, ancient mythology and astrology and the poet's own word:

> The harvest laugh of bright Apollo
> And the flint tooth of Sagittarius,
> Rhyme from the same Tau (closing cinch by cinch)
> And pocket us who, somehow, do not follow,
> As though we knew (those who are variants[)]

> Charms that each by each refuse the clinch
>
> With desperate propriety, whose name is writ
> In wider letters than the alphabet,—
> Who is now left to vary the Sanscrit
> Pillowed by
>
> My wrist in the vestibule of time—who
> Will hold it—wear the keepsake, dear, of time—
> Return the mirage on a coin that spells
> Something of sand and sun the Nile defends . . . [?]

The Tau unites Apollo and Sagittarius and even the poet whose word, Crane always hoped, would be one with the Word, written in wider letters than the alphabet, although the poet's verbal and magical charms often refused to be formalized in any system. Who will vary the Sanskrit, the holy word, the poem asks, and in the questions the poet affirms his own mission, described in "Cape Hatteras" as the "Sanskrit charge / To conjugate infinity's dim marge." Those who cannot be absorbed into the Tau's rhyme will make their own rhyme. But "Reliquary," as its name suggests, is an exhibition of holy relics, remnants of once living traditions which the poet feels himself to have inherited and which he must bequeath. His successor will be, like himself, one who knows "variants," who can read the ancient coins, and from the keepsake of time create his own conception of eternity. However interesting its subject, "Reliquary" falls short of a fully realized poem; its opening stanza about a ditch and a pillow is baffling, and the ellipsis in the remaining stanzas makes it possible to interpret the poem in mutually contradictory ways.[9]

"The Circumstance," dedicated to the Mexican god of games and flowers, Xochipilli, is another fragmentary poem. Here Crane expresses the immediacy of the religious impulse despite the "bloody foreign clown," the Christian conquerors who made of

9. For example, see Lewis's discussion of this poem, *Poetry of Hart Crane*, pp. 407–409. Lewis claims that in this poem Crane raises the issues of artistic and sexual heresies.

Xochipilli's followers "a dismounted people."[10] Still Crane's tribute is to this sacred power:

> If you
> Could drink the sun as did and does
> Xochipilli—as they who've
> Gone have done, as they
> Who've done . . . A god of flowers in statued
> Stone . . . of love—
>
> If you could die, then starve, who live
> Thereafter, stronger than death smiles in flowering stone;—
> You could stop time, give florescent
> Time a longer answer back (shave lightning,
> Possess in hale full the winds) of time
> A longer answer force, more enduring answer
> As they did—and have done . . .

Xochipilli's "coruscated crown" still shines with the life-giving power of the sun; only belief in the god can "stop time," can release us from the time-bound world. It is this awareness of the sacred quality of life that is Xochipilli's heritage, that the poet longs to express in his poem.

Compared with these fragments, "The Broken Tower," the last poem Crane is known to have put in any kind of final form, supports the assertion that Crane's imaginative powers were on the upswing in the last months in Mexico. It is not only that "The Broken Tower" is one of the best poems Crane ever wrote; the importance of this poem is in Crane's recapture of the original creative power of the word. This poem has been discussed earlier in terms of the salutary brokenness of its title and central image; at this point its religious meaning may be considered. The poem opens with a description of the church bells ringing at dawn, actually a poetic rendition of Crane's own ringing of the church

10. Weber omitted as incomplete "The Circumstance" from *The Complete Poems*. It may be found in Frank's edition of *The Complete Poems of Hart Crane*, pp. 150–151.

bells at Taxco, where he had participated in the festival of the local patron saint in January 1932:[11]

> The bell-rope that gathers God at dawn
> Dispatches me as though I dropped down the knell
> Of a spent day—to wander the cathedral lawn
> From pit to crucifix, feet chill on steps from hell.

The bell which calls the faithful to Mass and is rung at the most sacred point in the service, when the sacraments are consecrated, sounds in the poet's mind to force him away from the altar and into the world. But the contrast between the faithful and the poet is not simple; in the second stanza the poet's dispatch to the world is associated with the bells which also launch their message:

> Have you not heard, have you not seen that corps
> Of shadows in the tower, whose shoulders sway
> Antiphonal carillons launched before
> The stars are caught and hived in the sun's rays?

Antiphony is the central musical imagery of this poem: the church bells and the natural world, the poet's song and the "Word" of the "tribunal monarch," the poet's human love and divine love, all are responsive rhythms. In an earlier version the bells sound both the religious "clarion turn to God" and the natural "echoes of an ancient, universal hive." But even in the final version the antiphonal carillons of the church and the world play responsively in the poet's imagining. The bells and the poet will "break down their tower," and the result will be the release of religious celebration and music in the natural world:

> Oval encyclicals in canyons heaping
> The impasse high with choir. Banked voices slain!
> Pagodas, campaniles with reveilles outleaping—
> O terraced echoes prostrate on the plain! . . .

11. See Lesley Simpson's description of the occasion in Unterecker, *Voyager*, p. 722.

Here is the call for a new day of release and resurrection. The impasse between the divine and the natural worlds is bridged in the poet's consciousness, and in the church as on the plain the devout prostrate themselves at the holiest moment of the bell's ringing. The poet identifies his own entrance into the world with the launching of the bells:

> And so it was I entered the broken world
> To trace the visionary company of love, its voice
> An instant in the wind (I know not whither hurled)
> But not for long to hold each desperate choice.

In the next stanza the poet seeks to know if his word is "cognate" with the "crystal Word" of God. But he receives no answer, and so he shifts the direction of the question and asks:

> or is it she
> Whose sweet mortality stirs latent power?—

> And through whose pulse I hear, counting the strokes
> My veins recall and add, revived and sure
> The angelus of wars my chest evokes:
> What I hold healed, original now, and pure . . .

The response of the woman to the man is an answer, an antiphony that revives in the poet the music of the bell tower. The woman's pulse answering the man's own heartbeat has given him a sense of wholeness and purity which has healed his brokenness. And this new feeling restores to the poet a sense of awe and celebration; his human and mortal love receives an antiphonal response from the heavens:

> And builds, within, a tower that is not stone
> (Not stone can jacket heaven)—but slip
> Of pebbles,—visible wings of silence sown
> In azure circles, widening as they dip

> The matrix of the heart, lift down the eye
> That shrines the quiet lake and swells a tower . . .
> The commodious, tall decorum of that sky
> Unseals her earth, and lifts love in its shower.

Alone, tracing the visionary company of love, seeking some answer from God, he senses an uncertainty and asks, "could blood hold such a lofty tower / As flings the answer true?" The woman of sweet mortality not only exists as an answer to his human and mortal desires but, through them, she has revived the angelus. The tower he builds is contructed of earthly pebbles and heavenly circles. The sky that "Unseals her earth" is a divine power working in this world, the "tribunal monarch of the air / Whose thigh embronzes earth," whom the poet had addressed earlier in vain. The church bells that had gathered God at the beginning of the poem play again through the poet's own music. In the opening of the poem the poet had been wandering from "pit to crucifix." Now the pit has been transformed into the "quiet lake," shrined and made holy by the poet's human love, which has served as an intimation of divine love. The crucifix and the church bells that commemorate the crucifixion now become meaningful to the poet as a symbol that "lifts love in its shower."

The simultaneous sense of ascent and descent evident in these two stanzas expresses a consciousness that is traditionally religious. The "visible wings of silence" suggest the feeling of ascension, of spiritual elevation, of ecstasy. The apprehension of this symbol appears to move the poet away from the real world, to lift him far above the pit into which he had been dropped in the poem's beginning. Yet these wings "dip" to the matrix, the center from which all life and love originate, so that the ascension is a return, a descent. The return is not only to the heart's center but to a natural world which is still sacred. The lake, the sky, the earth are newly beatified; they are like paradise. The poet feels regenerated and renewed by this experience. The poet must "lift down the eye" because his ascending vision returns to the sacred and creative center of life.[12] Crane is expressing here in very condensed language an experience of transcendence in which the actual experi-

12. Mircea Eliade discusses images of ascension as they express the idea of transcendence in various myths. His comments are pertinent to this experience in Crane's poetry. See Mircea Eliade, *Myths, Dreams, and Mysteries* (New York: Harper & Row, 1960), pp. 99–122.

ence of space and time is replaced by the visionary experience of ascending to a center. Sensations of plenitude overpower the poet: the widening circles, the swelling tower, the unsealed earth, the lifting shower, all suggest an expansion of consciousness at this sacred moment. "The Broken Tower" is essentially a religious poem that moves from the traditional expression of faith in the church bells to the poet's own experience of transcendence, and in the movement of the poem the two expressions form an antiphonal response.

Church bells do not ring often in Crane's poetry. It was chiefly in Mexico that he was inspired by a religious atmosphere. The pattern of the Christian and pagan religious festivals which he witnessed and in which he participated, as well as their celebratory nature, aroused his imagination. The festive, wild, all-night ceremonies in honor of local patron saints and pagan gods revealed a side of religion that appealed to him in an immediate way. In the poems that he wrote in Mexico he dwells on the religious experience. Although he satirizes the church in "Imperator Victus" for its connection with imperialistic aims, he treats more frequently its forms and patterns and the mysterious force they represented.

Long before his Mexican trip, however, Crane had turned his poetic talents toward the expression of that impulse to mastery that can be described as a religious consciousness. He searched for words that would make it clear, and often he fastened on terms and concepts that are traditionally Christian, but he borrowed them boldly, used them freely, and aimed always to render them meaningful as new words. He wrote at least one poem in which he explained his frustration with traditional religious patterns; this was "Emblems of Conduct," a poem composed in 1924, early in his career, from snatches of lines from the work of another poet, Samuel Greenberg. Here Crane contrasts the good deeds of the apostle, giving alms to the meek, with the magnificent power of nature manifested in the volcano that burst "With sulphur and aureate rocks." The notion is Emersonian in its contrast between the lifeless institutionalization of religion and the glory of natural phenomena. "The apostle conveys thought through discipline" but, the poet concludes, his are "Dull lips commemorating spiritual gates." The poet prefers not commemoration but actual living, and he chooses not spiritual gates but a resting place in nature "Where marble clouds support the sea." There

> Dolphins still played, arching the horizons,
> But only to build memories of spiritual gates.

However, the poet's "spot of rest" beside the sea is oppressively reminiscent in its marble clouds of the dead weight of religious forms and customs. The dolphin, a symbol in early Christian art of love and swiftness, remains still playful to the poet, but the spiritual gates it arches are merely memories. In this poem the pattern that the poet sees being imposed upon experience is altogether deadening; it is something that he can neither understand nor yield to, although his escape from it is sadly in vain. Despite the eruption of the volcano and the playing of the dolphin, the world has been neatly disciplined and reduced to laws by orators, apostles, and historians.

Quite opposed to the lifelessness of the apostle is the overwhelming power of a feminine figure addressed in another poem of this period, "Interludium." This figure is called Madonna and associated with grace and the communicant cup, but her appeal to the poet is obviously more sensual and pleasurable than devotional. Here Crane reverses the method of "Emblems of Conduct." Instead of juxtaposing natural life and dead religious forms, he tries to associate religious patterns with a human experience that is meaningful. The woman he calls Madonna is not the mother of Christ in this poem but the life-giving center of existence, the eternal creative spirit. Both the poet and the natural world are fructified by her presence. Submission to her is submission to a vital force. The opening stanza renders her as all-embracing:

> Thy time is thee to wend
> with languor such as gains

> immensity in gathered grace; the arms
> to spread; the hands to yield their shells.

She is "illimitable and unresigned," a holy presence "that heavens climb to measure." Her mercy is "immensity," and the poet feels himself absorbed by her proffering arms and hands. As the poem continues, her presence overwhelms the poet:

> unfurling thee untried,—until
> from sleep forbidden now and wide
> partitions in thee—goes
>
> communicant and speeding new
> the cup again wide from thy throat to spend
> those streams and slopes untenanted thou
> hast known . . . And blithe
>
> Madonna, natal to thy yielding
> still subsist I, wondrous as
> from thine open dugs shall still the sun
> again round one more fairest day.

What the poet is describing is a sexual experience which is also associated with spiritual regeneration. In her unfurling and partition, this woman looses upon the man and the world a power so vast that it contains them. There is in this experience a sense of returning to the beginning when the man and the world were first created. The "communicant" and the "cup" lose all reference to the commemorative communion service; the poet actually experiences a moment in which the body, in sexual communion, is sanctified and the speaker is returned to that state of awe and ecstasy which is the desired spiritual state of all communicants. The poem celebrates the sensual force of the woman whose yielding and mastery has been "wondrous"; it is this very quality of wonder and joy that Crane found ground out of existence by traditional religious experience.

"Lachrymae Christi" is another poetic effort to master the religious pattern of the world, to render the immediacy of the creative

spirit at work in the springtime rebirth of nature. In this poem
Crane tries to connect various religious references. "Not penitence
/ But song," is the poet's reaction to the mysteries of the springtime.
The old monastic practice of mortifying the flesh with "vermin
and rod" no longer serves us as a fitting response to Christ's death.
As he is associated with Dionysus, the god of spring and rebirth in
the poem, Christ loses his special role as the divine sacrificial
offering; his death becomes merely the "Compulsion of the year."

Penance, the mortification of the flesh, confession, and a sense of
sin have no place in Crane's consciousness. In "For the Marriage
of Faustus and Helen," Part III, he emphasizes again the primacy
of praise and celebration:

> Delve upward for the new and scattered wine,
> O brother-thief of time, that we recall.
> Laugh out the meager penance of their days
> Who dare not share with us the breath released,
> The substance drilled and spent beyond repair
> For golden, or the shadow of gold hair.

The opening image of these lines anticipates the line in "The
Broken Tower" where the poet will "lift down the eye." The sense
of descending and ascending simultaneously is a sense of space
transcended, and his experience here is one of ecstasy and celebration. The new wine is an intoxicant, and it has the power to release
the poet from the time-bound world. It releases the poet's laugh,
as well as his breath and spirit, and thus, unlike the communion
wine, it is drunk not in remembrance but in celebration.

"At Melville's Tomb," written in 1925 and 1926, is a deepening
of the celebratory tone of "Interludium," "For the Marriage of
Faustus and Helen," Part III, and "Lachrymae Christi." While
these other poems appear at times to pass over too quickly the
darker facts of existence, "At Melville's Tomb" dwells upon them,
and its affirmation arises from them. Here the poet confronts the
pattern of life and death imaged in the powerful force of the sea.
The artistic imagination, overwhelmed by this destructive element,

"loosed" within it, is able to master its pattern, to read its "scattered chapter," "hieroglyph," and "portent."

In his tribute to Melville, Crane gives form to the visionary experience:

> Often beneath the wave, wide from this ledge
> The dice of drowned men's bones he saw bequeath
> An embassy. Their numbers as he watched,
> Beat on the dusty shore and were obscured.
>
> And wrecks passed without sound of bells,
> The calyx of death's bounty giving back
> A scattered chapter, livid hieroglyph,
> The portent wound in corridors of shells.

Because Melville had submitted to the destructive element of the sea, had been engaged to death's beyond and back, he could see the destructive sea as not totally annihilative. It is in its very destructiveness, in fact, that the sea grinds men's bones to dice and thus bequeathes a message from the dead men. It is a puzzling message which even as the artist observes it is obscured; still, it is a message, not to be sure the complete message that these drowned men were prevented from delivering by their death but some remnant of their former existence. The artist must create from this partial record the meaning of the voyage, the significance of life as voyaging, and the import of death. The men do complete their voyage homeward although they have been destroyed in the process; they deliver to the artist the message from eternity. In his apprehension of this mystery the artist experiences a strange sense of sight obscured and sound silenced. As he watches, the numbers are obscured and he feels the everpresence of death, "wrecks passed without sound of bells." Yet the obliteration of the artist's sight and hearing is a kind of awesomeness, a state in which he sees and hears anew. He receives the "calyx of death's bounty," a symbol of the destructive whirlpool that sends up the ship's wreckage from the deep, but also the cornucopia whose abundance suggests life. And he hears "portents wound in corridors of shells" as he holds a shell up to his ear, hearing perhaps only the sound of his own heart beating, but even at that hearing again and hearing the persistent and enduring rhythm of life.

Artistic vision is itself a sign of resurrection from destruction. From beneath the wave the drowned men's relics rise. The vortex of destruction tosses up a "livid hieroglyph." The corridors of shells wind around a message that is portentous, another word which opens, like the calyx, doubly into meanings of the foreboding and the marvelous. From these scattered suggestions the poem moves to its climax in the third stanza:

> Then in the circuit calm of one vast coil,
> Its lashings charmed and malice reconciled,
> Frosted eyes there were that lifted altars;
> And silent answers crept across the stars.

The imagistic pattern of circles which Crane had developed in the first two stanzas is here reconciled in one vast coil: the circular voyage in which the dead men return transformed, the calyx which is both the deadly vortex and the living whorl of floral leaves, the shell with its ominous and amazing warnings, death itself which is not the absolute end of the voyage, all are drawn together here in one integrative symbol. For Melville, as for Crane, the experience of death at sea becomes his most creative awareness of life's meanings. The lashings and malice of this overpowering element are charmed and reconciled by the artistic imagination, which will not see the sea simply as destructive. From submission to the sea's power and to the forceful tug of death, the artist, like the vortex, sends up his messages, but the artist's imagination ascends far above the coil of destruction to imagine that in the pattern of the heavenly stars the "calyx of death's bounty" is completed. From the very depths of his awareness of death the artist is lifted through his ascending vision to an ecstatic apprehension of life. "Stars scribble on our eyes the frosty sagas / The gleaming cantos of unvanquished space,"

Crane wrote in "Cape Hatteras," where his sight was also turned to "infinity's dim marge" and where again he writes of death and the vision that must be reclaimed from it.

Harriet Monroe, who finally published "At Melville's Tomb" along with her correspondence with the poet in the October 1926 issue of *Poetry*, questioned the image, "Frosted eyes lift altars." Crane's response was "that a man, not knowing perhaps a definite god yet being endowed with a reverence for deity—such a man naturally postulates a deity somehow, and the altar of that deity by the very *action* of the eyes *lifted* in searching."[13] What he is expressing in the poem, in language that was not meant to be visualized but which is highly visionary, is the sense of ascension which attends the release of the spirit from the fears and terrors of death. This transcendent release is not, as it is so often in Crane's poetry, the gift of a beatific moment. This vision arises from a confrontation with death; it is one with the experience of drowning and wrecks. What Crane eulogizes in this poem is Melville's mastery, his transforming imagination, his ability to see death as a bounty, to read the messages offered him in this world, to submit to the sea's rhythmic pattern, and to reconcile it with the process of life. The altar that he lifts is the new plane of awareness that he experiences. The answers that creep across the stars are "silent," but it is the silence of an answer which is ineffable.

These lines recall the ending of "Voyages II," where the poet prays:

> Bequeath us to no earthly shore until
> Is answered in the vortex of our grave
> The seal's wide spindrift gaze toward paradise.

The bequest which the poet seeks is the bequest from the grave; the seal's gaze, like the "Frosted eyes," is turned toward eternity. The circular imagery of the sea and the plane of the altar are combined again in the beatific ending of "Voyages VI," where the poet envisions

13. "A Letter to Harriet Monroe," *The Complete Poems,* p. 239.

> Still fervid covenant, Belle Isle,
> —Unfolded floating dais before
> Which rainbows twine continual hair—
> Belle Isle, white echo of the oar!

The floating dais arises out of the sea as a form of the poet's visionary awareness.

In the final stanza of "At Melville's Tomb" the poet returns to address Melville's tomb, the sea, which has been opened by the visionary powers of Melville's twentieth-century poetic heir:

> Compass, quadrant and sextant contrive
> No farther tides . . . High in the azure steeps
> Monody shall not wake the mariner.
> This fabulous shadow only the sea keeps.

Melville's writings were for Crane more accurate than compass, quadrant, and sextant in measuring the tides of the sea. When Harriet Monroe objected to these instruments contriving the tides, Crane said that instruments invented to measure some entity could so extend the concepts that they might even be said to have extended the original boundaries of the entity measured.[14] What is even more true is that Melville's treatment of the sea has so extended our awareness of it that he has actually contrived tides which mechanical instruments are powerless to fathom. Melville was for Crane the great fabulist, the artist who had conceived and yielded to the pattern of existence. It is "only the sea," the vast death-dealing and sustaining force, that can contain the spirit of this fabulous and mystical mariner. Although this poem is about death, the tomb of the sea, it celebrates the creative and inspiring mastery over death which is the highest aspiration of the artist.

"At Melville's Tomb" makes an explicit connection between artistic creation and spiritual awareness, and it is a connection which Crane underscored not only in his poems but in theoretical commentaries on the function of poetry. During the year that Crane worked on "At Melville's Tomb," he was also engaged in formulat-

14. *Ibid.*

ing the larger design of *The Bridge*, and this activity led him to consider the aim of his poetry. In a letter to Gorham Munson written in March 1926 and in an essay published posthumously as "General Aims and Theories" and written at this time, he states his conviction that there "are destined to be discovered certain as yet undefined spiritual quantities, perhaps a new hierarchy of faith," and that in this process the poet would play the primary role. He wanted to discover in his poetry "under new forms certain spiritual illuminations, shining with a morality essentialized from experience directly, and not from previous precepts or preconceptions."[15] In his letter to Munson he explains further that poetry cannot logically explain the "fact of man's relationship to a hypothetical god," but that it "may well give you the real connective experience, the very 'sign manifest' on which rests the assumption of a godhead."[16] The connective experience, or "the concrete *evidence* of the *experience* of a recognition*," as he explained, will be expressed in poetry that must become an effort to formulate a new word, a new religious language.

Crane felt that "new conditions of life germinate new forms of spiritual articulation," and in his poems he risked obscurity in "manipulating the more imponderable phenomena of psychic motives, pure emotional crystallizations, etc.," to express this spiritual sense. There were no "general denominators of speech that are solid enough or that ring with any vibration or spiritual conviction," Crane said, and so he not only had to discover the words and the forms to express the spiritual illumination which he felt at the deepest level of his consciousness, but he also had to pursue and understand that illumination itself which seemed so newly germinated and so unique in a poetic age dominated by the negations of T. S. Eliot's early poetry. Crane felt that the great mythologies of the past, among which he included the church, were no longer convincing and yet that "their traditions are operative still—in millions

15. "General Aims and Theories," *The Complete Poems*, pp. 219, 221.
16. *Letters*, p. 237.

of chance combinations of related and unrelated detail, psychological reference, figures of speech, precepts, etc."[17] Thus, while he sought to express the new forms of spiritual illumination, he also made use of traditional terms and references, not in an attempt to revive traditional religious language but in an effort to express in symbolic form the real conviction of his own spiritual experience. His problem was the obverse of Eliot's. While Eliot understood intellectually or rationally the power of traditional religious belief, he expresses in "The Hollow Men" and *The Waste Land* the agonizing inability of modern man to respond spiritually, to feel religiously inspired. Crane, on the other hand, felt a kind of ecstasy which he could only describe as spiritual illumination, yet he had only the faintest idea of a traditional religious heritage, scant knowledge of mythology, and no understanding of the dogmas of orthodox Christianity. But he felt, as he told Munson, that one could not ask "for exact factual data (a graphic map of eternity?), ethical morality or moral classifications, etc., from poetry."[18] What he was interested in expressing was the psychic experience of his religious impulse. And for an understanding of this experience, *The Bridge* is an informative document.[19]

Petition is the basic activity of Crane's religious consciousness in this poem. He sought always to know if he had mastered the pattern, if his word was "cognate" of "that tribunal monarch," if his sign was one with the Word, if God would descend to this world, and if the forms of this world could be illumined by poetry to reveal the spirit. What he is questioning here is his own power of perception. His need to lift altars and lend a myth to God arises from a powerful urgency to connect his experience with a world of eternal

---

17. "General Aims and Theories," *The Complete Poems*, pp. 222, 218.

18. *Letters*, p. 238.

19. Lewis calls Crane the most religious of modern poets. His discussion of the religious character of *The Bridge* is, however, at variance with my own. See Lewis, *Poetry of Hart Crane*, pp. 267–286. Hyatt Howe Waggoner has an instructive discussion of Crane's mysticism in *American Poets* (Boston: Houghton Mifflin, 1968), pp. 484–511.

values. The God to whom he addresses his petitions is a God of majesty and power and mystery whose presence can alone make meaningful the poet's deepest experience. He is also a God whose presence in this world must be discovered as it is revealed to the poet. The revelation of God in the Bible had no meaning for Crane, although he occasionally uses biblical references in his poems to expand his own point. The revelation of God through his creation is important in Crane's poetry only as that creation impinged upon the poet's consciousness as a dynamic force. What really interested Crane was the revelation of spiritual truths in the psychic experience of modern man. He longed to see his private dreams and visions verified in the universe. He desired to see his own spiritual illumination as evidence of a universal spirit. He tried to convert his vision into poetry that would endure beyond it.

In the opening poems of *The Bridge*, "Proem: To Brooklyn Bridge" and "Ave Maria," Crane juxtaposes two prayers, one uttered by the modern poet and the other uttered by the fifteenth-century navigator. As the poet looks at the bridge, he exclaims:

> O harp and altar, of the fury fused,
> (How could mere toil align thy choiring strings!)
> Terrific threshold of the prophet's pledge,
> Prayer of pariah, and the lover's cry,—

Earlier praised for its harmony with nature, the bridge now becomes a form of man's spiritual desires. It is the symbol of man's longing for a new life, of his petition for grace in his outcast state, and of his desire for unity and wholeness. The prophet, the pariah, and the lover all seek in their cries a response to their inmost needs, and in the bridge they experience the immediate symbol, the "Unfractioned idiom," that answers their prayers and reaffirms their hope that in this world God will reveal himself. In the final stanza of "Proem," as the bridge sweeps far above the world, vaults the sea, the poet sees it as a form of his own transcending power that must simultaneously "descend / And of the curveship lend a myth to God." It is in the curving circular form of the bridge that Crane sees the "sign manifest" of God. Emerson saw the circle as the most frequent image in nature, and in his essay on "Circles" he says, "The eye is the first circle; the horizon which it forms is the second; and throughout nature this primary figure is repeated without end. It is the highest emblem in the cipher of the world. St. Augustine described the nature of God as a circle whose centre was everywhere and its circumference nowhere. . . . Our life is an apprenticeship to the truth that around every circle another can be drawn; that there is no end in nature, but every end is a beginning; that there is always another dawn risen on mid-noon, and under every deep a lower deep opens." Although Emerson limited the circle to organic as opposed to mechanical structures and Crane purposefully extends it to mechanical structures, Emerson's conviction that the circle is the highest emblem because it most perfectly describes the nature of God is certainly shared by Crane. In the circle of the bridge Crane imagined that he gleaned the mystery of divinity.

"Proem" expresses the poet's apprehension of a natural world of movement and beauty overlaid or encircled by a mechanical world that reflects the same movement and beauty. The "inviolate curve" of the seagull, the sun's daily rounds, the "immaculate sigh of stars," are all related to the curveship of the bridge which in the modern world is the emblem of the eternal center. It is the poet's eyes, lifted in searching, that see in this profane structure a sacred emblem.

This God whose center is everywhere and whose circumference is nowhere is the deity to whom Columbus addresses his prayer in "Ave Maria." Not to Mary, but to God, Columbus offers his petition, and it is to a God who reveals himself in the circles of his sphere:

> Series on series, infinite,—till eyes
> Starved wide on blackened tides, accrete—enclose

> This turning rondure whole, this crescent ring
> Sun-cusped and zoned with modulated fire
> Like pearls that whisper through the Doge's hands.

Columbus prays for a sign from this majestic and terrible God:

> O Thou who sleepest on Thyself, apart
> Like ocean athwart lanes of death and birth,
> And all the eddying breath between dost search
> Cruelly with love thy parable of man,—
> Inquisitor! incognizable Word
> Of Eden and the enchained Sepulchre,
> Into thy steep savannahs, burning blue,
> Utter to loneliness the sail is true.

> Who grindest oar, and arguing the mast
> Subscribest holocaust of ships, O Thou
> Within whose primal scan consummately
> The glistening seignories of Ganges swim;—
> Who sendest greeting by the corposant,
> And Teneriffe's garnet—flamed it in a cloud,
> Urging through night our passage to the Chan;—
> Te Deum laudamus, for thy teeming span!

Columbus's God is a God who is manifested through nature and through the very elements of water, corposant, fire, volcanoes, that threaten to destroy the navigator; more, he is the God whose mystery and pattern Columbus has revealed in his own daring vision of the "turning rondure whole." He is the God Columbus makes known. The circular imagery in the poem reveals the centrality of God, but it also reveals the power of Columbus's imagination to penetrate the mystery of the universe. Columbus's faith is in the roundness of the universe, and as that faith is verified by the visible universe, God is made manifest to him:

> Of all that amplitude that time explores,
> A needle in the sight, suspended north,—
> Yielding by inference and discard, faith
> And true appointment from the hidden shoal:

> This disposition that thy night relates
> From Moon to Saturn in one sapphire wheel:
> The orbic wake of thy once whirling feet,
> Elohim, still I hear thy sounding heel!

In the circles of stars by which Columbus guides his ship, he sees the symbolic evidence of the first center, of God's presence in the universe from which all existence radiates. It is in the circular stars that Columbus receives his sign from God:

> In holy rings all sails charged to the far
> Hushed gleaming fields and pendant seething wheat
> Of knowledge,—

"Ave Maria" is a powerful plea to God for confirmation of the speaker's vision. It is a plea to visionary power as well. Columbus seeks not forgiveness but affirmation, and his faith is not in God's mercy but in man's own ability to apprehend the totality of existence and to make it manifest in his symbolic voyage. When in "Ash Wednesday" Eliot concludes his prayer to the lady, he prays:

> Suffer us not to mock ourselves with falsehood
> Teach us to care and not to care
> Teach us to sit still

The release from the sensual world, the purification from all earthly desire, for which Eliot longs in his prayer, are absent from Columbus's utterance; his is a care-ridden petition that his vision of this world will enclose God's holy purpose. Columbus seeks neither the release of his spirit nor the redemption of his soul but the return of his ships, for he has "seen now what no perjured breath / Of clown nor sage can riddle or gainsay."

Although Columbus's prayer is called "Ave Maria" and he utters a *Te Deum* and refers to the Angelus and the Word, he is in Crane's poem not a man sustained by a traditional faith but a man whose faith must be confirmed constantly by a sign from God, by his own sign. Columbus is another version of the speaker in "Proem," who desires to possess the world. Yet, in a way, the speaker in "Proem" is more truly devout than Columbus because he looks upon the symbols of his world with reverence and awe. Columbus, on the other hand, is impatient to prove that his vision has been affirmed; he is anxious to return to court with the good news. In his only address to the Virgin in the poem, he asks to be assured that "One ship of these thou grantest safe returning." Although his vision has been overpowering, he can never forget his quotidian mission to prove himself absolutely right. In fact, his interest in the voyage actually overcomes his faith in God's guidance when he puts a record of his discovery in a casque and throws it overboard. Unlike the speaker in "Proem," who is absorbed by the power of the bridge, Columbus is anxious to assert himself.

The longing for the pattern's mastery, the desire to yield to the powerful creative spirit at the center of the universe, are still at the heart of Columbus's plea even if his prayer is mixed with thoughts of Genoa and his anxiety about a safe return. And it is this longing that is absent from the twentieth-century world; now belief is simply a possession, something we have as we have commerce and technology, as Crane says in the opening of "The River":

> SCIENCE—COMMERCE and the HOLYGHOST
> RADIO ROARS IN EVERY HOME WE HAVE THE NORTHPOLE
> WALLSTREET AND VIRGINBIRTH WITHOUT STONES OR
> WIRES OR EVEN RUNning brooks connecting ears
> and no more sermons windows flashing roar
> breathtaking—as you like it . . . eh?

Such an accelerated version of the world is breathtaking because the inspiriting power has been removed from it. While God's "eddying breath" inspired Columbus with fear, it is absent from the modern world, and thus modern man lives with an illusory sense of mastery and security. In this hopelessly deflated world the Holy Ghost is no more meaningful than science and commerce. Even the natural world of stones and brooks reveals no message to the modern spirit. There are no signs in this world to point to a world of value and meaning; the only signs are billboards advertising "Certain-teed" and "guaranteed" products. But as this smug and diminished world passes into the "telegraphic night," the poet finds himself in the company of three hoboes who are in touch with a natural world of power and meaning. These men

> count
> —Though they'll confess no rosary nor clue—
> The river's minute by the far brook's year.

Underneath the diminished world of the twentieth century the poet discovers still the natural world where the "old gods of the rain" reveal their mysterious presence, and it is to this world that the poet descends to yield to the "ancient flow." As he succumbs to the "quarrying passion" of the river, he moves away from the actual world where stones and running brooks contain no sermons to a dream world of religious significance where, in the power of nature, he apprehends "The Passion," spreading "in wide tongues, choked and slow, / Meeting the Gulf, hosannas silently below." In the river's tortured movement to the gulf the poet sees an emblem of death and resurrection and of the soul's passage to God.

In the poem that follows, the poet's sensibility remains attuned to this world of mythic forces, identified in "The Dance" as the era of the Indian when the powers of nature were worshipped as sacred. As he participates in the Indian's fertility rite, he prays again for a sign that the world will be infused with the spirit of its creator: "relent, restore— / Lie to us,—dance us back the tribal morn!" Again it is the god of the "levin," the thunder and "firegall," the torrent, that is called forth, and although this god is identified as a feminine nature spirit, it is the same God of "Ave Maria" whose power inspired Columbus with fear and prayer. The poet desires to return to the beginning, to "all that's consummate and free / There, where the first and last gods keep thy tent," and to apprehend the world in the perfection of its creation. What he longs for here, and glimpses in the new life of spring, is the intensification of consciousness that is alone creative.

Not until "Cape Hatteras" does the poet take up his prayer again, and once again it is for "Sea eyes and tidal, undenying, bright with myth!" Like the "Great Navigator" who looked to the skies for some message of God's design, a pattern by which he could guide his ship and his soul, the modern air pilot must yield to the divine design of the universe:

> Stars prick the eyes with sharp ammoniac proverbs,
> New verities, new inklings in the velvet hummed.

Doom awaits the navigator whose vision fails to enclose these new verities, and the poet reminds the pilot of his holy mission:

> Remember, Falcon-Ace,
> Thou hast there in thy wrist a Sanskrit charge
> To conjugate infinity's dim marge—
> Anew . . . !

The pilot must move "Toward endless terminals, Easters of speeding light," and reclaim that vision of the world as endlessly creative which Emerson called in "Circles" the "moral fact of the Universe, the flying Perfect." In "Cape Hatteras" it is not Emerson but his disciple, Whitman, whose "span of consciousness" is evoked. It is the openness of Whitman's vision that the poet acclaims in the space age. Whitman's poetry, words themselves, contain the power to reveal the junction of "speed / With vast eternity," the spiritual force that animates the universe. Whitman is thrice anointed *Panis Angelicus* in this poem, and, despite the extravagance of the epithet, it points to Crane's conviction that the symbols of poetic vision are sacred, that they are the soul's nourishment in this world. What Crane celebrates in "Cape Hatteras" is the attitude of awe, a religious sense of newness. His references to Sanskrit, to the Veda, as well as to Easter and the eucharist, are indiscriminate references to the sacred consciousness which he longed to express.

After "Cape Hatteras" the poet descends to an urban world which he finds hopelessly degraded. Divine inspiration appears almost totally absent from this world, which is described most frequently as a dead garden. Eve in "Southern Cross" is "garden-less," Magdalene is a modern burlesque dancer in a place called "National Winter Garden"; in "The Tunnel" the speaker finds "the garden in the third act dead." The dead garden is the poet's mind objectified and its stupor revealed. "This was the Promised Land," the poet says in "Quaker Hill," but the promises now are only of real estate values. The stars which have throughout *The Bridge* symbolized the presence of divinity in the world become in "Southern Cross" "a phantom, buckled—dropped below the dawn."[20] This is a world of "lower heavens" in which man is conscious only of the profaned and real world. The modern world is a world in which the myth of creativity is absent both from nature and from human nature. Women, the great force of fecundity and creativity in the world, are chiefly objects of lust. Eve is a "simian Venus," Magdalene is known only in "the empty trapeze" of her flesh, and even the gentle Mary in "Virginia" must "Keep smiling the boss away," although this girl "leaning from the high wheat tower" with her golden hair does promise not only the return of spring to the city world but a return of love and devotion to womankind. But chiefly in the modern world human love is felt only as lust, "A burnt match skating in a urinal." The "inner being" of the Quaker, the still, small voice of peace and harmony, is drowned out by the radio, and the old Quaker meetinghouse has become the "New Avalon Hotel."

Yet even in this world the poet is moved to ask:

> Who holds the lease on time and on disgrace?
> What eats the pattern with ubiquity?
> Where are my kinsmen and the patriarch race?

---

20. Crane's use of the word "buckled" here is curious and may owe something to Hopkins's ambiguous use of the verb in "The Windhover." Of course, Crane needed no model for such usage since his own word choice was always original, but he did say of Hopkins, "I'm terribly excited about the poems of Gerard Manley Hopkins. . . . I have discovered that I am not as original in some of my stylisms as I had thought I was." See *Letters*, p. 317.

And his response is again that the artist, here identified as Emily Dickinson and Isadora Duncan and later in "The Tunnel" as Edgar Allan Poe, must speak the word, must discover the word that is the sacredness of life:

> Yes, while the heart is wrung,
> Arise—yes, take this sheaf of dust upon your tongue!
> In one last angelus lift throbbing throat—
> Listen, transmuting silence with that stilly note.

The angelus of the poet, like the Christian Angelus, is the music that will recall the inrushing of spirit into this world and transmute the deafness and dumbness of this fallen world into the awesome stillness that attends the sacred sense of peace and harmony.

Again, in the ending of "The Tunnel" the poet, like Lazarus, is brought back from the dead, to a natural world made meaningful once more and to a sense of his own creative powers. Out of his suffering and agony, he exclaims:

> O caught like pennies beneath soot and steam,
> Kiss of our agony thou gatherest;
> Condensed, thou takest all—shrill ganglia
> Impassioned with some song we fail to keep.
> And yet, like Lazarus, to feel the slope,
> The sod and billow breaking,—lifting ground,
> —A sound of waters bending astride the sky
> Unceasing with some Word that will not die . . . !

Near the "River that is East" the poet senses again the mystery of the universe where "far away the star has pooled the sea." Out of the trials of his experience the poet calls, in the same voice as Columbus, for divine guidance:

> Kiss of our agony Thou gatherest
> O Hand of Fire
> gatherest—

In "Atlantis" the poet returns to the ecstatic utterance of "Proem," to lift his voice in invocation to the creative spirit of his universe. Once again it is the bridge that serves as the symbol of his prayer. In the luminosity of his vision he sees in the bridge

> Sibylline voices flicker, waveringly stream
> As though a god were issue of the strings. . . .

The bridge is still the "prophet's pledge," and so the poet's hope remains still that it will "lend a myth to God." As the poet's vision is propelled upward along the "crystal-flooded aisle" of the structure, it becomes one in his "loft of vision" with the "palladium helm of stars." As the brightness of the bridge is fused with the glistening stars, the "cipher-script of time" is revealed as the "timeless laugh of mythic spears."

In this ecstatic and intensified moment the poet sees the bridge as the inspired pattern of the divinely creative spirit:

> Tall Vision-of-the-Voyage, tensely spare—
> Bridge, lifting night to cycloramic crest
> Of deepest day—O Choir, translating time
> Into what multitudinous Verb the suns
> And synergy of waters ever fuse, recast
> In myriad syllables,—Psalm of Cathay!
> O Love, thy white, pervasive Paradigm . . . !

It is not only the symbol of the bridge but the power of symbol-making that the poet extols, and his fervent desire to express the connective experience that will make the divine manifest in this world is closest to realization here. To translate, to recast, to conjugate infinity in this world is his prayer. In the final stanzas of "Atlantis" the poet's ecstatic supplication continues:

> Forever Deity's glittering Pledge, O Thou
> Whose canticle fresh chemistry assigns
> To wrapt inception and beatitude,—
> Always through blinding cables, to our joy,
> Of thy white seizure springs the prophecy:
> Always through spiring cordage, pyramids
> Of silver sequel, Deity's young name
> Kinetic of white choiring wings . . . ascends.

The deity whose presence Crane senses in this world through the bridge is a God of "inception and beatitude," of beginning and creation and beauty. It is a God who has not revealed himself once and for all in one creation but who continues to reveal himself in the forms and symbols of the poet's world. His presence is a "silver sequel," known to us in growth and movement and energy. The presence of this God, the intensification of consciousness, are felt as light and radiance, as "Unspeakable" and yet as "Answerer of all." The "orphic strings" of the poet are attuned to that "Everpresence, beyond time," whose "Whispers antiphonal in azure swing."

In "Atlantis" the real technological bridge gives way to a vision of bridgeship, the connective experience, the sense of totality, that will unite time with the timeless, the poet's creation with the creative spirit of the universe, the human world with spiritual illumination. The poetic imagination in *The Bridge* offers a constant supplication for divine inspiration, a long prayer for a sign that will verify its own inmost desires. Only by transmuting the forms of this world is the poet able to reveal the everpresence of the spirit working within it, and yet at the same time the poet seeks always a confirmation of his creative task. The power he glimpses in the curveship of the bridge, in the whirling heel of Elohim, in the Easters of speeding light, reveals hints, guesses, pledges, prophecies that glimmer and flicker through this imperfect world and verify the illuminations that inspire the poet. Still, this power is but a pledge, and the poet's apprehension of it is fleeting and ineffable. What the poet seeks in the exclamations and petitions of *The Bridge* is the means not only of perfecting his vision, which has been but a glimmer, but of symbolizing it. When in the course of the poem he falls into doubt, the poet doubts not only the divine presence in this world but also his own visionary powers. When his hope revives, it is because he has been made aware again of the "Word that will not die," not only the divine spirit but the song he must utter.

The poet in *The Bridge* is no mystic if we understand mysticism as a passive merger with the godhead. The poet here is an activist, a symbolist, longingly searching the cipher of time for the "multitudinous Verb" of eternity, fervently seeking evidence of the prophet's pledge not only in the forms of this world but in the forms of his own poetry. The poetic imagination longs to see its creation confirmed in the cosmos and its own symbols made eternally meaningful, but it does not long to merge itself with God.

The poet's most persistent mood is supplication, and the heart of his prayer is the evocation of the creative spirit. The sacred power that manifested itself in the creation of the world, in the "suns / And synergy of waters," that created form out of "abysmal cupolas of space," is the power to which the poet prays and the force which the poet feels working through him. The poet's charge is "to conjugate infinity's dim marge— / Anew," and his poem is an effort to express the sacred newness of life that emanates from the creation of the world and is evident throughout time when that world is envisioned anew. Yet the petitions in *The Bridge* and elsewhere in Crane's poems that arise almost at the very moment when the poet feels the influx of intensified consciousness serve to suggest the fleeting nature of that consciousness. Even when they are an expression of that consciousness, as in "Atlantis," the petitions include a hint that the all-suffusing power is even in its intensity momentary.

Crane's originality rests, however, in his persistent effort to give poetic form to those states of intensified consciousness in which the poet felt himself "possessed." The patterns traced in this study are fused into one pattern as they form the structure of that consciousness. The play between the impulse to violence and the impulse to possession, between stasis and flight, is the play in the architecture of Crane's consciousness, and in expressing it, he expresses the "pattern's mastery." It is a movement between extreme points, between decreation and creation, between fixity and flux, and yet it is a movement tautly controlled and powerfully restricted by the intensity of his feeling.

chapter seven: Conclusion

The patterns I have examined in Crane's poetry are the ones he repeated throughout his work. He uses particular words, images, and metaphors again and again, and rearticulates whole patterns. These recurrent elements in his work reveal the coherence as well as the complexity of his imaginative activity. They indicate the extent to which he continued to expand and explore in *The Bridge* the imaginative concerns that had interested him from the beginning. And they suggest the rich and intricate nature of the experience he sought to express. Opposed as Crane was to all preconceptions and predetermined systems, he started with none of his own. Yet there are subjects with which he was repeatedly concerned and ways in which he characteristically treats them, and they may serve to define his imaginative world. Such a definition is useful especially for Crane, whose work has seemed oddly disjointed, divided as it has been between his epic and lyric poems.

To be sure, Crane developed, but he did not alter so decisively as a study of his work by genre might indicate. A reading of his poetry as a whole must serve to revise the idea that he was a brilliant lyricist who mistakenly undertook to change the direction of his work by writing an epic and who thus failed. When Crane sat down to write *The Bridge*, he did not start with a blank page and an entirely new sensibility. He was perhaps motivated by a greater ambition than ever before, and that ambition was fired in part by what he imagined was the greatest achievement in modern poetry, *The Waste Land*, but he was also inspired by a sense of his own developing poetic powers, a sense that he could accomplish on an even larger scale what he had already achieved in his early poems. When he turned to the myth of America, he did not turn away from his already well-developed fund of imaginative resources; rather, he sought in American history and the culture of his times a scaffolding for his poetic concerns. The charge of his earliest critics that Crane simply did not know enough, that he lacked a coherent philosophy with which to underpin his epic poem, is misdirected because it denies the significance of what Crane did know and the coherence of his imaginative powers. Crane's earliest critics assumed that his long poem lacked a logical framework, but they missed the imaginative framework evident in his poetry as a whole.

Crane suffered neither from limited knowledge nor from restricted poetic means. His poetry is rich, complex, and often difficult. It reflects neither an unwilled surrender to sensations nor a willful attempt to fit everything, private feelings and public myth, into certain preformed systems. It is rather a persistent and rigorous effort to give form to the furthest range of his imagination. Crane did not move through progressive stages of intellectual and spiritual development toward some conclusive system. He knew himself from the start, and what he learned as he continued to write was how to express more fully that self. He remained from beginning to end extremely responsive to his sensations, to those moments of intensified consciousness which he felt revealed a truth beyond the logical, the rational, the already accepted order of knowledge. His poetry is a sincere and continuing effort to make accessible that intensity of apprehension, to find words and patterns that would articulate it. He told Munson that the tragic quandary of the modern world "derives from the paradoxes that an in-

adequate system of rationality forces on the living consciousness."
His desire was not to propose a more adequate system but to express
"in the more direct terms of physical-psychic experience" the open
ranges of his consciousness.[1] The patterns of his poetry are in
some sense the patterns of his consciousness. His work as a whole,
read self-referentially, reveals the areas that were open to him.

At the center of Crane's imaginative world is the poet. It is not
surprising that Crane was concerned with the activity of the poet,
since every major poet of his time was similarly concerned. However, while Eliot was interested in the poet's relation to tradition
and Stevens was concerned with what the poetic imagination
could achieve, Crane treats in his poetry primarily the nature of
the creative act. He explores the demands of creativity, the exigent
expenditure of self required by expression, the painful exposure
and rigorous performance that attend imaginative activity. He
details the uncertainty and self-doubts that corrode the necessary
confidence of the artist. At the same time, however, he emphasizes
the exalting and liberating effects of the imagination. He celebrates
the artist's triumph over suffering and loss, traces his powers of
endurance, asserts his freedom. These are psychological states familiar to both *The Bridge* and the lyric poems, to both the early and
the late work. Crane never lost interest in the creative power of
the imagination nor did he minimize its demands. He returned
to examine with exacting detail its requirements as well as its
rewards because he felt that the imaginative man had a peculiar
type of perception needed in the modern age. He did not believe
that every man could be a poet, but he was convinced that the poet
must reveal the revolutionary power of the word to the world. It
was not an easy task in an age which suffered, Crane felt, from the
limiting effects of an excessive rationality.

Early in his career he told Gorham Munson, "The problem of
form becomes harder and harder for me every day . . . I have
never, so far, been able to present a vital, living and tangible,—a
positive emotion to my satisfaction." The desire to give form to

1. *Letters*, pp. 238, 239.

emotion is the propelling force behind all his work, and its problems plagued him all his life. Crane explained to Munson the difficulties he encountered in this endeavor: "Oh! it is hard! One must be drenched in words, literally soaked with them to have the right ones form themselves into the proper pattern at the right moment. When they come, . . . they come as things in themselves; it is a matter of felicitous juggling!; and no amount of will or emotion can help the thing a bit. So you see I believe with Sommer that the 'Ding an Sich' method is ultimately the only satisfactory creative principle to follow."[2]

The direction of Crane's thoughts here owes something to William Sommer, an artist and friend with whom he shared discussions of literature and art during the formative period between 1921 and 1923. Some passages that Sommer copied or invented and left in his studio at his death may serve as a gloss on Crane's comments:

> Art is no longer a sensation that we take up with the eyes alone. Art is the creation of our spiritual, inward vision, nature just starts us off, instead of working with the eyes we conceive with the *subconscious* and thus the complete changing of nature.
>
> . . . I take my pen drawing home and start in with color, . . . prolonging forms that touch each other and in this way build a oneness that can be felt out of a Bach fugue or choral which has no beginning or end, just an arrangement of line and colour. Style can not be forced from our hand, it must come of itself as we see and drag the forms out of nature, the forms as we need them, not an imitation. . . .[3]

Sommer's emphasis, as well as Crane's, is on inspiration as the creative principle of the artist. Prolonging forms to build a oneness, the artist seems to be reponsive to nothing but the materials of his arts and the instincts they inspire. Style that must come of itself arises from an inner force that seems to operate independently both of the artist's will and of the exterior world. But as Sommer

2. *Ibid.*, p. 71.
3. William Sommer Memorial Exhibition catalogue, plates XXXIII, XLII (Cleveland Museum of Art, 1950), quoted by Unterecker, *Voyager*, p. 204.

admits, nature starts it off, and there seems to be in his mind a reciprocal relationship between the inward vision and the outer world, the imagination and the will. "Everything that happens," Sommer said, "is like the man it happens to. Intrinsic, inward, essential, real, inherent, within."[4] The inward shaping spirit is the storehouse of all that happens to it, of experience, sensations, sense perceptions absorbed from reality; but it also determines what it has stored. It is then doubly creative. It takes from the world what it needs, "the forms as we need them," and it gives to the world new forms, "the proper pattern at the right moment."

The act of the imagination is not, however, the simple transfer of past experiences into words, i.e., new forms or symbols; it is rather an esemplastic apprehension (to use a word from Coleridge and thus identify Crane's literary debt) of that experience, the creation of primary images, conception with the "*subconscious.*" Words that come as things in themselves are not important as references to something else; they are the primary equivalences of the patterns of the imagination. To be drenched in words is to be overpowered by the conscious and subconscious perceptions that are formed into a whole in these patterns. When Crane wrote to Munson about the problem of form, he expressed dissatisfaction with his attempts to present living and positive emotion. Everything he had done had been "mere shadowings," and what he wanted to create was not the shadow of the emotion but the emotion itself, the emotion apprehended by the imagination that is a new fusion of experience and a newly patterned whole.

The words with which Crane was soaked and drenched are the equivalents of this emotion. They carry a dynamic charge, come of themselves, find their poetic form to articulate the patterns of consciousness. For Crane, words are not simply signs and references; they are objects, centers of energy that form a poem as a matter of "felicitous juggling." The act by which words establish a dynamic pattern seems, in Crane's view, to be a matter both of chance and of skill. The poem is a movement of words, started by

4. Quoted by Unterecker, *Voyager*, p. 204.

chance articulations and combinations, and the life of the poem depends upon the trick that maintains the movement. It is there that the poet exercises his skill, balances the opposing forces of words, sustains their motion by working with it. Yet the poet who considers poetry an act of juggling must yield to the inherent necessity of the movement or his act will collapse. So, although the poet-juggler may be a manipulator of words, he is also their servant.

In Crane's poems words leap beyond their dictionary definitions and, as Leibowitz has said, "create a network of meanings, something akin to a chromatic scale of moods."[5] What Crane sought from the grouping of words was, he said, "an 'interior' form, a form that is so thorough and intense as to dye the words themselves with a peculiarity of meaning, slightly different maybe from the ordinary definition of them separate from the poem."[6] The form is the balancing act of the poet-juggler. In this act, words are used as parts of a pattern, and the pattern gives them their significance.

In these statements Crane separates poetic words from ordinary words, as in other places he distinguished between pure logic and the logic of the imagination. What he wants to emphasize is the way in which poetic words are charged with intensity and form

5. Leibowitz, *Hart Crane*, p. 53.
6. *Letters*, p. 77. In this passage Crane is actually talking about Donne's "The Expiration," but he claims to have achieved something similar in his own poem "Black Tambourine." By relying on the associational meanings of words and on the form of his poems to make these associations convincing, Crane sometimes baffled readers, who felt that he had bypassed completely the literal level of the words. He never actually dismisses this level of understanding, but he crowds his poems with meanings beyond it so that they become packed and jammed and as a consequence sometimes too complex and difficult. Occasionally the extrinsic meanings of words lead his readers away from their significance in the intrinsic form of the poem. For example, "Black Tambourine," about a black man in a cellar, elicited in some readers' minds sociological suggestions about the place of blacks in American life. Crane was impatient with this response because it seemed to indicate a misunderstanding of his artistic method. He said, "The value of the poem is only, to me, in what a painter would call its 'tactile' quality,—an entirely aesthetic feature. A propagandist for either side of the Negro question could find anything he wanted to in it." See *Letters*, p. 58. He went on to explain that in "Black Tambourine" he had achieved "an 'interior' form." Not everyone would agree with Crane here, but he persisted in his desire to give words more than their ordinary definitions.

imaginative patterns that extend their ordinary meanings. Words
that are dyed with a peculiarity of meaning, like the words with
which the poet was drenched, are saturated, filled with significance.
They do not serve to delimit or define an object; rather, they are
the object into which a multiplicity of suggestions has been absorbed. This gathering of meanings into words and patterns is not
an anti-rational process but a super-rational one in Crane's mind.
Ordinary meanings, pure logic, are limiting; they categorize, con-
ceptualize, divide, distinguish parts. Poetry, on the other hand,
unifies, harmonizes, patterns, balances, intensifies. It moves through
and beyond the boundaries of rationality to present new patterns of
perceptions. The act of the imagination is not opposed to reason;
it is rather an addition to it and perhaps its corrective. Reason for
Crane is conservative, and imagination is energizing and liberating.

If the effects of the imagination are liberating, its processes are
nonetheless exacting. The truly creative artist cannot, as Crane
said, "walk ably over an old track bedecked with all kinds of
signposts and 'championship records.'" He is instead almost driven
mad with the "intense but always misty realization of what *can*
be done if potentialities are fully freed, released."[7] The problem
of form, of giving form to potentialities, was hard for Crane because he felt he must work free from already evolved models. He
sensed that his aims were forever unaccomplished, "misty," but
he was driven by the intensity of his creative urge toward their
realization.

For that purpose, the imagination has the power of creative
thinking, the "superior logic of metaphor," Crane said. Those
who deny that logic are limited to "perfect sums, divisions and
subtractions," that is, to accumulations of what we already know.
They deny the possibility of a "new order of consciousness." Crane
made these comments to Alfred Stieglitz, whom he called an ac-
complice "in many ways that we don't yet fully understand. 'What
is now proved was once only imagined,' said Blake." And his
observations on Stieglitz's work shed light on the forward thrust

7. *Letters*, pp. 138, 139.

of his own creative aims. They were both trying, Crane said, to transform the "great energies about us" "into a higher quality of life."[8]

Their efforts were necessary, as Crane explained:

If the essence of things were in their mass and bulk we should not need the clairvoyance of Stieglitz's photography to arrest them for examination and appreciation. But they are suspended on the invisible dimension whose vibrance has been denied the human eye at all times save in the intuition of ecstasy. Alfred Stieglitz can say to us today what William Blake said to as baffled a world more than a hundred years ago in his "To the Christians":

'I give you the end of a golden string:
Only wind it into a ball,—
It will lead you in at Heaven's gate,
Built in Jerusalem's wall.'

The invisible dimension denied the human eye is the dimension of the imagination. The "baffling capture" of Stieglitz's photographs throws us, Crane said, into "ultimate harmonies." In the modern world, "the place of 'brokenness,'" there is without the artist "a foreshortening, a loss and a premature disintegration of experience." Only the artist can create a "new stage" of consciousness, a "higher tranquillity," "an even wider intensity."[9] It is Stieglitz's "intuition of ecstasy" that inspires his work and at the same time gives it its restorative force in the modern world. The artist, fully responsive to his inner powers, makes those powers accessible to the world through his art. Imagination is the power added to the world that transforms it. To imagine is, then, not simply to be overpowered by inspiration, to move out of the material world into an area of occult powers. To imagine is first to sense the limits of experience and to push them outward, to make them higher and wider.

The relationship of the imagination to the world is made clear in another comment. Crane said to Stieglitz, "you are gathering

8. *Ibid.*, p. 138.
9. *Ibid.*, pp. 132, 138.

together those dangerous interests outside of yourself into that purer projection of yourself. It is really not a projection in any but a loose sense, for I feel more and more that in the absolute sense the artist *identifies* himself with life. Because he has always had so much surrounding indifference and resistance such 'action' takes on a more relative and limited term which has been abused and misunderstood by several generations,—this same 'projecting.' But in the true mystical sense as well as in the sense which Aristotle meant by the 'imitation of nature,' I feel that I'm right."[10] In the reciprocity between the artist and his world, in the gathering of outside interests into a projection of self, the gap between the imagination and reality is closed. The artist identifies with life because the artist represents a new life. The objects he creates are not representations but transformations of energy into a higher quality. The projection of self is a projection of a higher energy into the world.

As we have seen, Crane's acquaintance with William Sommer and Alfred Stieglitz encouraged his belief in the transforming power of the imagination. He also sensed in another artist, Joseph Stella, an identification with life that he imagined was the liberating purpose of the truly creative individual. Stella's essay on the Brooklyn Bridge might have been written by Crane to describe his own poetic purpose:

> Brooklyn gave me a sense of liberation. The vast view of her sky, in opposition to the narrow one of NEW YORK, was a vast relief— and at night, in her solitude, I used to find, intact, the green freedom of my own self.
>
> It was the time when I was awakening in my work an echo of the oceanic polyphony (never heard before) expressed by the steely orchestra of modern constructions: the time when, in rivalry to the new elevation in superior spheres as embodied by the skyscrapers and the new fearless audacity in soaring above the abyss of the bridges, I was planning to use all my fire to forge with a gigantic art illimited and far removed from the insignificant frivolities of

10. *Ibid.*, p. 139.

easel pictures, proceeding severely upon a mathematic precision of intent, animated only by essential elements.[11]

Crane wanted to use Stella's painting of the Brooklyn Bridge as a frontispiece to the Black Sun Press edition of his long poem, and although in the end he did not use the painting, he was obviously moved by the striking analogy between the painting and the poem.[12] Both poem and painting transform the actual bridge into a dynamic image. In Stella's paintings it is presented in a series of geometrical and color patterns that suggest its verticality, its movement in stillness, its flight of cables, its massiveness rendered light. Although Crane had a less pure medium with which to transform the technological fact into symbol, he aspired to the same intensely new image forged with the same "gigantic art unlimited."

Crane responded in Sommer, Stieglitz, and Stella to the revolutionary ways in which they worked. The clarity and dynamism of Sommer's paintings, the precision and synthesis of Stieglitz's photographs, the severity and vision of Stella's work, seemed to Crane to express new areas of consciousness, open both to the actual and to the universal. Concrete observations led these artists into metaphysical speculations, as Crane himself felt at times moved toward the invisible dimension denied the human eye. All three artists were in some way influenced by Cubism. By breaking into the surface continuity of the picture, they sought a new form that would more adequately represent the total image perceived by the mind and the eye. For these painters as for the Cubists, the imagination is the active principle that transforms and extends the object by multiplying resemblances. In commenting on the

11. Joseph Stella, "The Brooklyn Bridge," quoted by George Knox, "Crane and Stella: Conjunction of Painterly and Poetic Worlds," *Texas Studies in Language and Literature*, XII (Winter 1971), 693. Philip Horton mentions Crane's interest in Stella in his biography, *Hart Crane* (New York: W. W. Norton, 1937), p. 111. But it was Brom Weber who first discussed the relations between Stella's essay as well as his paintings and Crane's conception of *The Bridge*. See Weber, *Hart Crane*, pp. 317–320. Since then, Knox's article has confirmed and explored the connections between Stella and Crane. See also comments by Irma B. Jaffe, *Joseph Stella* (Cambridge, Mass.: Harvard University Press, 1970), pp. 245–248.

12. *Letters*, pp. 333–334.

impact of Cubism on literature, Crane pinpointed this issue: "Analysis and discovery, the two basic concerns of science, become conscious objectives of both painter and poet."[13]

Unlike his fellow poets William Carlos Williams and Wallace Stevens, who were also influenced by Cubism and other developments in the arts, Crane did not try to transpose painterly techniques into poetry. He shared neither Williams's interest in the poem as an object nor Stevens's color symbolism.[14] What interested him in the work of his artist friends was their creative principles, their revolutionary views of the relationship between imagination and reality. Their ideas, revealed in both their art and their writing, were more important to him than the objective methods he could have borrowed from them. He was too interested in the logic of metaphor to abandon it entirely for visual precision in his work. However, he saw more clearly in the visual arts than in the poetry of his contemporaries the apprehension of new areas of consciousness.

In fact, Crane's comments on his fellow poets express a singular lack of enthusiasm and sympathy. He found the early Williams "fastidious," although he called *In the American Grain* "a most important and *sincere* book" and noted certain affinities between Williams's treatment of Poe and his own. Crane considered Marianne Moore "too much of a precieuse"; although he put Wallace Stevens in the same category, he liked him better, especially his "technical subtleties." Cummings was "quite ulta," and if he did some new and fine things in Crane's view, he would, Crane said, "never take the trouble to prune anything or discipline his genius."[15] Only Eliot and Pound were doing anything significant, Crane thought. For Eliot he had the highest praise at the same time that he felt his own direction must be different. Toward the end of his life, dejected by negative reviews of *The Bridge*, Crane

13. "Modern Poetry," *The Complete Poems,* p. 261.

14. He did, however, write one poem, "Sunday Morning Apples," which attempts to verbalize the subject of one of Sommer's paintings. See Paul's reading of the poem, *Hart's Bridge*, pp. 83–90.

15. *Letters,* pp. 37, 277–278, 25, 85, 375.

summed up his feelings about the state of poetry and critical taste in a letter to Allen Tate where he claimed that the critics were not interested in poetry any more; they were looking for "a cure-all." "Poetry as poetry (and I don't mean merely decorative verse) isn't worth a second reading any more. Therefore—away with Kubla Khan, out with Marlowe, and to hell with Keats! . . . I admit that I don't answer the requirements. My vision of poetry *is* too personal to 'answer the call.' And if I ever write any more verse it will probably be at least as personal as the idiom of *White Buildings* whether anyone cares to look at it or not."[16]

Crane, who had felt as a young man that only a creative genius could prevent the disintegration of consciousness in the modern world and who felt that he had that genius, was sorely tried to discover that he did not answer the requirements of his age. His self-assessment here is a fairly adequate reflection of the critical judgment of his times. Yet we may ask in what ways his personal vision of poetry, poetry as poetry, is new and significant.

His imaginative world is not entirely different from that of his contemporaries. He shares with Wallace Stevens, for instance, the awareness that the poet is not only a clown but that for him beauty is pain. The protagonist in "Esthétique du Mal" accepts and understands pain as an inextricable part of his union with reality:

> Reality explained.
> It was the last nostalgia: that he
> Should understand. That he might suffer or that
> He might die was the innocence of living, if life
> Itself was innocent. To say that it was
> Disentangled him from sleek ensolacings.

For Crane, too, to suffer was to live innocently. Crane's desire for possession of an elusive female figure, associated with the regenerating force of the landscape, finds expression in William Carlos Williams's *In the American Grain* as well as later in *Paterson*. Crane's interest in the dangers and intoxications of speed had been

16. *Ibid.*, p. 353.

explored in the manifestoes of Futurism, and his enthusiasms for the machine as a subject of poetry were elaborated by Gorham Munson in his study of Waldo Frank. His alternate vision of the modern metropolis as an inferno owed something, no doubt, to Eliot. The point is not that Crane borrowed from his contemporaries; it is rather that the new areas of consciousness which he claimed to explore were not totally unknown in the writing of his time.

What, then, did he contribute? His is a poetry of sensation, and, more than any other modernist poet, he expresses the intensity of feeling, its depths and its heights. The excessive emphasis placed upon *The Bridge* in assessments of Crane have led to a view of him as a visionary poet, straining for the transcendent. Yet no poet in his generation was more responsive to physical sensations, sufferings, and ecstasies than Crane, as a study of his poetic patterns should indicate. When he said he found it difficult to give form to emotion, he was expressing the central problem of his generation: the inability to express emotion. Insofar as he succeeded in exploring the range of his own consciousness, he broke new ground.

Crane's poetry is also more consistently affirmative and inclusive than his contemporaries who started out tentatively, carefully, precisely. Crane's charges of fastidiousness and preciosity may be well taken against a generation of poets whose first lesson of art was Imagism. The poetry of the 1920s was careful. Even the magnificent achievement of *The Waste Land* veered toward a perfection of means. There was a sense in his time, as Crane said, that "the fruits of civilization are entirely harvested." Against this mood and the technical skill and precision of poetry, he claimed boldly, "it interests me to still affirm certain things."[17] Crane went against the poetic grain of his time, and for this reason his work is in many ways new in expressing the frenetic quality of the jazz age, the exhilaration of speed and destruction experienced in World War I, the still fervent hope that the machine age might sustain the highest aspirations of mankind. But more than this, Crane's affirmations

17. *Ibid.*, p. 115.

and inclusions encompassed an emotional vitality that seemed forever destroyed. His poetry is intricate, varied, jammed with emotional power.

Finally, Crane is among modernist poets more heavily dependent upon the magic of words. He thought of his poems as a new word, and in a sense he did not claim too much. His ability to exploit the word, to use its overtones, to activate its associational meanings, to juggle it felicitously, was his great strength. His extreme receptivity to the dynamism of words freed him and made his poems not vatic effusions but tightly wrought patterns.

Index